PN
4888
.T4
T4
1982

Teague, Bob.

Live and off-col-
or

DATE DUE

Live and Off-Color: News Biz

BOB TEAGUE

Live and Off-Color: News Biz

A&W Publishers

NEW YORK

Published by
A & W Publishers, Inc.
95 Madison Avenue

New York, NY 10016
Manufactured in the United States of America
Designed by Regine de Toledo

1 2 3 4 5 6 7 8 9 10

Library of Congress Cataloging in Publication Data
  Teague, Bob.
    Live and off-color.
    Includes index.
    1. Television broadcasting of news—United States.   I. Title.
  II. Title: Live and off-color.
  PN4888.T4T4   070.1′9′0973   81-70459
  ISBN 0-89479-103-6   AACR2

To Jerry Yarus, Joe Gafa, and the rest of the "grunts"
on the NBC News team—the best in television, anywhere

CONTENTS

Live and Off-Color: News Biz

*T*HE KEY TO THIS BUSINESS is integrity and sincerity. Once you've learned to fake those things, you've got it made.

Sander Vanocur
NBC-TV NEWS

PROLOGUE

Indecent Exposure

*H*ERE I GO, committing professional hara-kiri in print. Before you finish these pages, my career as a broadcast journalist is nearly certain to be terminated. Why do I expect the ax? Because the soul of this book goes behind the glamorous facade of news biz, naming names and relating specific happenings that illustrate what is dreadfully wrong in this quadrant of television and what should be done to improve it.

Why would I, a rational person, take such a gamble, risking a job that pays more than enough to cover my alimony tab?

I confess to having chewed a lot of fingernails over that question before cranking myself up to type page one. My answer has almost as many facets as the tube itself. Something deep in my guts, too civilized to shout in the streets, tells me I have to write it all down and share it, no matter what:

Because I believe in solid TV journalism and the awesome potential of this marvelous electronic medium.

Because television news, as it is today, is a sort of schizophrenic prostitute—not the honest kind of whore I can respect.

Live and Off-Color: News Biz

Enormous swatches of television news are dumb, irrelevant, tasteless, and insulting to you as a viewer, to me as a reporter. I am reminded of a comment by WNBC-TV newswriter Robert White, a former *Herald Tribune* desk maven who worked for Channel 4's "Sixth Hour News" in New York in the late 1960s: "The only way news ever gets on this program is when the *gonsamachers* in charge don't recognize it."

In White's lexicon, a maven is a guy who knows his job and gets it done; *gonsamachers* spend most of their time faking it—passing the buck and covering their behinds with bullshit.

I am further galvanized because a gaggle of my colleagues from New York to California, when apprised of my decision to undertake this project, not only encouraged me, they also contributed generously, enthusiastically, to the mosaic I was constructing—which means that I am not relying solely on one man's piques and perceptions.

"Tell it like it is, Bobby," they cheered, then after a thoughtful pause, posed variations of this question: "Are you sure you want to do it now, while you're still working in news biz?"

My response was, if I don't do it now, before the tube chews me up and spits me out as it has so many others, I will certainly have a credibility problem. I don't want anyone to dismiss what I have to say as just another case of sour grapes; you know, as if I were trying to get even with a lover who had rejected me. By speaking out now, while still a bright star in the New York TV firmament, perhaps my true motives will be respected.

I feel uniquely qualified for this task because of my background as a print journalist and because you can count on one hand the number of TV newspeople with my kind of staying power: nineteen years at the same station in New York, the market universally recognized as the summit and crucible of news biz. I have witnessed and been part of many changes in the method and madness of broadcasting current events—as a scriptwriter, producer, street reporter, and anchorman. Some of the changes have been spawned by the times—simple expedients in a world where events become relatively unimportant an hour after they occur. Others have been downright ludicrous—gimmicks and guesses adopted for their

14

entertainment value that, sadly, fell short of the mark. In the process of change, the TV executives up there in what I call the "Golden Ghetto" frequently forget that their job is to facilitate getting relevant information to the public quickly and clearly, to bring contemporary history into millions of bars and living rooms. After all, that's what TV news is: a rough first draft of history just after it happens; sometimes just before.

All of which begins to explain why a television streetwalker like me occupies such a very special position in the experience of more people than I could personally meet in a lifetime. I am somewhat like the character of the messenger employed in Greek tragedies centuries ago. Momentous events were not shown on stage for moral or logistical reasons. A messenger rushed in to announce a betrayal, a violent death, a crucial battle, and the lives of all the other characters in the drama were altered by his reports.

So it is today as street reporters wade into the thick of life to broadcast triumphs and tragedies at five or six and eleven each night. Not everybody can be there to witness the cataclysmic eruptions. Most people are too preoccupied—each involved in his or her own personal concerns. The impersonal happenstances that affect their welfare are chronicled by us messengers. The nonparticipants depend on us to tell it like it is. In short, we are the eyes, ears, and, at times, even the consciences of our viewers.

Quite often, though, we fail to carry out our important mission as well as we could and should. We have a secondary responsibility, being required, at the same time, to inform and entertain in various ways that management thinks will make The Ratings jump a bit higher. These relentless dual pressures have blunted our effectiveness and sometimes crushed our morale.

Is it any wonder then that us "grunts" down here in the trenches think of the "star makers" who control our destinies as "Empty Suits"? They usually are more concerned about sponsors—the advertisers who pay about $2,800 for a minute of air time on local news shows in the Big Apple at 6:00 P.M., about $4,600 for a minute on the 11:00 P.M. newscasts. With one crass eye perpetually glued to the till, TV executives want their anchors and streetwalkers to do whatever it might take to keep the big spenders happy, eager

15

to come back for more. Only then can they rest easy in the catbird seats. They call us "Talent." What is most important in their eyes, however, boils down to cash and personality—hell, let's call it by its right name, sex appeal.

When you mix all those elements—the mandate to enlighten the public, the pressure to attract and hold a vast audience, the millions of dollars in advertising revenue at stake, and the stiff competition from news teams just a click away on the dial—you've got the god-awful mess that passes for broadcast journalism in the 1980s.

Up to now, network news programs have been less contaminated by the "infotainment" syndrome, but debilitating symptoms are certainly visible. Consider what has happened to ABC's million-dollar woman, Barbara Walters. In the 1970s, she made headlines with exclusive in-depth interviews of genuine newsmakers—Cuban President Castro, Egyptian President Sadat, and the Shah of Iran. In 1981, a print advertisement for a "Barbara Walters Special" promised viewers that former-Beatle Ringo Starr would talk about the late John Lennon; Linda Gray, J.R.'s wife in the "Dallas" soap opera, would introduce her real husband; Brooke Shields, the teen-aged model, would discuss sex appeal; and Loretta Lynn, the fabled country singer, would reveal "her latest heartbreak."

Another specious blending of news biz and show biz at the local level became apparent during the same season. When Dave Marash returned to WCBS-TV's "Newsbreakers" after a stint with the ABC network, the promos welcoming him back to Channel 2 featured bandleader Mitch Miller, folksinger Pete Seeger, basketball whiz Earl Monroe, actor Theodore Bikel, and choreographer Robert Joffrey. Why? Because, like Marash, they all wore beards.

This is not to imply an iota of disrespect for these talented superstars. It is my feeling, though, that the distinctions between newspersons and entertainers are important and should not be blurred by such frivolous associations in promos.

Here are further indications of show-biz thinking in broadcast journalism. The news director at Channel 4 in New York from 1979 to 1981, Ron Kershaw, has been striving to produce what he called "a theater of information, an upbeat show." His WCBS-TV counterpart at Channel 2, Steve Cohen, once said, "I believe I've got to make people simmer. I want them to simmer in their seats when they watch us. In a real sense, I want the newscast to be like Norman Mailer. I want to present the facts in the form of a novel."

In pursuit of their parallel goals, Kershaw and Cohen have recruited sexy-looking mannequins for their news teams, with little regard for their ability to tell the difference between a fact and a fandango. Both news directors, their old-pro holdovers complain, have gone overboard on live coverage of nonevents and meaningless live pictures from cameras carried by helicopters, mesmerized by the sophisticated technology at their command—as if to say they think the medium is more important than the message.

It is my guess that the journalistic obscenities they have fostered represented either shameless emulations of more successful news directors at Channel 7 or groping efforts to overtake them in The Ratings. News directors Al Primo, Al Ittleson, and Jim Topping of WABC-TV have, in sequence, managed to keep Channel 7's "Eyewitness News" at or near the top of the numbers game during most of the past ten years.

For example, Channel 7 presented a theater of information that probably made viewers simmer in their seats by sending reporter Anna Bond aloft in a chopper one Halloween night. Wearing a witch's costume complete with a broom, Anna enlightened millions as to what kind of flying conditions the errant goblins and ghosts could expect that evening.

At Channel 4, prior to Kershaw's arrival, a live bulldog named Winston participated in Dr. Frank Field's weather forecasts as a silent partner and comedy foil.

Channel 2 reporters frequently broadcast live from locations where absolutely nothing had happened or would happen in the foreseeable future—chitchat and nonreportage. "The live remote," said reporter Dave Monsees of Channel 2, "started out as a vehicle for covering important stories. It has now become a vehicle for making unimportant stories *seem* important."

Similar criticism has been voiced to me by local news bird dogs in Miami, Atlanta, Baton Rouge, Chicago, St. Louis, Denver, and San Francisco.

17

While I am criticizing local news directors at the three flagship stations in New York, I should also give them the praise they have earned. They have expanded coverage of the suburban precincts beyond the five boroughs of the city, and they have encouraged reporters to get involved in controversies where blatant injustices were apparent. They have spent impressive numbers of dollars to ship reporters and camera crews overseas to provide a special coverage of big stories of extraordinary interest to viewers in the tri-state metropolitan area—that devastating earthquake in Italy in 1980, for example, and the pilgrimage to Jerusalem by thousands of holocaust survivors in 1981.

My purpose here is not to throw brickbats at particular news directors who sometimes prevent me and other TV bird dogs from doing the best job we know how, nor is it to titillate readers with anecdotes and gossip about celebrities they have seen on the tube, although some of that is unavoidable. What I seriously have in mind is to zero in on the workings of the magic eye, to answer some questions about the public's wants and needs from my profession, to raise questions about modus operandi. I also have to deal with the ruses, the politics, the goofs, the trials and errors, and the dumb managerial tricks. That's the stuff the Empty Suits don't want to hear about.

Like many of my associates, I am convinced that people out there on the other side of the screen really want to know why they get certain information from us and why certain stories are ignored, especially on the local scene. They are curious and concerned because of our impact. If, for instance, we show a burning building only a couple of blocks from your home, it somehow means more than it would if you just happened to spot the blaze while walking down the street. With our all-seeing eye, we take community events and turn them into news—something important.

Suppose a hot controversy has flared up in your backyard— like an official proposal to tear down part of the neighborhood to put up a shopping mall or to introduce a halfway house for ex-junkies. If such imbroglios are dramatized on our local TV newscasts, people start talking about the pros and cons. A lot of hackles get raised. Everybody takes sides. Something happens one way or the other, colored to some degree by our coverage.

You also depend on newscasters as your surrogates. I mean, if you're the kind of opinionated viewer who has always wanted to give the mayor or the governor a piece of your mind, I am your alter ego. I ask the tough questions that you would ask, if given the chance, to make His Honor squirm. Vicarious satisfaction, right?

If you are over fifty, you perhaps began dreaming of that heady possibility when television made its public debut at the New York World's Fair in 1939. Although black-and-white TV began coming into our homes in 1946, that dream was still impossible until local TV news was invented in the middle of the 1950s.

In the early fifties, with rare exceptions, TV news dealt primarily with almost surrealistic occurrences thousands of miles from our hometowns. When John Cameron Swayze went "hopscotching the world for headlines" on the NBC network's "Camel Caravan of News," he concretized President Eisenhower's benign inaction, Premier Stalin's death, and Chairman Mao's Great Leap Forward. Everything dealt with "faraway places with strange-sounding names"; nothing to do with goings-on in the adjacent wards that would touch your life immediately. Swayze and the great Edward R. Murrow told you in solemn, stentorian tones about the postwar baby boom, the Cold War, and the so-called police action in Korea.

Your interest in it was of no small consequence as the infant medium flourished, burgeoning from a handful of commercial stations in the early fifties to 577 in 1963, when I entered the picture, to 738 in 1980. In the same time span, public TV stations grew from 68 to 254—a grand total of 992 at this moment.

As viewers became more sophisticated, more aware of their connection with the rest of reality, they demanded to be included in the miracle of transmitting pictures through the air. Television's response was a gradual increase in on-the-spot coverage, not only of the big stories like the Army-McCarthy hearings in Washington, but also important local events. This expansion, of course, opened a new source of revenue—local sponsors. At that point in the medium's evolution, the TV stations had to assemble their own local news teams. No longer did one man sit before the camera pontificating in splendid isolation. He was suddenly surrounded and abetted by a genial family of specialists—political analysts, consumer advocates, crime buffs, weather forecasters, business experts, sports enthusiasts, fashion watchers, and cracker-barrel comedians. The name of the game was teamwork, or, swarm all over the audience with something for everybody. So the definition of news evolved. An increase in local bus fares could command as much air time as a State of the Union message by the president.

The manner of presenting the news also changed, from aloof authority to offhand informality—a kaffeeklatsch on the air. The trendsetters, for the most part, were the major stations set up by the networks in New York, Chicago, and Los Angeles. All the news teams tried to give the impression that they identified with you and you could identify with them.

As local teams began popping up all over the map—two or three within the same city—the competition intensified to grab the biggest share of the audience. Being number two or number three was tantamount to being in the crapper, which led to excesses and ill-advised programming directives. At one point, for example, when my station, WNBC-TV, was number three in the New York local news ratings, executive producer Carole Clancy wrote a classic memo to associate producers, newswriters, and reporters. She urged us to order the word "Exclusive" to be flashed on the screen "where possible" during film and videotape stories on the air. "Even if everyone else has the story, we should use 'Exclusive' if we get good pictures or a sound bite [interview] that no one else got."

Clancy is not some charlatan who sneaked in through the back door of news biz. She is certainly a competent professional, and her sin in this perfidious instance was less corrosive than many others committed by her superiors in the Golden Ghetto. The devil makes them do it—the same devil who preys with equal ferocity on TV management everywhere. I'm talking about the force that compels them to sacrifice solid news reports for pieces of entertaining fluff, and to misuse our technology for meaningless live coverage of nonevents. The Ratings.

Should we nail their hides to the wall? I say no. Instead, we must let them know that there *is* intelligent life on the planet Earth, that while we appreciate the difficulty of the hand they have to play, we are hep to and weary of their jive. Only then can we enlist them as respected members of the ASPBJ—Aroused Society for the Protection of Broadcast Journalism. We need their cooperation to initiate a serious dialogue to explore what might be done to inject larger dollops of common sense and journalistic responsibility into our industry.

Let me emphasize again I am not saying that TV executives have not been daring, creative, and right on target in some experiments. With their guidance, we boldly exposed hidden faults in the bedrock of American society that triggered the angry black eruptions of the early sixties. They have also backed us up in the use of hidden cameras—at the risk of multi-million-dollar lawsuits—in many "newscam" exposés. The impact of these and other successful gambits, combined with the sheer power of the tube, have served to elevate broadcasters to a status rarely enjoyed by print journalists.

How else would you explain why CBS anchorman Walter Cronkite was more or less drafted to play a role in the selection of a vice-presidential nominee in 1980? Nothing could be more indicative of Cronkite's enormous power than the fact that former-President Gerald Ford sought an audience with him before talking to Ronald Reagan when the GOP presidential candidate asked Ford to accept second place on the ticket. That's clout.

No question about it, television has become a political tool as well as a social, economic, and educational lever. All you have to do is attend one news conference to see that. Politicians and almost everybody else in the power structure virtually ignore the writing press and radio bird dogs until they have finished preening for the cameras. They have learned that the consequences of telecasting to millions all at once can immediately affect the direction of political influence in this country. That's why David Garth of New York and lesser-known "image makers" collect fat fees from aspiring public servants who want to learn how to impress potential voters via television.

Getting back to the local level—my primary interest—I love the things I can accomplish as a streetwalker with a microphone and a camera. I sat in the local anchorman's chair for five and a half years; I have ad-libbed live, coast to coast on network newscasts, addressing maybe twenty million people at a time. There are worthwhile personal satisfactions in both of these arenas. Yet I always come back to the street, where I feel life is really going on, and where I have enough clout to do something about the things that roil me. The little movies I present on the tube each day can alleviate tension in a troubled neighborhood, initiate government action to ease the plight of a hungry family, bring heat to a cold tenement, launch official investigations of corrupt institutions, destroy popular misconceptions, reduce con artists' chances of fleecing unsuspecting sheep.

I taped a story a while ago about a hard-up couple in Brooklyn, unmarried teenagers with a sickly infant daughter. The guy had had a withered arm from birth and couldn't get a real job because of it, just handyman stuff here and there. Because they were teenagers with living parents somewhere, Charles and Terri were told by the Social Services Department that they were not eligible for welfare. After I introduced that couple and their baby on the tube, showed the miserable firetrap they lived in, and demonstrated on-camera how they cooked over a flaming tin can half filled with rubbing alcohol, the welfare agency suddenly found it possible to assist them. Several viewers mailed cash and checks to me to pass on to the needy couple.

More recently, I helped a distraught New Jersey housewife find her husband, who had disappeared after developing amnesia. A morning newspaper story had alerted my assignment desk, which sent me to interview the woman. Tearfully, she told a heartbreaking story on-camera. "Is there anything else I can do?" she asked, as I started to leave with my crew. "I've got to find him."

"My report," I said, "will include the photograph of your husband you showed us. It's my guess, based on similar cases, that if you call police stations in the neighboring towns and ask them to watch Channel Four tonight, they'll recognize him as somebody they've picked up in the past day or so."

Less than five minutes after my story aired, the woman got a call from the cops in nearby Newark. They had arrested her wandering spouse as a vagrant early that day. Happy ending.

When I choreograph a soulful dance like that, I feel more powerful and useful than any millionaire anchorperson. The problems they cover in the main—personally removed from the action—are much larger, more complex, and totally unyielding. Even Cronkite can't stop a war.

Prowling the streets gives me direct contact with all kinds of people, many of whom surprise me. A woman whose husband has been shot to death, a mother whose son has died of a drug overdose—mourners who, you might think, would prefer a decent interval of privacy—actually connive to talk with me on-camera. They yearn to share their heartaches with the rest of us. As Andy Warhol once observed, every man or woman—regardless of the scope of his or her life—still has a chance to be a star in this century, to be in the limelight for a fleeting moment.

To a large extent, Warhol was telling it like it is. I have been searching my soul for years over the question of how far I can go in rationalizing my Machiavellian approach to getting a story, deliberately taking advantage of an almost universal lust to appear on television. Yet very often when I suspect that I have gone too far, I have a close encounter with some true believers who willingly forgive my tresspasses, so long as I give them a chance to be embraced by the cold one-eyed monster at my command. They trust it. They trust the newsperson on the street. Why else would a FALN terrorist give himself up to Channel 4's Felipe Luciano? Why would a fugitive surrender on-camera to Channel 2's Chris Borgen? Why would a gunman holding a hostage in a church insist on being allowed to tell his woes to Channel 7's John Johnson? They did it because those newscasters and others like them have demonstrated on the tube that they are the kind of streetwise *mensches* who always get the story right; no bullshit. Their commentaries often reflect a healthy distrust of the establishment, and they are seen so regularly on the home screen that they are generally regarded as friends of the family.

I also have a few tales and observations about the off-camera

23

realities of that artificial family called the news team. On the air, we pretend to be closely knit kinfolk, with good old Dad the anchorman posing as the final arbitrator. Like real families, however, we are sometimes wracked by sibling rivalries, jealousies, and double crosses. When WCBS-TV's family learned that WABC-TV's hotshot sportscaster Warner Wolf was about to join their team at a salary of $450,000 a year—while most of them were hanging in there for less than a $100,000—it was hard to swallow their bile and say with a grin, "Welcome aboard, Mr. Wolf."

Another curious fact about the electronic family is our reaction when somebody among us is being threatened. If word gets out that a reporter or anchor is about to be eighty-sixed—jargon for "sacked"—we do not circle the wagons. Instead, the rest of us tapdance backward from ground zero. Fearing lethal fallout, or guilt by association, we rarely stand shoulder to shoulder with our brother or sister in trouble. Sad but true. The gold and the glory of news biz make cowards of us all.

Who encourages such rotten feelings? The deus ex machina in the Golden Ghetto. As one of my co-workers put it so bluntly, "To the big guys upstairs, we are just pieces of meat." They juggle our schedules, our work assignments, and lifestyles with godlike indifference, to see for themselves how each of us might bolster or weaken the family. They worry about and tamper with our haircuts, our diction, our clothes, our smiles. Being fat or homely is a no-no. The Empty Suits often seem a hell of a lot more interested in assembling a galaxy of sexy stars than they are in gathering news.

According to recent surveys, TV viewers watch more news than any other product on the air. Judging from the questions they ask me and my colleagues, in the mail and on the street, they'd like to know what goes on backstage. In the following pages, I will lift the curtain, revealing the funny, true, and ridiculous foibles that are inexorably linked with the creation, launching, and maintenance of broadcasting idols.

After giving you this detailed picture of news biz, I am also going to seize this opportunity to do something I've been burning to do for years: offer my own prescription—with passion and prejudice—for the sickness that afflicts this medium. My goal here is not

24

to effect an overnight cure single-handedly, but to provoke others to make thoughtful contributions toward that end. The time has come to stop offering alibis about "circumstances beyond our control."

Aside from a radical formula that would detoxify The Ratings, I also suggest less joking around in newscasts, less emphasis on the ghoulish details of a sadistic rape or dismemberment, more emphasis on the positive actions to improve the quality of life being taken by individuals, community organizations, and institutions, thereby encouraging others to follow suit. Also, I would like to see more in-depth follow-ups on the sensations we usually chronicle for two or three days, then drop forever.

WNBC-TV recently carried the kind of upbeat spot I'm plumping. It was a feature about unemployed teenagers who had been enlisted by the Harlem Rehabilitation Project. While being trained as stonemasons, they were helping to complete a neighborhood landmark, the unfinished Cathedral of St. John the Divine. Channel 4 also aired an inspiring piece about volunteers of all ages, races, and occupations who did a terrific job of cleaning up Central Park one day. Now doesn't that prove we can do it?

Local newscasting can and should become a much more relevant, informative, and positive adjunct to the democratic process. That is, it can give viewers the scope, depth, details, and perspective they need on current events to make intelligent decisions about their lives, their institutions, and their governments.

Viewers are entitled to good coverage of the chain reactions, small and large, that might affect their destinies, if not today, then maybe tomorrow or in the longer run. The kind of news show I am beating the drum for would grab you because it would mean something genuine to you. This kind of program, I submit, would not have to worry about The Ratings. If we do it right, the numbers will come. More importantly, no one would have an excuse for being uninformed or uninvolved. Only when we make these necessary renovations in news biz will we truly be doing our jobs.

1

From Print to Perversions

CONSIDERABLY WORSE THINGS had happened to me as a broadcaster—crazy things, by happenstance and design. But on November 20, 1980, I looked madness in the eye once too often.

For maybe fifteen minutes—while watching our 5:00–7:00 P.M. local newscast, "News 4 New York"—I ranted and cursed. "You bastards," I yelled to the world at large. I stood alone, shaking impotent fists, in my den on Central Park West. "You goddamn, no-good fuck-ups. You Empty Suits. Don't you know what the hell you're doing?"

Without warning, they had flushed a big story down the toilet—my story, an exclusive report, in the public interest, of a homicide in the Far Rockaway section of New York City. The Associated Press had Teletyped a version early that morning that suggested a racial vendetta. Radio reports, based on the AP synopsis, had charged the atmosphere in that neighborhood with fear, rumor, and suspicion. No other reporter—in print, radio, or television—had dug up the facts I had on my film, which would have lessened the tension between blacks and whites that developed that

27

day because of the killing. My report would have shown conclusively that the pizza baker who killed a black stranger with a 12-gauge shotgun the night before was not the triggerman in a white conspiracy, as widely believed—just one more lunatic in the naked city with a parallel history of violence against whites as well as blacks.

On the full-color screen in my brain, I saw hordes of misinformed blacks in Far Rockaway marching blindly toward Armageddon. Even if it didn't come down to that, I sensed, there was certain to be a qualitative, negative change in black and white relations. Snubs, insults, misunderstandings, and challenges would certainly develop in a thousand routine confrontations tomorrow.

Only a fraction of my rage was generated by the knowledge that most of these ugly probabilities could have been dispelled if my exclusive had been aired on Channel 4. Other sources of my discontent came into focus when I telephoned the WNBC-TV newsroom at the end of the two-hour news show on November 20. Associate producer Bob Campbell, explaining why my story had been eighty-sixed at the last minute, apologized. He said they definitely had been planning to run it, but while the show was on the air they discovered that they were seven and half minutes too long, and had to kill a lot of stuff.

With an effort, I suppressed an urge to reach through the phone and throttle the man. Two whole fucking hours and they didn't have time for my exclusive? I banged down the receiver, seething over the nonnews I had just watched:

A live interview with actor Larry Storch ("F Troop").
A live interview with actor Allan Fawcett ("The Edge of Night").
A live interview with author William Simon *(A Time for Truth)*.
A live interview with author Robert Massie *(Peter the Great)*.
A live interview with singer Vic Damone.
Videotape of Frank Rizzo, the former Philadelphia mayor, insulting a television newsman in Philadelphia.
Videotape of a $150 dollhouse being sold through alleged false advertising.
Videotape of athlete Ashrita Furman setting a world record for somersaults, covering thirteen miles in ten hours.

28

All of which made me ask myself for the umpteenth time whether a serious journalist could work in local TV news without eventually succumbing to apoplexy.

If my reaction strikes you as an overreaction, you may change your mind after I tell you some of the typical aggravations of my trade that I had managed to survive to get the story that never made the air.

On the phone, around 7:10 A.M., I learned from police at Central Booking in the 112th Precinct that our only chance to photograph the alleged killer would come at eight o'clock. He would be taken from his cell and put in a van with other overnight prisoners for a ride to criminal court for arraignment. My film crew—cameraman, soundman, and lighting tech—said they could not be ready to leave our headquarters in Rockefeller Center until eight—equipment problems.

Dammit. Central Booking was ten miles away, and I needed that picture. I appealed to assignment editor Jim Unchester to let me have the early videotape crew—Jerry Yarus and Joe Gafa.

Unchester explained that he had orders from the brass to save that crew for something else, and told me to just do the best I could.

My guts churned all the way to the police station as my cameraman-driver maneuvered the company sedan through rush-hour traffic. Hell, television news means pictures. If you are going to tell the story of a homicide, you need pictures of the victim and the alleged killer. A nightside crew, working without a reporter as usual, had filmed the body. No problem. I prayed that we would not be too late to get the gunman.

Luckily, he had not been moved when we arrived at the 112th Precinct at 8:25. Only still photographers from the *Daily News* and the *Post* were standing by with print reporters. No other TV crews. Rival TV stations had different priorities that morning, I supposed.

I had to beg four cops before I found one who could tell me how to recognize the alleged killer in the chained gang that momentarily would leave the station house.

We got him.

Somewhat relieved, I rode with my crew to the 101st Precinct in Far Rockaway, several miles east, to interview the arresting officer. He had gone off duty and was unavailable. Dammit, a key element of the story down the drain. I had to settle for reading his juiceless report, which didn't begin to answer the questions in my mind about the homicide.

After a few minutes of helpless fuming, I started combing the neighborhood where the shooting had occurred during the night, looking for witnesses. It took an hour and a half to find one. Yes, the guy said, he had seen the whole thing, but he wouldn't go on-camera. He didn't want to get involved in a race war. Off-camera, he told me enough to discredit the sketchy account that had come over the AP wire.

Minutes later, I found a woman who corroborated the first witness's version, but no on-camera. She also knew where the dead man's family lived, though she warned me not to go into the project without some kind of protection.

Dutifully, I apprised my crew of the potential risks. Wisely, they opted to wait in the car while I went in to check it out. Pulling a licensed automatic from my hip pocket—yes, I always carry a gun—I released the safety catch and pumped a .25 caliber round into the chamber. "If I don't come back in ten minutes," I said, "call the cops."

Climbing the dimly lit stairwell in the filthy, rundown tenement, I almost gagged on the stench of rancid garbage and urine. Between the second- and third-floor landings, my heart skipped a beat as I came upon a pair of scruffy-looking dudes just sitting there smoking marijuana. Their eyes smouldered with hostility. I hesitated, considering retreat, as my right hand tightened on the gun in the pocket of my trench coat. Without a word, the young toughs backed off, mistaking me, I think, for the fuzz.

On the fourth floor, I expressed my sympathy to the grieving widow. Gently, I cajoled her into locking her watchdog in the bedroom, silencing her parakeet by draping a tablecloth over its cage, going on-camera despite her unkempt appearance, and summoning seven neighbors, blacks and whites, who could tell me more about the pizza man who had zapped her husband. I went downstairs and returned with my three-man crew.

The pizza man, the neighbors told me, had been known to run

out of his shop with a gun, a hatchet, or a knife to threaten former customers as they walked down the street with takeout orders from his competitor just around the corner. In other words, the guy was a nutty shopkeeper with a short fuse, as the cops later confirmed by looking up old complaints.

With help from all of those sources, I put together a scenario that contained more facts and deductions than the police had at that point. I explained all of that to Campbell and to producer Mike Dreaden when I returned to the newsroom in mid-afternoon. They liked it—until they discovered that there were too many other elements, like interviews with celebrities, to fit into the show.

In my fury over their decision, I found no consolation in the fact that the same thing would happen to somebody else's solid story tomorrow and tomorrow and tomorrow. Over the years, I had listened to streetwalkers from all six TV stations in New York bitching about the higher priority given to fluff.

Furthermore, several other syndromes—equally hard to live with—had been gnawing at my guts since the sixties. Here, again, I was not alone. There was ample evidence of that from my travels across the country, from conversations with journalistic gypsies, from newspaper and magazine articles. Similar symptoms were debilitating local-TV news operations from St. Paul to Seattle, from San Francisco to Santa Fe, from St. Louis to Sarasota, from Savannah to Syracuse.

Coincidence had very little to do with it. The three networks' flagship stations in the communications capital of America are the bellwethers for affiliated and independent stations from here to yonder. Whatever any one of the "Big Three" does that succeeds in pumping up The Ratings coerces a legion of professional copycats. Thus it came as no great surprise when I learned that Al Primo, the *wunderkind* credited with creating the tremendously popular "Eyewitness News" concept for WABC-TV—a fun-and-games approach to local news—had since become a sought-after freelance consultant on television news to stations in fifteen other cities.

So what do you suppose would happen if one of the Big Three made an experimental leap forward by presenting the news in a circus format with the anchorperson dressed as a ringmaster?

31

   The operating dictum is, almost anything goes so long as it helps The Ratings. While fuming over my lost exclusive, I wondered whether that philosophy would ever fade. Would I ever get over the feeling of being a piano player in a whorehouse? Should I stand up on my hind legs and fight for reforms or walk away—back, perhaps, into the less-showy precinct of print? Gradually the answer came to me—piecemeal.

   There was no denying the facts of life. Sex appeal and gimmicks were inextricably imbedded in our sales-pitch culture—versatile, reliable come-ons for peddling anything from shoelaces to frozen vegetables. No wonder then that news biz was embracing them more and more, subordinating its original purpose in order to build numbers. Ergo, news biz and The Ratings were incompatible. A civilized divorce would be in order. True, almost any gambit, if examined by itself, could be excused, tolerated—like Winston the weather dog and the bearded promos. Unfortunately, each slice of such compromises bred escalating extravagances among competitors in pursuit of higher ratings, which often meant lower standards of professionalism. And bad taste.

   Against that background I began giving serious thought to trying to come up with a proposition (spelled out in the final chapter) for getting rid of The Ratings in news biz without being judged insane.

   Ironically, I had been nominated for the loony bin a generation before, for quite different reasons, by pragmatists on the University of Wisconsin football squad. Otherwise, they deemed, I would not have dropped out of criminology to major in journalism. Mine had been the the only dark face in the journalism class of 1950. I was going to become a newspaper reporter, of course, not a TV star. Hell, television had scarcely been born. And the doors to every branch of the media were virtually sealed and booby-trapped against nonwhite intruders. The smart ones chose more promising academic avenues—medicine, law, education, engineering, or social work. Although the odds were stacked the wrong way, I told my skeptical teammates I had to gamble. They were flabbergasted when I won.

Football made the difference. As an all–Big Ten running back—number two in ground gaining in the Western Conference in my senior season—I was offered a by-line on my hometown paper, the *Milwaukee Journal,* about four months prior to graduation. Over the next four years, I wrote sports, news, book reviews, and editorial-page features. After a two-year hitch in the army during the Korean War, I joined the staff of the *New York Times,* starting in the fall of 1956. I had figured on staying there forever, unless something truly extraordinary came along. Then one day in the spring of 1961, I got a call from WCBS-TV. Somebody wanted to know if I might be interested in switching to television reporting on Channel 2.

"I'd certainly like to talk about it," I replied noncommittally, not at all eager to surrender a comfortable berth on one of the most respected sheets in the country.

On the following Tuesday, I met vice-president Ernie Leiser in a roomful of executives at CBS headquarters over Grand Central Station. Leiser did most of the talking. He was a tall, gaunt man with a somber face and down-to-earth manner that made me think of old woodblock prints of Honest Abe. Leiser had been admiring my prose in the *Times,* he said. I seemed to be just the bright young black they had been scouting for to break the color barrier. (WABC-TV had put Mal Goode on the air a year or so earlier, but Goode's hair was so straight and his skin so white that his arrival had been virtually unnoticed.) After referring quite parenthetically to a starting salary of $200 a week, Leiser waxed long and eloquently on the sociological significance of the daring move his station was prepared to make. The time had come to ignore the wrath of unenlightened elements who would object to my presence on the tube. "A wonderful opportunity for you, Bob."

He also made it sound exciting. I wanted the job. I was not swayed, however, by his Lincolnesque rhetoric on peripheral issues. After ten minutes of listening, I interrupted the vice-president. "Could we stop talking sociology for a moment and talk about money?"

The eight or ten faces in the conference room turned red and sour. Jaws dropped in disapproval and astonishment.

"Now the hard fact is," I plowed on bluntly, "I'm making two hundred thirty-four dollars a week at the *Times*. It's the best paper in the country and I'm really quite happy over there. So any move I make would have to be up, not down, as you suggest, or lateral."

I don't recall Leiser's exact words. He made it perfectly clear, though, that he and his colleagues regarded me as an arrogant, ungrateful upstart. He terminated the job interview right there.

Nearly two years after my interview with Leiser at Channel 2, I more or less sneaked through the color barrier at Channel 4, by accident, with a solid assist from sociology. I mean, getting the job was subtly related to television's inadvertently persuasive coverage of black demands for a piece of the action in the early sixties. After seeing countless examples of unconscious racial bias reported on their own screens, news-biz executives were beginning to realize that they were equally unconscious.

Now for the accident part. In December 1962, all seven newspapers in New York City were shut down by a printers' union strike. During the print blackout, which lasted over four months, the flagship stations of all three networks expanded their local news coverage. They also beefed up their staffs by hiring out-of-work reporters whose by-lines were familiar. I was part of a so-called Young Turks movement at the *Times*. Along with John Corry, Gay Talese, Robert Lipsyte, and John Pomfret, I had been brought to the paper to enliven the drab print skirts of the Great Gray Lady of Times Square. Our reputations, at the time of the strike, were impressive. So WNBC-TV hired me and forty other print refugees—over the telephone—as temporary Channel 4 newswriters. The fact that my skin resembled dark-brown leather didn't come up, you see, since print journalists aren't pictured in the *Times*.

Quite frequently during the long strike, the TV assignment desk was forced to use some of us temporaries as streetwalkers to back up Gabe Pressman and the small all-male staff of regulars. That didn't happen every day; sometimes there was a week between excursions with a TV film crew. After finishing our writing stints for radio and television newscasts, we camped around the central newsdesk, praying, waiting for assignment editor Bob McCarthy's beckoning finger. It was agonizing when he looked past me to someone else hunched and poised in the starting blocks. The rules of the game allowed no overt protest. Frustration with a capital F.

Eventually, though, with help from Pressman, Bill Ryan, and Joe Michaels, I developed enough skill to become one of McCarthy's favorites. A local news executive, Elmer Lower, summoned me to his office one afternoon. "I've been watching you on the tube," he began expansively. I could almost feel a pat on the back. "I want you to think about not going back to the *Times* when the strike is over. You're green as pickles, but you've got presence on-camera, and you know how to tell a story. You could have a real future in television; maybe double your newspaper salary in a year or two."

I told him I would think about it.

A week or so later, having discussed it with close friends and the woman to whom I was then married, I made up my mind. First, I paid a visit to the *Times,* which was still feeding copy to its Paris edition, unaffected by the strike. Editor James Roach, expressing personal regrets over my defection, wished me luck. Then I went to Elmer Lower's office off the newsroom at WNBC-TV. "What did you want to see him about?" his secretary, Bobby, asked, a bewildered look on her face.

"About . . . well, Mr. Lower offered me a permanent job here the other day. I came back to tell him I'm accepting it."

Bobby looked down at her typewriter, embarrassed. "I'm sorry. Mr. Lower isn't here any more. He went over to Channel Seven yesterday."

I felt myself plunging feet-first into a deep, dark abyss.

Sympathetic to my plight, the young secretary made a couple of discreet inquiries on the telephone. Mr. Lower, she reported afterward, had not informed anyone else of his offer to me; nothing had been left in writing.

I wondered if I were eligible for welfare.

During the next few weeks, trapped in a valley of depression, I must have kicked myself a thousand times. Inspired by pain and disillusionment, I formulated an iron-clad rule: in TV news, never hitch your wagon to a rabbi; reach the stars or the pits on your own.

Fortunately for me, the newspaper strike continued well into

April. Just before it ended, I got the accolades I had been hoping for. My air work had impressed news manager Buck Prince, news director Dick Kutzleb, and producer Henrick Krogius, among others. So in the spring of 1963, I became a proud card-carrying member of the NBC News team, one of three black journalists on the tube at different stations that year. (By March 1980, racial minorities were on the tube almost everywhere, holding 2,052 professional jobs in commercial TV in a work force of 13,471 surveyed by the Federal Communications Commission.)

Although blessed with a staff position in 1963, nothing was said at the time about signing a contract—the only real talisman in the trade. I remained in the writers' pool, preparing radio and TV copy for established stars to read—Frank McGee, Edwin Newman, Bob Wilson, John K. M. McCaffery. After a full day on the copydesk, I worked a second shift on the street, beginning well before sunrise. I did not complain. Hell, I was becoming a New York celebrity. And every spot on the air I managed to get meant twenty-five extra dollars in my paycheck.

Pretty soon I was spending more time in the field and less time in the newsroom. I was on my way. Then one of those built-in booby traps blew up in my face.

It happened at the end of a typical fourteen-hour grind. I was leaving the shop when Kutzleb stopped me to say there was a big story breaking on Staten Island that he wanted me to cover.

Jesus H. Christ. "Have a heart, Dick," I groaned. "I've been at it since four A.M. I'm bushed."

"Okay," the man said equably. "I'll get somebody else."

Now, there, I told myself with a sense of relief, was a real human being, not one of those executive bullies. Like my college football coach, Kutzleb understood that the best way to get the most out of a man was to treat him like a man.

Boy was I dumb. For the next six weeks, I couldn't buy an assignment on the street; I was reassigned to full-time chores in the writers' pool. After my writing stints, I spent long empty hours at Bob McCarthy's feet, day after day, week after week, puzzled. Why had the assignment editor changed his mind about me? In my naiveté, I never guessed that I was being punished. Kutzleb finally explained—after my six-week sentence in limbo had been served.

Something in my personal computer whirled and clicked. The printout in my head was frightening. Having fled from print, I had stumbled into a brave new world run by men who had perfected the art of pissing in your face while telling you it's raining.

A lot of unpleasant, unfair things had also been happening to many of my teammates at the time, like unreasonably long hours and sudden changes in the work schedule that bounced them from one odd shift to another. This was something you learned to live with. Even when you are a star, you can be presented with a pink slip. Things change so rapidly in news biz, you come to expect the worst, and you are pleased when you manage to get by in spite of it. I theorized in my first year that I could perhaps protect myself by working harder than my peers and by keeping a low profile in the newsroom; by regarding TV executives as potential sources of trauma; by trusting no one above the rank of reporter.

Walking away from it all never crossed my mind in those days. The money was just too damned good. Fame was downright seductive. I am reminded of what Sander Vanocur wrote in *Esquire* magazine after resigning from NBC News several years ago. He characterized NBC television as "a very paternalistic" corporation. "Big Mother," he called it, switching genders. "She feeds you rather more than you need for your own good . . . and punishes you . . . you tend to feel that you must not do anything or say anything that she will not approve. The result was that commentators became subordinate to producers, who in turn were being second-guessed by the management."

I can't tell you all the reasons why I managed to survive in that environment for so many years—how much of it was my talent and dedication and how much was luck or sociology. Anyway, I finally signed a $30,000 contract about a year and a half after joining the news team. How did I nail down that elusive, coveted piece of paper? With the assistance of the Republican convention in San Francisco in the summer of 1964. I was on loan to the network team, and most of my assignments were live.

If you remember your insecurity the first time you made love—like a tightrope walker with the hiccups—you have a good idea of what it is like to do your first ten live telecasts from the trenches. One of my maiden ten came *that* close to aborting my career on the tube. What saved me, I think, was the fact that I didn't have too much time to brood about the possibility of coming off like a nerd.

We had two live units on location at the St. Francis Hotel one day during the prenomination phase of the convention. Correspondent Elie Abel was on the third floor of the hotel for the hearings being conducted by the GOP platform committee. My unit was on the sidewalk near the main entrance. I was supposed to cover threatened demonstrations by San Francisco radicals aimed at intimidating the policymakers inside.

As Chet Huntley and David Brinkley opened the live telecast from their glass anchor booth in the Cow Palace miles away, my location was practically deserted. Not a single picket in sight—only a handful of cops and pedestrians. What a relief. All I had to do was enjoy the show on the TV monitor sitting on the pavement near my TK-41 camera.

Maybe seven or eight minutes into the show, something went wrong. Huntley called for a live switch to Elie Abel. On the monitor, I saw the picture change. Elie was mouthing words that were not going out over the air. Somebody in the NBC control van parked near the hotel had forgotten to give him a mike.

"We'll have to come to you in about ten seconds," director Chet Hagan advised me over the telex stuck in my ear. "Just keep talking for three or four minutes. That'll give us time to run a mike up to Elie's location."

"But there's nobody here," I protested. "Absolutely nothing going on."

Ignoring my bleatings, the director counted me down to air. "In five, four, three, two . . . you're on!"

I felt trapped, wired to an electronic monster that wanted to destroy me, with literally millions looking on, which made me angry enough to fight back. I took one deep breath and started talking, calmly, deliberately, giving myself a chance to think—to dredge up everything I had heard or read about the San Francisco radicals who had advertised intentions to disrupt the platform hearings and everything I had learned about the various planks being measured for the Goldwater platform.

Half a lifetime later, the director cooed in my ear. "Okay, Bob. You can wrap it up now. Elie has a mike."

Without skipping a beat, I announced, "We switch now to correspondent Elie Abel at the platform committee hearings inside the Saint Francis Hotel."

Elie came on. I was off, feeling limp and drained but elated. I had ad-libbed three and a half minutes without a flub!

"Attaboy, Bob," the director said with a chuckle. "You saved our ass."

Music, music, music. I admitted to myself that I craved that kind of approval. It meant a lot to me to be the kind of person who could be relied on to save his teammates' asses in the clutch.

Back in New York and under contract, my air time and reputation grew. Wherever I went, people recognized me, made a fuss. Important men wanted to hear my opinions. Women suddenly found me sexy. Headwaiters always managed to find a good table. Sometimes the adulation was cloying. The lack of privacy in public can be a pain in the rump. But what could I do? From my fans' points of view, they had a right to intrude, as I had done in their homes almost nightly. I also came to appreciate that their interest in me had much to do with how well and how long I might maintain my position among the stars. As some wise old head summed it up long ago, "If you want to take credit for the sunshine, you gotta take credit for the rain."

Through the eyes of my fans, I began to perceive that being a television newsman gave me the kind of glamour generally associated with talk-show hosts and actors. My shadow, appearing so regularly in their living rooms, had created what they regarded as an intimate relationship. As Norman Mailer said when we bumped into each other at a restaurant, "I feel I already know you. That's the trouble with television. It takes all the impact out of meeting somebody in person."

The rewards of recognition and trust are counterbalanced by

the heights of bullshit you have to scale in this business. The Empty
Suits are forever setting up hurdles and roadblocks because, in their
eyes, whatever you are doing has to be wrong if The Ratings aren't
right. No part of any failure is ever attributed to bad decisions by
management. They see no harm in promoting the notion that covering the news is less significant than persuading more viewers to
tune in, as if news coverage were a mere by-product in the process
of building up The Ratings—like our sterling coverage of the crash
of Flight 66 at Kennedy Airport. Reporter Anthony Prisendorf, taping a less important story near the airport, beat the opposition to
the grisly scene—bodies all over the place in bits and pieces.
Reporting live from the edge of the smouldering wreckage, he
showed and described the efforts of rescue teams as they picked up
the dead and tried to bring comfort to the dying. A superb job; a
legitimate use of the live camera. "All I had to do," Prisendorf said
later, "was tell what I saw and keep myself from vomiting." The
executive producer, congratulating the reporter, said, "Do you know
what your coverage did for our ratings? If we had a plane crash like
that every day, it would put us over the top."

If you think that's an odd assessment of a tragedy, let me tell
you about one of the WNBC vice-presidents and The Ratings. He
came storming out of his office into the newsroom one morning with
a copy of the latest local news ratings in hand. Our "Sixth Hour"
newscast was languishing at 2.8, the equivalent of maybe no viewers
at all except our immediate families and Nielsen's tattletales.
Approaching assignment editor Dick Lobo, he growled like a
wounded bear. "Have you seen this? We've got to do better than
this," he bawled. "From now on, I want you to get more blood and
guts, more sex and violence on the program. But if you tell anybody
I said so, I'll deny it."

I do not subscribe to NBC superstar Tom Snyder's theory that
all television executives are clones from some live-remote island in
the South Pacific. It is my belief that when they come into news biz,
they are much like the average above-average human being—intelligent, knowledgeable, competent, determined, and forthright. By
his or her second or third day on the job, however, the neophyte is
conducted to an arcane ritual in the Golden Ghetto. An exorcism.

Somebody with unlimited corporate power shows him a printout on The Ratings while explaining the numbers in the funereal tones of an undertaker. Presto! He is diminished. The first thing to go is common sense, then vision, taste, initiative, and guts. What's left is an Empty Suit, a slave to the A. C. Nielsen Company and the American Research Bureau, better known as Arbitron. The Ratings compiled by their computers are statistical estimates based on the number of homes, locally or nationally, having television sets. Thus, a rating of 20 for a network sitcom indicates that 20 percent of the seventy-six million American homes with TV sets were tuned to that particular program. A share, on the other hand, is the size of the audience compared with the number of homes actually watching television at that hour. Thus, a 32 share means that 32 percent of all homes watching television at that hour were tuned to the program in question, a respectable share of the available audience.

Nielsen monitors twelve hundred households with its infamous "black box"—the Storage Instantaneous Audimeter. The audimeter is wired to the on-off and channel selector buttons on the household television set. The black box records the programs watched by the household. It does not take notice of how many members of the home may be watching at any time. A telephone number is assigned to the audimeter. Nielsen's computer dials the number in the middle of the night to retrieve the information about household viewing habits. For three cities—New York, Chicago, and Los Angeles—ratings are available overnight, national figures somewhat later.

In addition to the electronic rating system, Nielsen also pays twenty-four hundred households to keep weekly diaries of their viewing habits. The information they provide is more detailed, giving age, sex, and viewing times for each family member and each TV set in the house. The families are selected at random from the telephone book, but they are forbidden to reveal their Nielsen connection to television stations, the press, or almost anybody else.

The three major networks each spend up to $2 million a year for Nielsen ratings. Advertisers and ad agencies also pay for the service. The company has annual revenues of $35 million from its TV rating service, enjoying a monopoly at the network level.

Local television stations use Arbitron as well as Nielsen, or

Arbitron alone. That company does electronic monitoring in 208 so-called market areas, defined as "Areas of Dominant Influence" of television stations. For the most part, the ADIs correspond with the Designated Market Areas used by Nielsen. New York City is the number-one market in both systems, with an estimated 6.4 million TV homes in the metropolitan area, which means that each rating point represents about 144,000 viewers. The larger the audience, the larger the advertising revenue.

The arithmetic of news biz had never occurred to me at the time I got sucked into the tube. Even when I learned, numbers of that magnitude seemed incomprehensible. I was too busy making money and becoming famous while doing something I believed in, something important. I didn't notice at first that television news was going crazy to the point of being an embarrassment, like a situation comedy with a laugh track that giggled at the wrong punch lines. There was just so much for a new bird dog to learn.

In the early sixties, there really wasn't much formal training. You had to pick it up out there on the street. Once in a while, an old pro would take you aside and coach you on how to get the story and how to film it. "Wait a minute," he would say. "This is all wrong. The idea is good, but you need less of that and more of this." In local news coverage, the guiding maxims were dump and jump, grab and stab (with a microphone). You did not have time, with rare exceptions, for full preparation and research. The story was happening right now. You had to improvise as you went along, enlisting strangers to aid and abet your purposes at the scene. It is still like that today.

One of the trailblazers on the streets of New York, Gabe Pressman, had given me pointers in my early days. Gabe had started at Channel 4 in 1953. He taught me, for example, the advantage of talking with the interviewee off-camera for a couple of minutes when feasible. "That way," he said, "you find out what the guy has to say, how he thinks, where the bullshit is. Then you tell your cameraman to start rolling, and you limit your questions to the areas where you know the good stuff is. Of course, in the heat of a story that's unfolding at the moment, you don't have time for a preinter-

42

view. You don't even want it. I mean, if a guy has just come running out of a burning building, staggering and gasping for air, you roll the film right off the bat—catch him while his juices are still boiling. You simply shove the mike in his face, asking the simplest questions: What was it like in there? What happened? What went through your mind at that moment? And right there you have the guts of the story in a matter of seconds."

Under Pressman's guidance, I learned the difference between the kind of news coverage that grabs people and what he called cosmetic journalism: the difference between detached announcements by well-rehearsed anchors reading TelePrompTers in the studio and the hurly-burly of personal involvement on the street. In national news coverage, the network correspondent is of necessity more of a bystander, a stranger far from home among strangers. Not for me. I chose Pressman as my role model, without the privileges that went with his seniority. As a beginner, I had to be as flexible as a rubber doll—going wherever I was sent and doing whatever I was told. It took several years to reach Pressman's status where I too could say, "Hell, that's not a legitimate story."

Why would anyone want you to do nonnews in the first place? Because high stakes spawn high anxiety in the Golden Ghetto, especially during the "sweeps" every February, May, and November when Nielsen and Arbitron make their audience surveys. The results determine how much money local TV stations in over two hundred cities may charge advertisers for a thirty-second spot—big bucks or bigger bucks—which cause Empty Suits to develop greater appetites for audience-grabbers like sex and violence, a week-long series if possible. NBC producer Steve Friedman told a *New York Times* critic, only half facetiously, that the ideal promotion for a feature story during the sweeps would go like this: "Rape, pillage, and destruction. Details at eleven."

The 1980 November sweeps were exactly in keeping with that formula. The WCBS-TV 6:00 P.M. and 11:00 P.M. newscasts advertised the following series:

"Incest—The Last Taboo"
"Battered Parents"

43

"Beyond the Pill"
"Teenage Suicide"
"Child Molesting"
WCBS-TV finished first at 11:00 P.M. by a skinny one-tenth of a point in The Ratings and narrowed WABC-TV's first-place edge at 6:00 P.M.

During the February sweeps of 1981, WABC tried to regain lost points with similar offerings. Ernie Anastos did a series on "Walking Time Bombs," about the violence committed by mentally unbalanced New Yorkers. In a series on "Gambling," Roger Grimsby explained how anybody could make an illegal bet. Storm Field did a series on how to recognize and prevent heart attacks. Rose Ann Scamardella delineated the tragedy of old age in a series called "The Life and Times of the Elderly in America."

WNBC, my station, fought back on the same level. Pia Lindstrom explained "How Crime Affects the Elderly." Connie Collins delved into psychic healing and life after death in a series entitled "Is There Something There?" Gabe Pressman played back a lot of file footage of major fires in a series on inadequate safety codes for high-rise buildings.

I am not quarreling over these subjects or their contents on the air. What I object to is the practice of deliberately overloading local news shows with such material during the sweeps, for reasons that have little or nothing to do with the higher tenets of journalism. The decision to run a series on such subjects ought to be closely related to current happenings that give them timeliness and perspective. Furthermore, the week-long emphasis on such lengthy features— from four to seven minutes per segment—invariably means drastic cutbacks in hard-news coverage during the sweeps.

Regardless of whether those "grabbers" made the whole difference in any station's ratings, there is no escaping the reality that what is aired during the sweeps does not reflect the true nature of the news program, nor the true number of viewers for the regular newscast between the sweeps. Among other reasons, each New York station spends about $100,000 to advertise their grabbers during that period. Secondly, entertainment shows are juggled and hyped, affecting the newscasts that precede or follow them in the lineup. In the November 1980 sweeps for example, WCBS-TV's 11:00 P.M. news show undoubtedly benefited from the "Who Shot J.R.?" hype for the "Dallas" soap opera that aired in New York at 10:00 P.M. WCBS averaged 755,000 homes at 11:00 P.M. that month, compared with 736,000 for WABC and 710,000 for WNBC. At 6:00 P.M., WABC averaged 704,000 homes, followed by WCBS with 640,000 and WNBC with 563,000.

It's a very big game indeed, compounded by the fact that TV viewers are so fickle. As Richard Salant, the former CBS News president, once observed, "Television is a superficial medium, made so by the short attention span of a peripatetic audience."

Salant, subsequently moved over to the NBC network as vice-chairman, continuing to heed The Ratings and that peripatetic audience!

The wary TV newsperson, I decided early on, treads a careful line between being a nuts-and-bolts reporter and being an entertainer. By giving them a little razzmatazz from time to time you can boost what I call your Survival Quotient. One of my gimmicks was being the first air man in New York to cover soft-news stories in rhyme.

I further bolstered my SQ by periodically doing feature stories as parodies of soap operas and sitcoms, complete with their theme music. As a rule, I received more applause from management for my clever stuff than I did for genuine hard-news exclusives. I got the message. They will love you for being witty and entertaining. They will love you for winning small crusades for human dignity. But they subtract a lot of points if you try to tell a truth that might compel viewers to reevaluate a conventional piece of nonsense.

One of my unforgettable defeats on that front occurred during the gasoline shortage. I did a piece about the long waiting lines and the hundreds of service stations that had posted No Gas signs at the pumps. This was the day President Jimmy Carter dumped James R. Schlesinger as secretary of energy. When the camera zoomed in on me for my closing stand-upper, I said, "Schlesinger's departure may not necessarily mean more gasoline for your car. His successor's claim to fame is peddling nonoctane Coca-Cola in large quantities." That was not exactly a revolutionary comment, just a reminder to the viewers that some of the games played by politicians are a mixture of placebos and bullshit. Before I could put it on the air, however, Carole Clancy objected. "That's commentary," she cried, making it sound like something subversive. Since Clancy was a newcomer at WNBC-TV, I tried to reason with her.

"I know," I said patiently. "That's why I'm telling you in advance. There's a company rule on commentary, but we are allowed to make fair comment and poke a little fun so long as we don't libel anybody."

Clancy still wouldn't buy it and urged me to do another stand-upper saying something else.

In spite of my long-standing vow to keep a low profile in the presence of heavy-hitters, I lost my cool. I growled at the woman, flatly refusing to cosmeticize my scenario. I was mad as hell. Why should I put up with that? At that point in time, I had been cranking out news spots and commentaries for over sixteen years without incurring a single lawsuit.

The executive producer brought up reinforcements: Jeff Rosser, number two in the newsroom chain of command. When he echoed Clancy's suggestion, something inside me ducked and cringed. "Okay, I'll be happy to do a new stand-upper," I conceded through clenched teeth, "though I have to admit that I can't think of any other way to wrap the story. Just tell me what you guys want me to say. I'll go back out with the camera crew and say it."

Neither Rosser nor Clancy could offer a single alternative. After staring blankly at each other, they erased the problem by cutting me out of the tape altogether. It went on the air as silent pictures of gas lines, voiced over by anchorman Chuck Scarborough. Nobody was irritated by that bland piece, inside or outside of the medium, except me.

Admittedly, the question of how much latitude a reporter should be allowed in a given situation is tricky and complex. I think a reasonable approach would be to insist that producers keep young pups under close surveillance; challenge them to verify their facts and justify their commentaries prior to going on the air. If they do so consistently over a span of, say, three years, treat them like seasoned bird dogs: turn them loose. Sooner or later, news executives should either trust their reporters or replace them with ones they can. I am reminded of the Woodward-Bernstein Watergate exposé in the *Washington Post*. In the early stages, when other newspapers and government officials were trying to knock down those shocking allegations, Ben Bradlee looked at the team's track record and decided "to go with the boys."

Of course, there are a few television honchos who are not conscientious cowards or mercenaries. I had the privilege of working under a couple of them during the sixties: Robert Kintner, then president of NBC, and William McAndrew, then president of NBC News. They cared about solid news coverage rather than gossip, wisecracks, and sensationalism. They were not afraid to make decisions that cost money or put the network's reputation on the line. They gave us grunts the respect we earned as professionals and backed us up with the resources we needed to get the work done. Kintner was widely known in the business as "the managing editor" because of his preoccupation with news, having once been a grunt in print himself. Significantly, both Kintner and McAndrew had extensive backgrounds as working newsmen in broadcasting as well as print.

There was a telling incident in the mid-1960s. Frank McGee just happened to be in the corridor that skirts the executive suite, waiting for an elevator, when he overheard a primeval shouting match between NBC chairman Robert Sarnoff and Kintner.

"Sarnoff was saying the stockholders were unhappy about the size of their dividends, and he was going to cut the budget for the news division [of the RCA conglomerate]. Kintner wouldn't hear of it. He reminded Sarnoff that it was the news division's integrity and credibility that had bailed us out in the late fifties when the quiz show scandal damn-near ruined NBC. The next think I knew," McGee went on, "Kintner came charging out of the chairman's office like an angry bull. Through the open door I could see Sarnoff standing there with blood all over his face. 'What happened?' I asked. Kintner answered without breaking stride. He said, 'I had to punch that sonofabitch in the nose.' "

It was reassuring to see Kintner and McAndrew walking among us in the newsroom, asking intelligent questions, making helpful suggestions, dispensing praise and rebukes where deserved. Then in 1966 Kintner accepted a White House appointment as special assistant to President Lyndon Johnson. McAndrew died in 1968. Without them, effective control of our network and local-news operations shifted to a different breed in the corporate structure—anonymous committees of cost-accounting overseers. They seldom deigned to visit the newsroom. According to scuttlebut, they didn't even know where it was. Unlike Kintner and McAndrew, they guided us primarily on the basis of the numbers they read on profit-and-loss statements, slide rules, computers, and The Ratings. Justly, we gradually lost our number-one position in television news. By February 1970, our local six o'clock broadcast had slipped to second place with a Nielsen 9, compared with WCBS's leading 13 and WABC's trailing 7. In the same month two years later, WABC led with a 12, followed by WCBS at 8 and WNBC at 5. From then into the fall of 1980, that pattern persisted with the two rival stations jockeying for the lead while we played "Tailend Charlie."

Throughout those long seasons of ignominy, a death wish developed in the pits—a perverse desire to see our ratings plunge even faster, in the hope that the Empty Suits who had maneuvered us into a tailspin would be wiped out in the crash. Pride in ourselves and our profession ruled out sabotage. However, a number of disenchanted grunts in the newsroom, the editing rooms and among the camera crews in the field lost some of their zest, giving much less than the customary 110 percent to the team.

So why did an old bird dog like me keep coloring his gray hairs and tackling every assignment as if it were the biggest story of the year? Personal pride was certainly a factor, along with the feeling that good work was my shield. Beyond that, out there in the field, I was still having fun chasing corpses, controversies, and catastrophes with a camera crew. What an intoxicating ego trip. I was the screenwriter, director, narrator, and the star in hundreds of mini-movies a year. I was amazed, amused, and adrenalized by the menagerie of personalities I encountered. I was also a sex symbol with clout.

2

A Star Is Porn

ON THE WAY TO BECOMING A STAR in the firmament of news biz, you are constantly amazed at what it takes to negotiate square one. And, once there, what is required to avoid sudden pratfalls through the exit chute, nearly all of which come under the heading of circumstances beyond your control, totally unrelated to your ability or productivity. Sadly, little can be done about changing all of that so long as everything else in news biz is subordinate to The Ratings.

If a news director has a choice between job applicants—one with brains and experience, the other with less expertise but more raw sex appeal—you'd better believe he will go for the person most likely to sex-ceed. How you look, how you come across on the tube is twice as important as anything else about you. That simple criterion can be complicated, however, by conflicting, changing perceptions of pulchritude among fickle viewers and fickle Empty Suits at your station. One may decide that your hair is too long. Another will suggest that you wear contact lenses because your eyes are too blue for the camera. I am not making this up. I was there when reporter Marjorie Margolis—a raven-haired "ten" by any reasonable standard—was ordered to hide her long tresses under a short, matronly wig. Mary Alice Williams was the reporter with the eyes too blue. More recently, I was there when reporter Dave Gilbert responded to a memo directing him to the executive suite for a private evaluation by Ron Kershaw and Ray Meyer.

"I was expecting something really heavy," Dave said later. "Like maybe they were going to tell me I wasn't digging up enough to give my stories more depth. Or that my stand-uppers didn't have enough punch.

"Anyway, when I got in there, they ran one of my stories on a playback machine. It looked okay to me. Then they told me what was wrong, saying absolutely nothing about my reporting. 'Dave, we both agree on this,' Meyer said very seriously. 'That part in the middle of your hair—it ought to be a couple of inches to the left.' End of critique. I couldn't believe it."

Yes, Dave moved his part to the left.

I was also there when Bill Ryan was ejected from the anchorman's chair in 1965 because somebody decided that his ears stuck out too far from his head. Ryan's ears looked exactly as they had when he first sat in that chair in 1963; neither did they change during the next two years while he and co-anchor Gabe Pressman dominated the local news ratings on "The Pressman-Ryan Report." His ears were simply reappraised in 1965.

Thus began the convoluted evolution of our 6:00 P.M. newscast—sometimes for the better, usually for the worse. Next came "The Sixth Hour News" anchored by Robert MacNiel and later Jim Hartz (1965–71); followed by "News 4 New York" anchored by Sander Vanocur (1971–72); "The Sixth Hour" anchored by Lew Wood (1972–74); then "Newscenter 4," a two-hour format anchored by Paul Udell and former Cleveland Mayor Carl Stokes (1974–76); Tom Snyder and Chuck Scarborough (1976–77); Scarborough and Tony Guida (1977–78); Scarborough and Jack Cafferty (1978–79); Scarborough and Sue Simmons (1980); revised a few months later to "News 4 New York" with Scarborough and John Hambrick (1980).

Meanwhile, the 5:00–6:00 P.M. segment of the two-hour program and the half-hour 11:00 P.M. newscasts were undergoing similar shake-ups. (Ours was the only New York station with a two-hour newscast until late 1981. Channel 7 joined NBC in a two-hour format between 5:00 and 7:00. Channel 2 followed suit several weeks later. All three networks broadcast a half-hour show at 11:00 P.M.) Some of the same anchors listed above bounced from show to show, along with Pia Lindstrom, George Page, John Palmer, Felipe Luciano, Will Spens, Carol Jenkins, Ralph Penza, and me.

Only our 11:00 P.M. show was strong enough in head-to-head competition to periodically wrest the lead from Channels 2 and 7 in the 1970s. Our 6:00 P.M. show floundered in third place, which made management nervous and capricious.

NBC's headquarters are in the fifty-two-story RCA Building in Rockefeller Center. If you rode an elevator down from the top, stopping on each floor to read the departmental directories posted on the walls, you would get the impression that there were very few Indians among the fifteen hundred occupants of our teepee—mostly chiefs. Beneath the board of directors for the parent corporation, RCA, there is an NBC board of directors, 7 presidents, 9 executive vice-presidents; 112 vice-presidents, and a boatload of managers, supervisors, and producers who run the news operation. In other words, if you are lucky enough to land a job as a news reporter or anchorperson, you have to keep an awful lot of heavy-hitters happy.

As a rookie streetwalker in the early sixties, I had no idea of what I had stumbled into. To a large extent, some of the protocols, professional standards, and expectations I had learned in print had bent my mind into the wrong shape for television.

When I started back in the early fifties as a cub reporter in Milwaukee, I was a one-man band, so to speak. All I needed was a ball-point pen, a notepad, enough *chutzpah* to walk up to strangers and ask questions, and the ability to type forty words a minute. A piece of cake. Then in sixty-three, I was suddenly tossed into the maelstrom. I had to learn what could and could not be done with 16mm movie cameras, 600-watt quartz lights and Frezzolini lamps, RFM wireless and lavaliere microphones, film and videotape, live remotes, writing for the ear instead of the eye, plus a whole bunch of technical stuff. I had to learn how to coordinate whatever I did with a battalion of support personnel, in the field, the newsroom, and the studio control complex.

Furthermore, I had to adjust my thinking to the fact that in this medium, words mattered a hell of a lot less than pictures. That meant finding ways to show the essence of the story as well as tell it. As I observed or heard an important scrap of information, I had to think simultaneously of what kind of pictures I could ask my camera crew to take to illustrate it. This often meant climbing four flights of stairs to the roof of a cold-water tenement in Flatbush; wading knee-deep in the flooded streets of Lodi, New Jersey; descending into sewers; or waiting four hours for morgue attendants to remove a body from the murder scene.

During my ten years in print, at the *Milwaukee Journal* and the *New York Times,* the rule had been objective reporting: keep yourself out of the story. Just the facts, ma'am. In news biz, the rule was get involved. Show yourself in the news-gathering process; poke through the rubble of a collapsed apartment building; offer comfort to a bereaved widow; walk through the scene of a crime and recreate the events you are describing; demonstrate with your own head how a new gadget or a different technique is supposed to kill people or save their lives. In short, I had to become a credible performer, a movie actor.

And great God in the foothills! I had to learn how to talk all over again. Once or twice a week during my first two years at Channel 4, I spent a couple of evenings with a famous speech therapist, Liz Dixon, at the station's expense. Several of my teammates were getting the same training, including a few with much more experience than I, among them Gabe Pressman, Lew Wood, Edwin Newman, and Frank Field. Even now, a decade and a half later, I still have to find time to run through the voice exercises Liz taught me—ten or fifteen minutes every morning to reinforce the habit of speaking from my diaphragm instead of my throat; to consistently buzz my plural endings, elongate my vowels, chop off my consonants, vary the color and pitch of my tone.

The Big Three flagship stations in New York still provide that kind of coaching for talents deemed to have the rest of what it takes:

a strong personality, aggressiveness, sex appeal, credibility, and a certain naturalness on-camera that can scarcely be described, only perceived.

Gloria Rojas, a dark-haired, copper-toned Puerto Rican beauty, obviously had it all—until reevaluated by management at Channel 7. She told me of her experience with a highly touted consulting firm hired by WABC-TV—Frank Magid Associates in Cedar Rapids, Iowa. "They sent us out there one at a time for one day of lessons; flew us out. God knows what that must have cost the station for eight or ten of us. I could understand why they might send some of the new reporters, like Peter Bannon and Anna Bond. But at that point, I had been on the air at Channel Seven for almost ten years. Anyway, when I got to Cedar Rapids, I never met Frank Magid himself. My instructor was a kid about twenty-two years old, a guy who had never worked in television. He took me into a studio equipped with videotape cameras, lights, anchor desk, playback monitors—the whole magilla. He gave me some copy to read, then critiqued my performance, saying I had to start making love to the microphone. I thought that was dumb and said so. Then he showed me videotapes of Jane Pauley [NBC's 'Today' hostess] and a few other sweet middle-America girls who were doing it right. Of course, there was no way I was going to come off as middle-American WASP. That's not me. So what did I do? I cornballed it the next time around; you know, the old goodness-gracious Howdy Doody bit. The kid bought it, gave me a passing grade. I flew back to New York and tried to forget the whole thing."

Let's revisit Dave Gilbert at Channel 4 for a moment. Prior to being advised that his hair was parted in the wrong place, the handsome blond bird dog, imported from Atlanta, got a terrible shock. Like Bill Ryan's ears before him, Dave's face was downgraded to unacceptable. The same news director who had hired him, Ron Kershaw, called him in about six months into his contract and said point-blank, "I don't like your mustache. I don't like the way you look on-camera." Kershaw didn't explain why the man's looks had been A-OK on the audition tapes from Atlanta. No, Gilbert didn't shave his mustache or consult a plastic surgeon. "Hell, if I did that, they'd find something else to bitch about. It does make me worry, though, about what might happen when my current contract expires."

Dave had been through a similar situation before. "I guess I'm getting used to it by now. Like when they hired me at WXIA in Atlanta, they took me out to lunch and said, 'Dave, you're just what we've been looking for—an upbeat, fast-talking guy from a big city [Chicago]. What you did up there was great.' A couple of weeks later they called me in and said I had to tone down my style on the air. I had the image, they said, of a fast-talking, upbeat guy from Chicago. No good in the Deep South. I guess I did tone down a little, but I never did develop a drawl."

A less extreme but equally absurd reappraisal shook up Chauncey Howell, the witty court jester on our early-evening newscast. Chauncey is a rather portly, moon-faced elf, and utterly charming. He was brought up short in the hallway by one of our managers, Sheldon Hoffman. "I've been watching you on the air," Hoffman said. "You need glasses."

"But I see perfectly well," Chauncey protested.

"Not for your eyes," Hoffman countered. "For your face."

Chauncey fretted about it for a few days, then forgot it. Hoffman never mentioned glasses again.

The "Silver Fox" of Channel 4, reporter Jim Ryan, startled all of us in the seventh-floor newsroom with his new hairdo—wild and frizzy but fashionable. He called it a permanent. We called it an Irish-Afro—a fright wig, a big mistake. Ryan accepted our putdowns with a tolerant smile until finally confronted by assistant news director Jeff Rosser. "Jim, I'll give you three choices," Rosser said mildly. "Either get a haircut, get a hat, or get a job in radio."

Ryan went back to the barbershop.

Even lovely anchorwoman Sue Simmons was found physically imperfect at the start of her New York career. The numbers watchers who brought her in from Washington, D.C., at a salary in six figures had the notion that NBC's dismal digits could be jacked up to respectability by pairing a sexy black woman with a sexy white man, Chuck Scarborough. After their first broadcast on "Newscenter 4," just about everybody was favorably impressed. Walter Cronkite of CBS telephoned Sue to say how terrific she was on the air. A couple of nights later, however, general manager Bob Howard kept Sue and Chuck on the new studio set for hours after the show. The technicians, under Howard's supervision, kept experimenting with various lighting combinations. Sue has very light skin. The general manager wanted her to look "more black."

The point is, somebody up there in the Golden Ghetto is always tinkering and tampering with you, especially if The Ratings or your personal Q rating is low. The Q is a super-secret yardstick, rarely revealed to news personnel. It comes from Marketing Evaluation Inc., in Port Washington, New York. Eight times during each television season, those anonymous experts rate each talent's likability in the eyes of TV viewers. It is a costly service bought by television stations, film companies, advertising agencies, and advertisers. Each talent is rated with two scores: percent of public familiarity (FAM) and likability (Q). A sample of one thousand viewers is used to make these crucial determinations. The Q number is found by dividing the percentage of people saying the talent is "one of my favorites" (FAV) by the percentage saying they are familiar with said talent. Thus, $Q = FAV/FAM$. The scores are broken down by demographic categories based on the sample audience's age, sex, education, family income, geographic location, and hours of viewing time in the average week. At one point, *New York* magazine pried some Q numbers loose from the networks, reporting that Walter Cronkite was the reigning doyen with a 92 FAM and a 33 Q.

Aside from these endless make-or-break Q ratings, we are also graded periodically on sex appeal, by a machine.

Reporter Mary Alice Williams came to my desk one day with a bad case of insecurity. At that time, in the fall of 1979, Channel 4 boasted nine female anchors and reporters. MAW, as everybody called her, was one of the most accomplished. She was also impishly seductive, with a voice that must have triggered countless fantasies among male viewers every time she appeared on the screen. Roughly three months after her marriage to a United Press International newsman, MAW confided to me that she was worried about holding her job. "The Empty Suits take away points from any of us who get married," she explained gloomily. "Our galvanic skin tests don't come out right. Marriage lessens our sex appeal."

I hadn't the foggiest inkling of what she was talking about, but in my heart, I celebrated the divorce that I had not wanted in 1974. "I thought the galvanic skin test was one of the elements they use in lie-detector tests. Cops-and-robbers, who-done-it stuff. It measures emotional responses by the amount of sweat on your skin at a given moment under questioning. If you're lying, you sweat more, right?"

MAW nodded. "Right. It's also being used, in a different way, by television stations all over. Do you remember that big bloodbath at station KNXT in Los Angeles a couple of years ago? Well, that was done, I'm told by friends out there, on the basis of galvanic skin tests. They fired about twenty-three people who flunked.

"What they do is bring a pilot audience into the screening room—sort of a cross section of the viewers they're trying to reach. After wiring them into this machine, they show tapes of various newscasters. The machine records their reactions—good, bad, or indifferent—which means that at almost any moment, any one of us talents, male or female, may be eighty-sixed on the basis of other people's sweat."

What made this kind of pressure all the more difficult to ignore was the knowledge that none of us was irreplaceable. Audition tapes came in from the hinterlands daily. Some of the more aggressive candidates for stardom walked in off the street every week. Out of the corners of our nervous eyes, we appraised each one of them, privately calculating our individual chances of surviving yet another challenge. One factor weighing heavily in our favor was an unwritten rule that more or less bound news directors to maintaining a racially, ethnically, and sexually balanced staff—sort of a cross section of the population in the market area they must court. Altruism? Not a bit of it. They want to avoid discrimination suits and demonstrations by equal-opportunity advocates, and to keep the Federal Communications Commission off their backs. All of which meant that if you were one of the two Hispanic males on the team, you worried twice as much about job applicants with names like Gonzalez and Rodriquez. By the same token, good-looking women like Mary Alice Williams and Connie Collins got the jitters whenever blondes and redheads showed up in the newsroom.

There was a nagging suspicion among us, males and females alike, that many of the sweet young things getting off the bus every day would sell their souls or bodies for a television job in the Big Apple. In response to my question about that, one of our talented women reporters said, "The sex thing? Yeah, it happens—mainly when they know you're kind of desperate for the job. Like the day I had an audition at Channel Seven. That part went fine. The news director praised everything I did on the studio set to show my stuff.

"Nothing was said about sex up through my audition. Then he leads me down the hall into an office. The whole 'Eyewitness News' team is sitting in there, like a bunch of hanging judges, wondering, I supposed, which one of them I might replace. Rose Ann Scamardello, Anna Bond, Milton Lewis—the whole gang. None of them smiled. They just looked at me.

"The director says to them, 'Okay, you've seen her. Now you can leave.'

"As they trooped out, a couple of ABC star makers came in. After introducing me, the news director takes both of them into a corner at the far end of the room. I'm sitting there all alone at the other end, and I can hear them talking about me, like I was a piece of meat. One of them stares at me and says to the others, 'Nice face, but the legs aren't too good.' I felt like crawling under the rug.

"They went on like that for several minutes, discussing my anatomy. Eventually, the news director walks back to me. He comes right up to my face, nose to nose. That's when he said, 'Do you fuck?'

"I went into shock. I was only twenty-three at the time, and still a virgin. I was not prepared to handle that. I recovered as fast as I could and said, 'Not very often.'

"He said there was no opening on the staff at the moment, but to call him back next Monday. He might have something for me—if I could accept the fact that fucking would be part of the deal."

Which reminded me of a parallel tale. After filming a story in Buffalo, I paid a visit to our affiliate station WGR-TV, where I met weather reporter June Bacon-Bercy. Over lunch in a nearby coffee shop, I asked the inevitable question, "What's a nice girl like you doing in a place like this?"

June caught my drift right away. She knew she had the necessary credentials to make it big in New York, where all the good ones come sooner or later. "Thanks for the compliment. Buffalo *is* the pits. I'm here because when I applied at Channel Two and Channel Four in New York, they made identical offers I had to refuse."

At WNBC-TV, she recalled, it went like this. She had a perfect on-camera audition in the studio. Reaction from the heavy-hitters was so positive, "I just knew I had the job. Then I went to a final interview with one of the big wheels."

After praising her abilities, June said, he zeroed in on her physique. "He said he wanted me to go to bed with him. And if I wanted the job, I would have to."

Another friend was anchoring at an independent TV station in New York when she explained how she failed to connect with "Eyewitness News" at Channel 7, the number-one team in The Ratings. "I really wanted that job; just knew I was going to get it. They didn't have anybody like me at the time. The news director said my writing was very good, though I did need work on brevity—telling the guts of the story in fewer words. And he really liked my audition on the "Eyewitness" set in the studio.

"Okay. So now I go with the news director into his office. He says a lot of complimentary things about how good I look on-camera. On and on and so forth. But the bottom line was, he had changed his mind about hiring me. I said 'Why not?' He says because I had already shown an attitude that meant I didn't want to fuck. That's what he said, just like that. I was floored; couldn't get my breath for a minute. Then I went into my little dance about being a grown woman with the right to decide if and when I want to have sex with somebody, somebody I liked. He said, 'What's the difference? What difference does it make as long as you get what you want?'

"I told him I didn't need the job that badly. I could always go back to teaching. He said that's probably what I should do, because I wasn't going to make it in this business unless I'm willing to fuck."

Confidential testimony from several females—on- and off-camera grunts—made it clear that a former news director at Channel 4 was one of the worst sex offenders in the industry. They called him Dr. Demento. The disgust they invariably expressed when his name was mentioned eventually prevented me from taking his kind of advantage of my position and power in a different context—stopping me short a block and a half west of my bedroom.

As a television star and part-time instructor at the Columbia University School of Journalism in the seventies, I soon realized that some of the young women in my class would do almost anything to enhance their chances for getting on-camera some day. At the end of one seminar, one student lingered after the rest had departed. "I hope you have a few minutes to spare," she began. "I really want to be a star, and I need your help." Her problem, she said, was in the street-reporting class taught by Professor Harry Arouh, a former WCBS-TV bird dog who knew his stuff. "I always say the wrong thing in my closing stand-uppers. Maybe you can straighten me out. This evening?"

At my suggestion—deviously planning ahead—we straightened her out in Mikell's bar on Columbus Avenue, conveniently close to my apartment. Over martinis on the rocks, I previewed a lecture I already had in mind for the entire class. "The stand-up closer is not something separate and apart from the story you're covering. Neither is it a soapbox for your personal opinions, particularly in your neophyte years. Every news story should consist of related facts. You simply string them together with words and pictures in a sequence that makes sense. Some facts go into your opening narration over pictures, your opening stand-upper, or whatever piece of business you choose to kick it off." I was undressing her with my eyes, fantasizing the denouement. "Additional facts should be brought out in your sound bites, that is, statements by people involved in the story. Whatever important facts that have not been covered in those elements should then be spelled out in your closer."

While I talked, she kept looking at me in a way that projected sexational pictures in my brain. Inexplicably, though, my train of thought was suddenly derailed by total recall of Dr. Demento's latest infamy. A good-looking woman reporter, having finished a summer stint as a vacation relief replacement, went to Dr. Demento's office to press her case for a permanent job. She pointed out that the producers and editors had all praised her work.

Seated at his desk, Dr. Demento spread his legs and pointed to his crotch. "Yes, but you have not done anything for management."

In Mikell's, I seemed to be heading down the same road. So I made up some flimsy excuse to desert the young temptress from Columbia. Walking home alone, I outlined what I should tell all my female students about libido pressure in news biz.

This is not to suggest that TV personalities have to abstain from all emotional and sexual attachments with their fans or with one another. Hell, it can scarcely be avoided. Nearly all of us are physically attractive and surrounded with the glamorous aura that comes with being on the tube. We meet so damn many equally attractive and available members of the opposite sex, both in and out of news biz. But, I hasten to point out that our vast opportunities for fooling around off-camera only partially account for the high divorce rate among us. At one point in time, eleven of our twenty-three anchors and reporters were either divorced or in the process. As far as I knew, only four or five had wound up in Splitsville because of extramarital activities. In most cases, the grounds had to do with hassles unrelated to hanky-panky, like the long, odd hours of our profession. That is what had put my marriage on the rocks. There was a five-and-a-half-year period between 1965 and 1971 in which I anchored or co-anchored the half-hour 11:00 P.M. newscasts on Saturday and Sunday nights, plus the fifteen-minute 1:00 A.M. roundup Monday through Wednesday, immediately following Johnny Carson's show. That kept me away from home during the evening hours when normal families watched television together or otherwise did things to bolster their solidarity. "You're never here when I'm awake," my lonesome wife pointed out. I usually left our four-acre retreat in suburban Westchester—fifty-five miles from Rockefeller Center—around 4:30 P.M., returning well after midnight. "My husband exists only on the tube," she complained.

I only half listened, showering her with expensive status symbols instead—a car of her own, a forty-foot swimming pool, and a $5,000 sauna. What was most important to me at that time was sitting in that chair, proving to myself and to the world that I could hold my own with the elite of broadcasting. Every show I anchored was number one.

After approximately three years of reading copy on the TelePrompTer, however, I began to miss the excitement of the street, which has happened to many anchorpersons. The president of ABC News, Roone Arledge, once told the *New York Times,* "There is nothing sadder in life than to fight for a goal, and then find that it isn't what you expected. I think a person who can both report and anchor would find anchoring very routine and stultifying."

Anchorwoman Kai Maxwell of WVTH-TV in Syracuse voiced similar sentiments when she applied for a go-anywhere reporting job with NBC's Atlanta bureau. "I've also anchored in New Haven, San Francisco, and Detroit, in that order. The Syracuse station is no problem. I could keep on sitting there pulling in the numbers and developing hemorrhoids, but that's not enough for me any more. I want to get out there and do something that really matters for a change."

At KNXT-TV in Los Angeles, anchorwoman Connie Chung was flirting with the same idea when she said, "I think anchorpeople who are real journalists often feel guilty about just anchoring. If they don't go out and do some reporting, they become just readers. No journalist want to be just that."

As a rule, you see, anchors are only minimally taxed in the daily effort of putting a newscast together. Journalistic expertise has almost nothing to do with the job. You read what they put in front of you, trying to shade the copy in the solemn or gay spirit in which it was composed. You don't have to be an authority. You simply give the impression of being authoritative. In other words, it is an acting gig.

After you've settled on that throne, however, you are reluctant to abdicate, because you are at the top. And that is where the big money is. Practically every local anchor at flagship stations and major affiliates across the country earns well above $100,000 a year. More than a few count on chauffeured limousines, hired by the company, to deliver them to and from the studio every night. In New York, salaries of $300,000 are not uncommon. Network anchors, of course, are paid more than twice that amount. The current record, held by Dan Rather of CBS, is $8 million for five years. There are two main reasons why anchorpersons can command megabucks. First, the newscast doesn't work unless the person in that chair is verbally agile, authoritative, and interesting. Second, audience surveys indicate that 40 percent of all news watchers in America choose their program on the basis of their feelings about the anchorpersons.

In my case, the bucks had not been that heavy—$42,000— when the thrill of anchoring began to fade in the late sixties. That's when I made a belated effort to save my marriage, begging to go back to the street. Dick Graf, who was news director then, looked at me as if I had oatmeal on the brain. Because my shows were number one, he tried to cajole me out of making the change. Nearly two more years passed before management found it convenient to grant my request during a major revision of the news-show formats and a general expansion of the staff. My liberation came too late, though, to lift my marriage off the rocks.

My voluntary step down automatically elevated me to a comfortable, respected position in the newsroom. I no longer was a threat to any other grunt. Suddenly I was everybody's favorite elder statesman. They dumped their professional problems on my desk and invariably heeded my counsel.

Felipe Luciano, a former street-gang leader and reformed convict, came to my cubicle one day in a state of acute agitation. For several weeks, he had been locked in a bitter contretemps with Carol Jenkins, his co-anchor on the weekend eleven o'clock newscasts.

"She acts like she hates me," Felipe muttered fiercely. "She won't even look at me on the set. So we sit there at separate desks, not relating to each other at all. Like we're working on two different programs."

Carol had already told me her side of it. "Felipe keeps asking me when am I going to disappear. He says they promised him he would have the weekend shows all to himself. How can you work with somebody who wants to get rid of you?"

Having weighed the testimony, I rendered an opinion to Felipe: "Once upon a time, when you were doing your macho number with the Young Lords up in Harlem, I shared the weekend anchorchair with a couple of guys—first, George Page, then John Palmer. I never had any trouble with either of them. The reason was we each took the attitude that it was not my show or his; it was ours.

"Aside from taking turns reading the lead story, we didn't worry about how much or how little we did on a given broadcast. What the hell, some stories take longer to tell than others.

"Now, getting back to you and Carol, I think you're both behaving like prima donnas. Which also means you're not sure of yourselves, each afraid that the other will somehow come off better on the show. The fact is neither of you can be your best on the air until you understand in your guts that each of you has unique talents. Nobody can make either of you look bad. You can only do that to yourselves. There is only one Felipe Luciano, one Carol Jenkins. All you guys have to worry about is being the best Felipe and the best Carol that's in you.

"If you both concentrate on that, you'll simply be professionals working together and helping each other in a common cause. Whether one of you is taken off the show will depend on The Ratings. Nothing else.

"So my suggestion is that you make the first move; cut off your own bullshit. Smile at Carol for a change. Pay her some compliments. Let her know you think she's a dynamite lady—which she is in my judgment, on-camera and off. Take her out to dinner after the show. Give her the idea that you are damn proud to be working with such a great lady.

"Show some admiration and respect. I guarantee she'll eat it up. And five will get you ten if she doesn't start feeding your ego with some of the same delicious stuff."

Exactly two weeks later, Felipe—well aware of my unabashed addiction to dry martinis—placed a quart of Beefeater's gin on my desk. "For the elder statesman," he announced, embellishing his salute with a wide, wide world of a grin. "I've been trying the advice you gave me about Carol. It's working."

Being back on the street meant longer days—ten and a half hours on the average. The switch was nonetheless worth it. All my evenings were free. I could make extra money on speaking engagements. And—no longer constricted by a wedding ring—I could take full advantage of the personal magnetism gratuitously conferred upon me by the tube. I wish every player could have at least one season like that. Believe me, it heals the raw edges and mellows the soul.

One amorous adventure I'll never forget enabled me to break the hottest political riddle of the month, scooping the five other TV news teams and the entire New York press corps.

She was already ensconced at a midtown hotel for our rendezvous when I breezed in forty minutes late. I'll call her Greta—a lovely paper shuffler in city government. "I was just about to give you up for dead," she chastised.

It was five minutes after six. "Come on, Greta. You know this business. They ran me ragged today."

Roughly thirty minutes later we took a break. Greta said, "Now what about this ran-you-ragged bullshit?"

"No bullshit," I said, "they stuck me with the job of trying to find out who the mayor is going to name as the new black deputy mayor. I flubbed it. The best I could get from my sources all over town was that Mayor Beame is considering three prominent blacks. No names. I just hope to hell the guys on the other channels couldn't come up with anything better than that."

64

Greta giggled. "I could have told you all about it, lover. Why didn't you call me?"

"Sonofabitch," I exclaimed. "You know?" I glanced at the radio clock on the nightstand next to the bed. Six-forty. The early newscast was still on the air. "Come on, baby, tell me."

She took her time, enjoying watching me sweat. "Well, it's like this. When the mayor realized he couldn't go with David Dinkins because of the income-tax scandal, he . . ."

"I know, I know," I pleaded. "Just give me the names, for Christ's sake. The names."

And she did: State Senator Joseph Galiber of the Bronx, and Dr. Eugene Callender, chairman of the Urban Coalition, and Paul Gibson, an American Airlines vice-president. "Gibson is the guy who's going to get it."

I lunged for the phone. Within seconds after reaching the producer in the control room, I was broadcasting live on a two-way audio hookup with anchorman Lew Wood. "A reliable source in the Beame administration told me just minutes ago . . ."

3

Doing It
On-Camera

WHEN YOU WORK THE STREETS instead of the studio, you feel like an urban cowboy—home on the range. Back there at the ranch in Rockefeller Center, Empty Suits are in the saddle. But out there in the wide open spaces of the New York metropolitan area, you can forget about the 7 NBC presidents, the 9 executive vice-presidents, the 112 vice-presidents, and all the other ramrods above you. On your own, with good old boys in the camera crew, you are forever playing the role of the errant good guy—galloping into trouble spots, facing challenges head-on, shooting from the lip to win the day.

Ah, give me the life of a cowboy. That's how I felt upon returning to street reporting, free at last from the weight of the anchor. Although my reflexes had been somewhat dulled by five and a half years in the Channel 4 bunkhouse, I quickly resharpened them, aided by a string of tenderfoot cowpokes sent out with me to observe the top hand on a news roundup or two. Betty Rollins, Mike Jensen, and David Diaz were among my young wranglers who later rode tall in the saddle for the NBC spread. In schooling them, I regained my own savvy and toughness.

The first thing I tried to teach them was the variety and difficulty of the obstacles they would have to overcome, not only in the field but in themselves—like the insecurity I had not handled too well on my first TV assignment. It was an interview with the general manager of the basketball Knickerbockers, Ned Irish, about his club's prospects in the coming NBA play-offs. Intimidated by my inexperience and unfamiliar with the tools I had to work with, I asked the man every question I could think of, paying little or no attention to his answers. I was swarming all over the story and surrounding it in the hope of coming up with something worth putting on the air. Almost everything I had learned during ten years in print seemed to fall away. I was no longer a working journalist; I was intent on becoming a star.

When my 16mm footage came out of the soup, film editor Clay Cassell studied the fat reel in disgust. "Eleven hundred feet for one interview? What the hell kind of story is this—the Second Coming?"

Cassell was a hard-boiled veteran with a gravelly voice and an air of surly indignation. He reminded everybody of Humphrey Bogart. Underneath all that, however, he was a thorough professional and a pussycat. Patiently, Clay explained how much time it was going to take him to roll through all that spaghetti, screening it on a miniature viewing box electrically attached to a sound amplifier, to find whatever twenty- or thirty-second segment would be selected for the newscast. He pointed out that a minute of film runs thirty-six feet, and few interviews go more than forty seconds on the air, usually less. Unless you have one hell of a complicated story to tell, you should figure on holding the average interview to a couple of minutes, seventy or eighty feet. If the guy you're talking to is one of those hard nuts to crack, you keep it going for maybe two hundred feet. His advice was that if you can't get what you're after in that much footage, forget it. Interview somebody else.

You have to be equally judicious and economical when orchestrating a news "package"—using sound bites, narration over pictures, and stand-uppers to tell one story in detail. On paper, your end product should read like the script I prepared for a package on deteriorating subway service in New York. In Channel 4's style, the left side of the page is used to indicate which pictures should be spliced in sequence with the sound track spelled out on the right side of the page.

TEAGUE/SUBWAY DEFECTS/DEC. 12

	When people say, "I love New York,"
TEAGUE WALKING ON	they're not talking about the subway
SUBWAY PLATFORM	system. Only a masochist could be in
TOWARD CAMERA	love with a dirty environment,
	defective equipment, delays, discomfort,
	and danger. The New York subway
	has it all. . .
STALLED SUBWAY TRAINS	Yesterday during the morning rush, the
	Transit Authority pulled 96 trains out of
	service—mechanical breakdowns. On the
	average day, the Authority says, 80
	trains break down.
IDLE R-46 IN SUBWAY YARD	The R-46 is a case in point. A multi-
	million-dollar disappointment. The
CAMERA PULLS BACK TO	Transit Authority bought 754 of these
TEAGUE	subway cars before discovering that the
WITH SAME TRAIN IN	R-46 can be hazardous to your health.
BACKGROUND	And right now, R-46s are barred from
	the tracks during rush hours. To partially
R-16 TRAINS IN BARN	make up the loss, the TA is taking these
	older cars out of mothballs and putting
	them back into service. The R-16—built
	in 1955.

Jim Miller	SOUND BITE
Maintenance Supervisor	(Miller talks about shortage of cars and maintenance problems)
	(NARRATION RESUMES)
(COVER LAST HALF OF INTERVIEW WITH SHOTS OF MEN FIXING TRAINS) DIFFERENT MECHANICS WORKING ON DIFFERENT TRAINS	The preventive maintenance program in the subway system suffered a major cutback in 1975, a casualty of the city's budget crunch. And not until last July, when the fare went up to sixty cents, did they bring that program back in order.
George Fisk	SOUND BITE
Subway Mechanic	(Fisk explains necessity of preventive maintenance, comparing it to regular check-ups for your own car.)
	ON-CAMERA CLOSER
TEAGUE EMERGES FROM TROUGH UNDER DISABLED TRAIN WHERE OTHER MECHANICS ARE WORKING ON THE UNDERCARRIAGE. TEAGUE WALKS TOWARD CAMERA AND STOPS	With the maintenance program back up to par, the mechanics say, they still need time to catch up with the backlog—a backlog of neglect. So the daily average for subway breakdowns—very high at the moment—may continue well into the summer of eighty-one. Bob Teague News 4 Brooklyn.

Putting a tight, informative screenplay together was the easy part. Other exigencies of my calling made it necessary to grow a callus on my heart. When covering a murder, for example, you have to delve into the gruesome details of the bloodletting. If at all possible, you must also show the victim's friends or family, preferably in a rage or in tears. If you are covering a political campaign, you must goad the candidates into spitting obscenities at each other, like, "He said you're incompetent and unqualified. What's your reaction to that?"

Even when you feel that you are doing something disgusting,

70

or merely in bad taste—displaying insensitivity to the point of being inhuman—you have to hang tough and follow through; like sticking a mike under the nose of a weeping old woman whose grandson has been stabbed to death in a rumble. I did all that and worse. It came with the territory. Had I failed to do it for dear old Channel 4, some other streetwalker made of sterner stuff would certainly do it for dear old Channel 2, Channel 5, or Channel 7. And if my masters saw that kind of pathos on a competing station—they all had a shelf full of TV monitors in their offices—they would ask me, "Where the fuck were you when Channel Blank was getting the good stuff?" No one has yet devised a satisfactory answer to that one.

My friend Gloria Rojas of Channel 7 says that's exactly what happened to her in covering the aftermath of a plane crash. While other members of the "Eyewitness News" team blanketed the crash site, Gloria was sent to the nearest hospital. "What a scene," she told me. "In the confusion of all those victims being brought in, the hospital's security and communications broke down completely. Chaos all over the place. I just walked into the emergency section with my crew, and nobody tried to stop us. We took pictures of the injured, some of them barely conscious, struggling to live. I didn't want to bother any of them. Just being in there meant that we were increasing their chances of infection. So we just took pictures, talked with one of the surgeons, then packed up to leave. That's when a reporter from Channel Eleven showed up with his crew and started interviewing some of the victims, including this guy who's obviously dying. I said to myself, this is an abomination. I am not going to sink to anything so gross. I'm going to leave.

"Back at the station," Gloria went on, "our executive producer saw Channel Eleven's exclusive on the ten o'clock news. He wanted to know whether I'd interviewed the same guy or even somebody else who was dying on the spot. When I said I had decided not to do it as a matter of decency, he damn near had a fit. He said I should have done it, too. So what finally happened was, our station called Channel Eleven and begged a copy of their tape. We ran the interview on our program at eleven with a credit line that said 'Courtesy of WPIX-TV.' I was so mad I couldn't even cry."

The fact is, you never know which of the many damned-if-you-do-damned-if-you-don't choices you will have to make on a given day.

You walk into the newsroom at 7:00 A.M. ready for anything. A couple of assignment editors and two or three desk assistants are already seated at the sprawling central news console. They are poring over AP and UPI copy from the endlessly clacking Teletype machines in the adjoining cubicle; answering phone calls from tipsters, flacks, and people with problems; making calls to set up interviews; reading publicity releases; monitoring emergency calls coming in on police and fire department radio channels. Based on this input, they make their decisions as to where they should send you with a camera crew—the scene of a rape, a subway wreck, a gangland execution, a circus parade, a City Council hearing, a spelling bee, a stickup.

Assignment editors are also required to develop the outlook of ghouls, within fifteen minutes of taking the job.

As I slouched into the newsroom one morning—hung over and minus a heartbeat—our new deputy assignment editor Gail Yancosek was glum. "I don't see anything on the wires or in the papers worth covering," she griped. Roger Higle had called in sick; she was anxious to prove that she could handle the desk on her own. She ticked off the news items—a two-bit stickup in Yorkville, a dinky two-alarm fire at an orphanage with nobody hurt, another mugging in Central Park—wondering how the hell were we supposed to make a news show out of stuff like that.

Desk assistant Al Branam came in from the Teletype room to the rescue—a young man with a mission. Waving a fresh sheet of wire copy in triumph, he relieved Gail's anxiety with the news that the AP just sent an update on the orphanage fire, saying that it was deliberately set.

Yancosek beamed.

From the moment you hit the street in the morning, regardless of your assignment, you are vaguely insecure, afraid that some bird dog from another channel will come up with a better angle, a better picture, or a more dramatic sound bite on the same story. It is axiomatic that management never misses the other guy's superior scenario on the banks of TV monitors that show and tell around the clock, which explains why I was close to a state of mild hysteria when cameraman Joe Kamfor lost his way in Brooklyn en route to a major story in the slums of Bedford-Stuyvesant.

By the time we arrived, all the other newsreels—except the absent Channel 5—were packing up to leave. They had just finished a hectic session with Congresswoman Shirley Chisholm after an unrelated ground-breaking ceremony. Chisholm had been accused in the morning headlines of diverting campaign funds to her personal bank account.

"I'm sorry, Shirley. We couldn't get here any faster," I apologized, one on one. "I'll have to ask you to take it once more from the top."

She smiled recognition and sympathy.

"Speed," said my audioman, Jerry Goldman, meaning the 16mm film in Kamfor's Auricon was running fast enough to record sound and pictures without distortion.

I warned the feisty politician that I would have to play the devil's advocate. Shirley nodded. She knew the drill.

"Let's start with the sixty-four-dollar question. Did you use the campaign money for anything other than campaigning?"

"Of course not." As Shirley rambled on, blaming the discovered discrepancy on sloppy bookkeeping by inexperienced campaign aides, I was nagged by improbable possibilities. Had somebody else managed to get something out of her that I was missing? So I began fishing, asking dumb, irrelevant questions to keep her talking, just in case.

My third banality hooked a nerve. "What would the late Adam Clayton Powell say about this mess you're in?"

About four sentences into her response, the toughest woman in the House of Representatives—reacting to fond memories of the dead Harlem congressman—began weeping. She maintained just enough self-control, however, to keep talking, comparing Powell's legendary tribulations with her own. I was flabbergasted and elated. Hell, I had Shirley Chisholm crying on-camera—a television first.

The other reporters began flogging their crews, herding them

73

back to the scene of my coup. They were sensible enough to keep their mouths shut to avoid disrupting the mood she was in. She wept long enough for all of them to get close-ups of her tears.

When it was all over, the crew from Channel 5 arrived. Gabe Pressman, my former mentor at Channel 4, wanted to know what had happened.

"No sweat, Gabe," I told him. "Shirley is still here. She said she didn't take the bread. And she cried." I delivered the last line as a throwaway, knowing the impact it would have.

Gabe's eyes expanded into circles of disbelief. "Shirley Chisholm? Honest-to-God tears? You've got to be putting me on."

The other bird dogs, enjoying the entertainment, backed me up.

Gabe's agony surfaced in his face. The rest of us, appreciating his dilemma, watched from the sidelines as he went to work. He badgered, bullied, and blustered for twelve minutes, exhausting a four-hundred-foot roll of film. He did everything but trample on the woman's toes. Shirley had regained her celebrated rocklike composure, however. She refused to weep for Gabe.

The old pro finally trudged away, muttering less-than-flattering opinions of the Brooklyn lawmaker.

Leaning on public officials, as Pressman did, is de rigueur in news biz. I learned that in my first semester on the street. There I was, with the Harvey Weinstock film crew, covering a massive brushfire in the boondocks of Staten Island. By the time we had captured the fire-fighting action and wrapped it up with my on-camera stand-upper against a background of flames, our deadline was bearing down upon us like the sword of Damocles. And the best story in the world is absolutely worthless if you can't get it on the air.

A Channel 4 motorcycle courier was standing by, waiting for our film. Camera crews and reporters were not allowed to bring the film back to the lab. Union regulations.

I groaned, realizing it was after 4:30 and there was no way the courier could hustle back to Rockefeller Center, get the film developed and edited in time for the six o'clock show.

My cameraman, having been around longer, did not share my

pessimism. He assured me laconically that we could make it, pointing out that the fire commissioner had landed a few minutes ago in a helicopter. All we had to do was get him to fly it back to the Pan-Am Heliport just a few blocks from the studio. We could call the assignment desk on the car radio and tell them to send another courier to meet the commissioner there.

I gaped at the man. I wouldn't dare suggest it. The commissioner was here on official business.

Weinstock nodded confidently. All I had to do was interview the commissioner first. All politicians loved to see themselves on television.

I objected that there was no room for the commissioner in my story. I'd already interviewed the firefighters and civilian volunteers on the job. They were the real story.

Weinstock conceded that, adding that there was no law saying I had to put the interview on the air.

Still skeptical and somewhat chagrined, I approached the fire commissioner. He readily consented to an interview. A couple of minutes later, I carried our can of film from Weinstock to him and asked if he could fly it back to the city, ten miles way, explaining that otherwise we wouldn't make it in time to air.

The commissioner agreed to take it, and the chopper lifted off. I turned to Weinstock, accusing him with my tone of voice and eyes as I asked what was going to happen when the commissioner didn't see himself on the show.

Weinstock told me not to worry about it. He said that the commissioner was a regular player in this game. He'd given a lot of interviews that had never showed up on the tube. All he wanted was a shot at it, and his batting average was pretty good.

How can we get away with such questionable gambits? The irresistible pull of the magic cathode-ray tube, when we have the imagination to exploit it. That's what enabled me to solve a very tough problem while on loan to the NBC network team at the 1968 Democratic convention in Chicago.

Late in the afternoon on the first day of the nominating process, I was staked out with a live-remote unit in the lobby of the Sherman House. The elephantine TK-41 camera I was wired to trailed only twenty-five feet of cable, limiting my field of operation. The telex in my right ear came to life. An urgent message from the network command miles away at the convention site. They wanted me to find Mike DeSalle, the former Ohio governor, and put him on the air live at the top of the "Huntley-Brinkley Report."

Producer Chet Hagan informed me that I had exactly twenty-five minutes to get him. He was staying somewhere in the Sherman House with the Ohio delegation. The producer didn't care how I did it as long as DeSalle was in front of that camera by seven o'clock. They were going to switch to my location for two or three minutes at thirty seconds into the show. He wished me luck and I knew I would need it. Unplugging my telex line from the TK-41's sound cable, I told the stage manager, Freddie Lights, what I had to do. He raised his bushy eyebrows and whistled, "Go get 'em, Tiger. Bring 'em back alive."

DeSalle was not in hiding. Being a practical politician with a limping cause—the Draft Ted Kennedy Movement—he needed television as much as I needed him. In fact, as I reached the elevator bank on the far side of the lobby, the hotel's public-address system began announcing that Governor DeSalle would hold a major news conference in the third-floor ballroom, starting at 6:45 P.M. I glanced at my watch. It was going to be awfully close. I refused to consider for a microsecond that I would not be able to pull it off.

A predictable complication reared its ugly head as I stepped into the self-service elevator and turned to face the front. Rival correspondents from ABC and CBS shouldered their way through the closing doors to join me. They, too, had been staked out with live units in different areas of the vast Sherman House lobby. I groaned under my breath. Their orders undoubtedly conflicted with mine.

"What do you think?" CBS asked me. "Can we get him downstairs live by seven?"

"Your guess is as good as mine. We'll have to play it by ear, I suppose."

"It's my guess," ABC chimed in, "that DeSalle—if he got anything solid out of today's conversation with Teddy—will *want* to go live."

None of us said so, but each was thinking about how to screw the others to get to DeSalle first.

When we reached the ballroom, DeSalle was surrounded by newsgatherers and pleased with himself. At least forty reporters and half a dozen film crews were firing questions at the paunchy little man from Ohio. He ignored the questions, pointing to his wristwatch. It was not quite 6:45. He waited until a dozen radio spot men had affixed an additional cluster of microphones to the lectern directly in front of him. It was 6:47 when DeSalle finally opened up.

His statement ran nearly four minutes. He said more and more convention delegates had let him know that they were ready to vote for Senator Kennedy. They simply wanted assurances that Teddy would accept the nomination if it came his way on a draft. DeSalle played it like a pro, hinting a great deal more than his words conveyed, winking slyly and pausing dramatically between cryptic phrases. "I talked with the senator by phone this afternoon, as most of you know. While Ted didn't give me a flat yes or no, he left me with the distinct impression that he would in fact accept a genuine draft."

At 6:51, I felt excitement and anxiety mounting. I forced myself to sit still for two questions from the floor: Exactly how close was the draft movement to the 655 votes required for nomination? What were Teddy's exact words when the governor popped the big question?

I scarcely heard his response, too busy watching the clock.

An incoherent babble of follow-up questions all but drowned DeSalle's last few words. I deliberately waited three beats, then addressed the man on a lower, calmer note that cut through the high-pitched bleats all around me—a trick I had learned in New York's gang-bang brigade. "You've covered the substance of it, Governor," I declared. "You can only confuse things by going along with a fishing expedition."

Realizing that it was I who had the man's attention, the other bird dogs broke off their questions and listened—against their wills.

"I'm with the 'Huntley-Brinkley Report,'" I continued calmly, trading on the prestige of the number-one team in news biz. "I'd like to take you downstairs to my camera in the lobby for a coast-to-coast interview at seven o'clock." I consulted my watch theatrically—6:54 P.M. "We'll have to leave right now to make it. CBS and ABC also want you live after that."

Howls of protest threatened to rupture my eardrums. The cursing couldn't have been louder or angrier if I had set off a stink bomb. I knew from experience, however, that it would take the mob several long seconds to figure out what they could do about it. So I moved rapidly, displaying as much savoir faire as possible. DeSalle—eager for a Maine-to-California forum—let me usher him to the nearest exit. The objections grew louder and uglier. "Nobody can just walk into a press conference and break it up," a disgruntled voice complained close to my ear. "You can't do a thing like that. We've got deadlines, too."

DeSalle's smile remained genial as I maneuvered him through the cursing, jostling throng. "I'll be back in a few minutes," he promised again and again. "This won't take long. I'll be back."

By then the mob was beginning to get physical. We wouldn't have made it without an unexpected assist from ABC and CBS. They ran interference and helped us into the elevator, holding the irate posse at bay. Both had accepted the reality that being second and third with DeSalle would be better than not getting him on their news programs at all. They followed us down on the next elevator.

We reached my hot camera at 6:59. My stage manager tripped on a cable in his eagerness to put an NBC mike into my hand and wire me into the camera. He dried my sweaty face with a powder puff. I took a deep drag on a borrowed cigarette, then moved into position under the garish brilliance of the flood lamps. The governor came with me.

As Freddie gave me a silent countdown on his fingers, I looked into the Howitzer-like barrel of the TK-41 and smiled. At exactly 7:00:30, DeSalle and I were on the air.

Maybe you think the assist I received from ABC and CBS in Chicago was a breach of the bird dogs' code, a once-in-a-lifetime fluke. Not at all. While competing, we also cooperate almost daily, unless the story we are working on is an exclusive. We band together, for example, to persuade adamant bureaucrats to let us enter forbidden premises with our cameras. We lend spare reels of virgin film or spare camera batteries to a rival team caught short. We swap scraps of information on stories that are difficult to piece together. No, we do not give away everything we know, holding back two or three juicy tidbits that add a special flavor to the bare bones of the stew. Each of us knows that sooner or later he or she will be the bird dog in need of assistance. So what we have is sort of a mutual defense pact. There is enough carnage among us in The Ratings wars without deliberately zapping one another.

The most common act of mercy is pointing a bird dog arriving late on the scene in the right direction to sniff out the basic facts before all of the essential elements and sources disappear.

One time I showed up tardy at a Brooklyn home where a guy had gone berserk and killed his parents with a shotgun. The five other New York reels had been there for over an hour. J. J. Gonzalez of Channel 2 immediately advised me that if I hurried with my crew to the rear of the house, I could get pictures of the bodies in the family's garage; the coroner's meat wagon was going to remove them momentarily. We made it just in time.

Gonzalez never said a word about the delicious sound bites he had filmed. I had to scurry like hell to come up with my own. All he had wanted to do was save me from the untenable position of going on the air with a homicide story that did not include the key picture that everybody else would show. I had done as much for him a number of times over the years.

Unavoidably—the human condition being what it is—all of us eventually have occasions to regret our handouts to certain inimical allies who either fail to return the favor or otherwise violate the unwritten parameters of our mutual defense pact.

Once upon a time in the Bronx, police discovered several tons of toxic chemicals illegally dumped on scattered vacant lots—a menace to youngsters in the neighborhood. It was a sensational whodunit that every newsreel in town tried for weeks to resolve.

An enterprising Channel 2 reporter, poking through an isolated

79

pile of glass and cardboard containers being collected by sanitation trucks, found a ledger. It gave away the manufacturer's name and address, with a catalog of the lethal compounds in that load.

The WCBS man said later that after doing his stand-upper with the ledger, he planned to turn it over to the cops. Then a WABC reporter showed up with his crew and he decided to share the ledger with him, figuring some day he'd be the guy playing catch-up and need a clue from a competitor.

He couldn't believe it when the other reporter put the ledger back in the pile, hiding it under some boxes. Then, with his camera rolling, he started prowling through the stuff. All of a sudden he picked up the ledger, turned to the camera, and said, "Look what I've found."

The WCBS reporter was furious, but knew there was no point in trying to talk him out of it. So after giving the ledger to the cops, he called the WABC reporter's boss, Ron Tindiglia, at Channel 7. Tindiglia thanked him and said he'd take care of it; the staged discovery scene never got on the air.

The line between creative coverage and faking the news is sometimes a thin one, but in this case the reporter had clearly gone too far.

Conflicts between streetwalkers rarely involve questions of that magnitude. A more typical hassle developed between Heather Bernard of Channel 4 and Arnold Diaz of Channel 2 on the hottest story in New Jersey at the time.

When Heather reached the home of Karen Ann Quinlan's family, several competing reels were standing in line at the front door awaiting their turns to shoot. The Quinlans were in a legal battle with the state for the right to disconnect the life-support apparatus that prevented their comatose daughter from "dying with dignity."

"Arnold Diaz was next in line ahead of me," Heather recalled with rancor. "The other crews ahead of us took only fifteen or twenty minutes each. Arnold was in there for over an hour. I was furious. Finally, I went inside to see what the heck was taking so long. I couldn't believe it. His crew was all packed up. He was sitting at the table with the Quinlans having lunch.

"Okay. The family had to eat anyway. No harm done. Then as they finished lunch—Arnold and his crew were starting to leave—I noticed a stack of letters on a table in the corner. I made the mistake of asking Mrs. Quinlan about all that mail. She said it was the letters and cards they had received in recent weeks expressing sympathy for their daughter and the family. Arnold had missed that angle completely. Now he tells his crew to unpack their gear. He wants to do another sound bite and shoot the letters. I grab him by the arm and say, 'Arnold, come on. Enough is enough.'

"We had such a big argument about it that Mrs. Quinlan butted in. 'Now, children. No fighting in this house.' Arnold backed off and I did my piece first.

"The next day he called NBC and told Earl Ubell that Heather Bernard had been bitchy and obnoxious, very unprofessional, on the Quinlan story. When I saw Arnold again a day later, I thanked him. I said NBC had been threatening to fire me because they said I'm not aggressive enough in the field. 'You've saved my job.'"

If your zeal propels you into conflict with another streetwalker, you can huff and puff with reckless abandon, being wrapped in a cloak of immunity. You know the other guy does not want to risk damage to his money-in-the-bank profile or risk a multi-million-dollar lawsuit for damaging yours.

The physical dangers you have to worry about have to do with getting too close to somebody else's action—like an archery exhibition I covered in Central Park. "The World's Greatest Archer," the program said, would amaze us. And he did. Shooting steel-tipped hunting arrows, Darrell Pace punctured bull's-eyes and popped balloons without a miss. Then he called for a volunteer to assist with his version of William Tell's celebrated feat.

Now, here was a chance for a TV reporter to get involved in the story, as news directors are always urging.

"All you have to do," Pace said, "is hold this apple in your hand, waist high."

I thought about getting involved. I thought about getting hurt. No thanks.

Josh Howell of Channel 7's "Eyewitness News" team took a bold step forward. With his camera rolling, he stood there, a small apple in his hand, a larger one in his throat. The World's Greatest Archer took aim from thirty yards away. All of us held our breaths. Swish. A clean hit that carried the apple downrange.

Everybody applauded the intrepid reporter. Josh was all smiles—until his cameraman approached with a hangdog look in his eyes. "I'm sorry, Josh. I didn't get it; had a problem with my viewfinder. Could you do it again?"

All of us on the street have lost stories, as Josh did, through no fault of our own. Rolland Smith of WCBS came back from the field with an epic saga of misfortune.

While trying to do a piece about parachuting as a sport, Smith jumped from a rented plane about three thousand feet over the nearest real estate. His cameraman, an eager volunteer for the mission, was supposed to leap behind him and film the brave newsman floating down. At the last second, however, the cameraman sprouted chicken feathers. He slammed the door behind Smith, sat back down, and buckled his seatbelt. No pictures.

Descending without a mishap, Smith looked up into the empty sky. He guessed what had happened and consoled himself with the thought that he could make a good story with the pictures being taken by his backup cameraman on the ground.

When Smith landed, however, the guy on the ground looked embarrassed. He apologized, explaining that he'd seen the plane, but not Smith. The sun was in his eyes.

The most constant health hazard you face on the street involves the coverage of violence—shootouts between cops and robbers, looters on the rampage during blackouts, and race riots.

From their perspective in the Golden Ghetto, TV executives saw black violence in the ghettos as the biggest story of the 1960s, aside from the conquest of space. They also saw news personnel as invulnerable, fearless zealots. Cameraman Mike Clark and I did not quite fit the mold.

I led Mike's crew into the heart of Harlem one evening to cover a Black Muslim civil-rights rally. It was an ugly, articulate, rousing harangue by Malcolm X on Lenox Avenue at 125th Street. "The white man is a blue-eyed devil," the black firebrand screamed to a restless crowd of perhaps a thousand. "We must stop turning the other cheek. We must arm ourselves and fight back. Kill the white lackeys of capitalism and oppression. An eye for an eye, a tooth for a tooth."

A platoon of white cops was fidgeting at the edge of the gathering. We fully expected them to swoop down and haul Minister Malcolm away, which would have been the case years earlier. Times had changed, though. The black movement had gained enough respectability and sympathy to avert such punitive measures in the city of New York. The cops simply did their best to look like something other than blue-eyed devils.

Eventually, the Black Muslim leader shouted something that incensed a number of blacks in the crowd. A bitter exchange of epithets and accusations developed among rival factions. Beer bottles and fists began flying.

"Let's get the hell out of here," Mike yelled above the din, hoisting his camera off the tripod.

"Shouldn't we film some of this action?" I asked against my better judgment.

"You're out of your fucking mind," Mike countered, sprinting for the company car. Our audioman and lighting tech were close behind, dragging cables, quartz lamps, and the sound amplifier on the pavement. I followed them, on the double.

Several minutes later, heading downtown through Central Park, we got a call from the assignment editor over the two-way radio in our glove compartment. He had just heard via the police radio that the cops had put down a riot at the Malcolm X rally and wanted to confirm that we had some footage of it.

"Riot? What riot?" the cameraman blustered. "We're in Central Park heading back to the base. We ain't seen no riot."

Several weeks after that incident, with racial tension rising once again in Harlem, I returned with an all-black crew. Management had the theory that the color of our skins would protect us. Our job was to film man-on-the-street opinions. *Vox pop.*

Emerging from our car, we were half expecting trouble. The night air was muggy, suffused with belligerence. An ugly-looking crowd gathered around, muttering darkly among themselves, as we assembled our gear.

83

The first direct challenge came from a scroungy black beggar pointing a rusty tin cup from the fringe. The old man jeered about Uncle Toms coming to spy for the white man, telling us we ought to be ashamed to be working for the enemy.

Amid murmurs of agreement from the mob, the rest of us in the film crew sort of ducked our heads, trying to ignore the troublemaker. Our audioman, Eddie Bones, was aloof and loose as a goose. Flicking ashes from his cigar, he called to the beggar. Bones was not a commanding figure, a middle-aged stump of a man. But his voice was strong, intimidating, as if accustomed to being obeyed.

Our tormentor approached uncertainly. The crowd quieted down. The wary panhandler stopped about five feet in front of us. Bones reached into his own pocket and pulled out a quarter. He held it high between thumb and index finger. "You know what this is, pal?" he asked loudly. "It's money. If we didn't work for the white man, we wouldn't have no two bits to put in that fucking tin cup you got." He dropped the quarter into the cup. There was no more heckling after that.

That confrontation in Harlem was a marshmallow roast compared to what happened to me later at the 1968 Republican convention in Miami Beach. Never before had I come so close to losing my job and my life.

NBC had assembled about twelve hundred of us working stiffs in Miami Beach from the various stations in its web—auxillary legs, eyes, and ears for anchormen Huntley and Brinkley. Most of us were quartered at the luxurious Harbor Island Spa. On the night that Nixon was being nominated by the GOP delegates in Convention Hall several miles away, I was in the hotel's huge swimming pool with other off-duty grunts. I got a call from assignment editor Van ("Mr. Big") Kardish. His desk was at the NBC command post in Convention Hall. A riot had erupted in the South Miami ghetto called Liberty City. I was to rendezvous with the Dexter Alley crew to cover it. Kardish reminded me that it was still early in the evening, and I'd have plenty of time to get back with the film and make air before NBC signed off coverage for the night.

Ugh. I had to do what the man said, but what a gut-wrenching scare I got. The whole of Liberty City seemed to be in flames.

Screams and sirens filled the night. Guns and Molotov cocktails were exploding everywhere. Bricks and bottles sailed through the darkness. A bottle grazed my temple. A UPI still photographer was disfigured—blinded in one eye—when a rock smashed the windshield of his car.

Cautiously, moving no closer to Armageddon than we had to, we shot enough scenes of looting and destruction to tell the story. My film made air without a hitch.

"A great job," I was told by several chiefs at the command post. "We really beat the opposition with your coverage. You look beat. Go back to the hotel and get some rest. You've earned it."

They were telling me!

My stature as a hero was rescinded the following afternoon. While lounging around the pool with a few other heroes of the night shift, I received another urgent call from Mr. Big. The riot had flared up again and he wanted me to cover it.

I didn't want to hear any more. I was replaying the tape of last night's close shave on the screen inside my head. I told him I wasn't going. The assignment editor spluttered in disbelief.

Flatly refusing an assignment was practically unheard of—a cardinal sin. I told him that covering the riot in Liberty City had scared me shitless. I'd seen all the riots I wanted to. I hung up the phone and stretched out once again by the pool. I had been borrowed from the anchor desk in New York for the big story in Miami Beach. And with three little words, "I'm not going," I had virtually kicked myself out of news biz.

As I expected, the phone rang again. Kardish said he was sending Jack Perkins to Liberty City. I was to report, on the double, to Mr. Wald at Convention Hall.

Vice-President Richard Wald was no Empty Suit. He was tough, unafraid to make hard decisions. Behind his back, we called him the "Iceman Who Cometh with an Ax."

Facing me in his private office, Wald's eyes were like ice cubes. He asked me to explain why I had put myself in this awkward position. His voice was equally cold and brittle.

I took the deepest breath any man could manage and, forcing myself to look him in the ice cubes, I told him that I was physically afraid. Remembering what I had seen the night before and what could have happened to me, I had started thinking about living and decided I hadn't had nearly enough. No television story was worth the rest of my life.

The Iceman was not impressed. He mouthed the popular fiction that my color would surely protect me in a black riot.

I tried to explain that the kind of folks who shoot guns and throw rocks in the night were not necessarily sharpshooters. Besides, any black man seen wearing a shirt and tie could as easily be mistaken for an Uncle Tom or a cop.

Wald brushed my rebuttals aside, lecturing me on the responsibilities of my profession. My brain went blank for a minute or so. I felt in my bones that he was reciting one of those unanswerable memos from the Golden Ghetto. Somehow he got around to a hypothetical question, prefaced with the information that some militant civil-rights groups were beginning to insist that only black reporters be sent to cover their news events. He asked if I would be afraid to cover a story on those terms.

I told him I'd rather not; that no organization should have the power to dictate our coverage. Once we went down that road, there would be no end to it. The Jewish Defense League would demand only Jewish reporters, and the DAR, etc., etc. I said I thought we should boycott groups that made those demands.

Wald said I was wrong. He believed in doing anything whatsoever to get the story.

Clearly the jig was up, so I decided to take my punishment like a man. "I know I can't justify what I did, but you're saying things now that, well, condone dishonesty and cheating; the ends justify the means. I don't believe in sacrificing people or principles so readily. To my way of thinking, that's immoral."

Wald bolted upright in the chair behind his desk, like a cobra getting ready to strike. "Immoral? What do you think this is, Sunday School? I don't make decisions on the basis of morality. I make decisions on the basis of what it's going to take to make NBC the biggest, the best, and most respected news-gathering organization in the field."

My chances for survival had dropped to zilch. So I fired the other barrel at my executioner. "All I can say is, I'm glad I don't work at your level of this business. You, sir, are the most corrupt human being I've ever met."

He glared at me, tight-lipped, for several seconds. My heart tried to hammer its way through my shirt. With an effort, I willed myself not to blink.

"That's all for now," the vice-president said coolly. "You'll be hearing from me."

A few hours later—still sitting on death row—I deliberately got bombed out of my skull at the traditional farewell party for the NBC News team as the convention ended. I promised myself not to think about where I might go from there until the next day.

Man, what a party. On the broad concrete deck around our hotel's swimming pool, scores of us ate, drank, gossiped, joked, laughed, and flirted. That is to say, everybody else did all that. I mostly drank. Nobody would talk to me or even acknowledge my presence. The word had gone out. They knew I was going to get it. They therefore kept a safe distance from the condemned man, afraid that my sorry condition might be catching. When I went to the free bar, everybody else backed away. When I jumped into the pool, they scrambled out. A buffer zone, perhaps ten feet in diameter, surrounded me wherever I went. I laughed to myself without bitterness. A couple of years earlier in New York, I had been part of a similar conspiracy of silence when NBC eighty-sixed sports reporter Lou Boda to make room for Kyle Rote, the former football star. Now it was my turn in the barrel.

Shortly after midnight, a gaggle of *gonsamachers* arrived at our gala by the pool. They had finished my court-martial behind closed doors at Convention Hall. No one ever told me, then or later, exactly what had transpired at my trial. I can only assume that some NBC executives defended me on the grounds that I had done good work over the past five years, and perhaps on the grounds that during that era, a competent black talent could not be easily replaced.

In any case, one of the big shots arriving at the party, producer

Robert Northshield, quickly calibrated my lonely position in the midst of all that festivity. He spoke up in a very loud voice. Bless him. "Hey, Bob. Are you under the impression that you're in some kind of trouble?"

The party suddenly hushed. Hundreds of eyes swiveled to me. I took a thoughtful gulp of my fifth or sixth martini on the rocks and chuckled mirthlessly. "Well, gang, in a word—yes."

"Well, you're not," the great man said with finality.

A lot of grunts stopped holding their breaths. A cheer went up, then applause. I was instantly surrounded, slapped on the back, hugged, and kissed.

It was nice to have friends once again.

Ethical differences between the Iceman and me—I admitted to myself years afterward—were not as great as I had pretended, practically no difference at all. From square one of my career in news biz, I had bent my personal rules of good conduct, decency, and integrity again and again to get news stories on the tube. Sure, I worried about it some, but I kept on doing it.

Was I justified in rationalizing my opportunistic approach to streetwalking with a microphone? Was I evolving into an Empty Suit?

The more I mulled over those questions, the less proud I became of myself. One particular incident left me with a churning knot of self-loathing. In Coney Island, covering the suicide leap of a twenty-three-year-old man, I flimflammed the victim's mother into giving me the exclusive sound bite I needed to flesh out my scenario. My excuse was, who knows what Channel 2 or Channel 7 might have filmed before I reached the scene some three hours later?

After picking the brains of neighbors who had known the dead man, I questioned a woman who had witnessed his plunge from the roof of a twenty-one-story apartment building. I still had no idea why he did it. I gathered from the cops they were baffled, too. No suicide note. My cameraman, good old Harvey Weinstock, saved my ass again. He suggested that somebody in the family might be able to fill in the blank, and added that they also might have a picture of the guy that we could put on film.

I didn't hesitate. Nothing seemed more important than getting those elements on film.

The man's mother, a middle-aged, red-eyed widow in a blue-and-white flower-print kimono, cracked the door only an inch or so when I rang her bell. She did not want to go on television. "Go away," she sobbed. "I'm in mourning."

In my best phony sympathetic manner, I advised her that neighbors were saying that her son had killed himself because he was heavily into hard drugs. "They're claiming he started selling it, then got hooked on scag himself. I'd hate to put that on the air if it's not true. I'm sure your son was a decent guy. Unless I get the real story from you, I'll have no choice." The truth is, only one person, speculating off-camera, had suggested any such thing. Nevertheless, it worked.

The woman launched into an anguished tirade against people who will say anything to get on TV. Weinstock's camera was rolling. Then she told me that her son had been depressed for several days. His nineteen-year-old girl friend had been devastated by his confession that he also liked to have sex with men occasionally; she had broadcast this to their friends.

That interview—plus an exclusive snapshot of the dead man—boosted my stock in the trade, but not with my girl friend at the time. As the two of us watched that story on TV later, she accused me with her eyes and with the question of whether it might not have been better to let the reason for his suicide remain a mystery; to spare his mother that kind of useless humiliation.

I didn't know the answer at that point. I was trying to come to grips with that problem.

It was a different young woman—a stranger—who later assisted me in coming to terms with myself and the ethics, or lack of them, in my profession. "Just how far will you go to get a story?"

She was naked when she posed that challenge. So was nearly everybody else in the room except me and my film crew. This was our first experience with a hippie commune—a huge loft in Greenwich Village. It was dirty, sparsely furnished with cots, sleeping bags, wooden crates, and broken tables. Tattered blankets draped over ropes served as partitions between individuals, couples, and families. A special effort was required to hide my disgust and anger over the unchosen plight of several kids toddling about the bare wooden floor.

Focusing on my adversary's smoky blue eyes, I said I would go as far as necessary to tell the story. I felt compelled to pick up the gauntlet.

"Good enough. So have breakfast with us." She offered a marijuana joint and a can of warm beer. I accepted. The three Archie Bunkers in my crew looked on in transparent disapproval.

The woman, a pale, slender, taut-breasted blonde about twenty years old, smiled at me. Everybody in the commune called her Rocky. "This is how we start our day," she explained, sucking on a joint. "If you want to understand what it's like living in a setup like this—I mean, really understand—you have to open up your mind, let some different vibrations come in."

It was 10:00 A.M. Everyone except the toddlers—twenty-three men and women of various races—was lighting up and nursing a can of Rheingold.

Actually, the pot had very little effect on my mind, until later. At the time, I was preoccupied with all those bodies around me, and with the story I had come to shoot. The grass relaxed me just enough to lose my sense of discomfort in that strange environment, enabling me to put together one hell of a feature, filming the naked bodies only from the rear or in silhouette. Their sound bites, defending their dropout lifestyle, were surprisingly articulate and interesting.

What surprised me even more, though, was the delayed effect the marijuana seemed to have on my psyche. I was alone in my apartment after midnight, reviewing ideas and arguing with myself. In one corner of my mind was a suppressed hedonist with no interest in facing my responsibilities, possessing things, or getting caught up in ambition—like Rocky and her friends. In the other corner was an aggressive, pragmatic, hard-nosed reporter who kept my career on the up track—to support my habits, pay the rent, alimony, and taxes. That night, Rocky's side seemed to be winning the sparring match. How had she put it? "What the hell, man. You only go around once. If you don't do it now—if you back off from every gamble that doesn't fit in with middle-class mediocrity—you miss the best of this gig called life. And don't forget, fifty years from now, all new people."

The parts of her that had rubbed off on me made a difference. I felt less certain of my approach to things in general, less committed to ideas that I had accepted for many years as hard-core certainties. I felt the weight of all the downbeat chapters of my history—the disappointments, betrayals, lies, failures, frustrations, misunderstandings, and pain. For the first time in my life, I began to grasp why some people don't want to live forever: Heaven and hell were childish myths. Justice rarely triumphed. And the American Dream was a lie.

With those revelations came a sense of relief. I began to feel less guilty about doing whatever it was I had to do. I simply promised myself that I would contribute as little as possible to the madness that cripples humanity, to help where I could be helpful or walk away.

Morally rearmed, I went back into the trenches, determined to keep my promises. A perfect test presented itself almost immediately.

The assignment editor sent me out to Queens to interview this guy who was involved in an unprecedented lawsuit against the city. When I knocked on his door and identified myself as a Channel 4 newsman, he said his lawyer had advised him not to talk to the press. "Besides," he added, "I don't watch Channel Four. I watch 'Eyewitness News' on Channel Seven. They're number one."

An ingenious piece of flapdoodle came to mind—a reflex action. Remembering my vows, I gambled on the truth instead. "That's right. They're number one. We're number three. That's why I need all the help I can get."

He looked at me closely, then nodded. "Okay. Come on in. I know what it's like to be a loser." And he gave me one hell of a sound bite.

Eureka! There was a better way.

Subsequent experience—my own and that of my colleagues

with similar misgivings about our standard procedures—soon persuaded me that I probably would have to compromise my new principles. A lot.

A bunch of us Channel 4 bird dogs—Ken Alvord, Robert Potts, Mary Alice Williams, Barry Cunningham, and Liz Trotta—discussed our dilemma one evening over drinks at our favorite oasis, Hurley's bar, on the corner nearest to the newsroom.

"If I had played it straight yesterday," Cunningham said, "I would have come up empty on the biggest story in town." He went on to tell us about the funeral service for Vinnie ("The Horse") Giralamo, a 275-pound motorcycle gangster.

A couple of days earlier, Giralamo had died in jail mysteriously, while awaiting trial for murder. He was accused of flinging a screaming young groupie from the roof of the Hell's Angels' clubhouse on the lower East Side of Manhattan. Whatever she might have done to trigger such a primitive response was known only to Giralamo.

When Cunningham and his crew arrived at Provenzano's Funeral Parlor on Second Avenue, an intimidating assemblage of Hell's Angels—husky, bearded thugs with gold earrings, scummy teeth, foul mouths, leather jackets, and ass-kicking boots—and their gaudy motorbikes filled the street.

"Get the fuck outta here," they warned all the news teams hovering uncertainly on the fringe. The other reporters gave up. Not Cunningham. He was on a six-month tryout, having lost his berth at Channel 5. He dared not come back empty. So he asked for an audience with the thug-in-chief, Giralamo's successor. "What we'd like to do here," he began, "is take pictures of the body inside the funeral parlor and the mourners filing past the coffin to pay their last respects to Mr. Giralamo. We will certainly be discreet and cause no disruption in there. After shooting the eulogy, we'll leave, okay?"

The gang leader gaped, astonished. "You're out of your skull, man. Nobody goes in there but us. This is private."

Cunningham managed to look utterly defeated. "You mean you're taking it upon yourself to restrict the entire television news industry to taking pictures only out here on the public street?"

"That's it, man. Out here on the street, okay. Don't even try to come inside."

Exactly what Cunningham had in mind all along.

"Hell, even when you don't play it like a Boy Scout, you can blow it," Ken Alvord told the gang in Hurley's. "You *have* to be devious in this game."

Alvord and his crew had been blocked at the door of a homicide scene. "You can't take no pictures of the body," said a towering chunk of granite disguised as a New York cop. "No pictures. Period."

Alvord tried the old we-only-want-to-shoot-the-scene-not-the-body gambit. It worked. His cameraman walked around the tiny room alone, focusing his Auricon here and there, dissatisfied. He rejected every angle without taking a shot. "Goddamn room is too small. I can't shoot it without showing the body. No way."

As Alvord, feeling faint, buckled at the knees, the cop caught on. "Get the fuck outta here."

The point made by Alvord and Cunningham in our discussion was reinforced by my own recollection of what had happened to a Channel 7 reporter, Betty Adams, when she tried to do it on-camera without subterfuge.

Every newsreel in the Big Apple, along with radio and print newshounds, had converged on the overseas gateway at Kennedy Airport. Senator Ted Kennedy would soon arrive by limousine from Manhattan, scheduled to fly to Ireland. The security blanket— Secret Service agents, Swat teams, Port Authority police, and city cops—was tighter and heavier than any we had seen since Fidel Castro came to town.

They corralled the mob of us behind maroon velvet ropes attached to stainless-steel stanchions near the entrance. "Here are the ground rules," one of the crew-cut feds announced. "You can take all the pictures you want. The senator will not stop for interviews. One more thing: you will not be allowed to move beyond these ropes."

Our pleas and grumbles failed to move them. There were so

many guards around us, determined men with guns on their hips and muscles in their faces, we could see no chance of getting a sound bite.

Dammit.

Senator Kennedy emerged from his limousine with a small entourage, and walked leisurely toward the entrance. Having no other choice, we stood there like a pack of dumb animals. Our cameras rolled and clicked. As the senator came abreast of us, Betty Adams was suddenly overcome by her professional reflexes. With microphone in hand, she jumped the velvet rope and lunged to reach him. "Senator Kennedy, would you please . . ."

That was as far as Betty got. The whole security blanket came down hard on the woman, as if her mike were a pistol.

While Kennedy's protectors struggled with the Channel 7 reporter and hauled her away for interrogation, the rest of us moved in on the now defenseless senator, firing questions. He stopped and answered in detail. All of us shot the story we had come for—all, that is, except Betty.

A willingness to defy authorities, as Betty Adams did, is one of several personality traits you have to develop to be effective as a streetwalker. In many instances, the story you're out to cover is not just lying there for the taking. It is hidden by vested interests, protected by protocols. To circumvent them and get the story, you may, for example, imply to a stubborn, tight-lipped district attorney that you already know more than he has told you—to draw him out at least far enough to confirm your hunches. You may ignore No Trespassing signs and sneak into a mental hospital where you have reason to believe that the patients are being mistreated. You may walk into someone's home or office with a concealed microphone and a camera that appears to be inactive, to catch a person off guard. Deceitful? Yes, but morally correct in my judgment. Long before my time, society gave journalists the right to play by a slightly different set of rules. Some white lies and deceits can be justified if perpetrated solely for the purpose of digging up the truth and airing it, but not for the purpose of sensation mongering as I did with the poor woman whose son committed suicide. That was an abuse of my mandate to be somewhat devious. Realizing that, belatedly, I never again went that far.

Wouldn't it be wonderful if all the conflicts and hassles a TV bird dog has to face in the field were created only by authorities, strangers, and rival journalists? Forget it. On a given day, your most formidable antagonist may be your producer.

Riding back to the studio from Queens with my crew, I got a call on the car radio from Jeff Rosser, who was then my producer. He wanted to know the content and length of the story we had covered. Basically, it was a one-on-one interview with City Councilman Eugene Mastropieri.

"It starts with a walking stand-upper outside his office. My entrance into the building sets up his sound bite. Mastropieri says he's innocent; explains the circumstances that made him look guilty; says he has paid the overdue parking tickets and the taxes he owes, and he's going to fight to keep his seat on the council. I close with an on-camera stand-upper, giving the date the council plans to vote on his expulsion. Time: about one forty-five."

"What about the interview we set up for you with Councilman Katz?" Rosser asked.

I explained that putting Katz into the bag would make it too fat, well beyond 1:45—Rosser's explicit span of tolerance for news stories. Rosser wanted Katz in, insisting that it be done in 1:45 nevertheless, even if that meant trimming Mastropieri.

"It's my judgment, Jeff, that we don't need Katz today. We've let him blast Mastropieri on the air several times already. This is the first time the accused has opened his mouth on-camera. And— what the hell—he's desperate to clear himself. He does not speak in simple sentences."

"One forty-five," the producer repeated. His tone conveyed the rest of the message: case closed.

Knowing that further negotiation would be futile, I responded like a short-order cook. "Okay, you got it. Two pounds of sausage in a one-pound bag coming up."

95

The radio was silent for perhaps ten seconds. "See me when you come in," Rosser commanded.

In the end, he let me do it my way. My experience with a long string of producers before him told me, however, that this had been only a preliminary skirmish. We would clash again. And again.

Connie Collins, in the newsroom cubicle next to mine, overheard me grousing to myself as I walked back to my desk from an infuriating test of wills with Rosser. I had lost.

"They want the fucking story covered ten ways from Tuesday," I muttered. "Every angle under the sun; all of it in a minute thirty, a minute forty-five. What bullshit."

"I know, honey," Connie said sympathetically. "They ask us for miracles every day. And they get them."

"Yeah. But this time I'm mad as hell. I'm not going to take it any more."

So I tromped into the editing maze and put together a videotape package that told the story the way I felt it should be told, in 2:25. When I finished, five or six minutes before air time, I telephoned the producer to give him the news, a fait accompli. The story was worth every bit of 2:25 and it was too late to recut to his time specifications.

Now it was Rosser's turn to grouse. Since my story merited the lead slot on the 6:00 P.M. newscast, however, he had no choice; he went with it, grudgingly. He accused me of always coming up with excuses for running long, ignoring his standing order that—with rare exceptions—news stories should be under two minutes.

I argued patiently that very few of my stories were two minutes long, that most of my stuff ran less—even if I had to kill what I thought were key elements to do it. He threatened to have the logs checked, and told me to see him after the show.

At 7:00 P.M., as Chuck Scarborough signed off the newscast, I walked over to the producer's desk. He had a single sheet of paper before him—a list of my stories for the past five weeks, compiled by a desk assistant.

President Lyndon Johnson, accompanied by press secretary Jack Valenti, pauses for an exclusive TV interview the morning after his nomination at the 1964 Democratic convention in Atlantic City.
(Photo by Dan Farrell)

Anchoring the weekend "Eleventh Hour News" at WNBC-TV in 1969, number one in The Ratings.
(Photo by Jacob Patent)

Starting a typical day at 7 A.M. in the spring of 1981, getting marching orders from assignment editor Jim Unchester at the central news desk. Jim's deputy, Larry Schulz, is on the phone lining up someone else's story for the day.
(Photo by Charles Thomas)

Comparing assignments with reporter Jane Hanson at her cubicle in the WNBC-TV newsroom.
(Photo by Charles Thomas)

Before leaving Rockefeller Center in mid-Manhattan on assignment, tape-man Joe Gafa (left) and cameraman Jerry Yarus load their hardware into the trunk of a company car. *(Photo by Charles Thomas)*

At the scene of a suspicious fatal fire in the borough of Queens with reporters J. J. Gonzalez (left) of WCBS-TV and Maxene Black (center) of WABC-TV. *(Photo by Charles Thomas)*

Wrapping up the fire story with an on-camera stand-upper under the expert direction of Joe Gafa (left) and Jerry Yarus. *(Photo by Charles Thomas)*

Back in the newsroom preparing a detailed script that tells the show producer and the videotape editor exactly what pictures should go with which words to tell the story. *(Photo by Charles Thomas)*

In the videotape dubbing room with editor Howard Froimovitz, cutting a twenty-minute field cassette down to one minute forty-five seconds of the best words and pictures to tell the story. *(Photo by Charles Thomas)*

Sharing a joke with anchorwoman Sue Simmons in her office off the WNBC-TV newsroom. *(Photo by Charles Thomas)*

Entertainment reporter Chauncey Howell expressing his gratitude for a suggested feature story that enhanced his reputation as one of the funniest personalities on the tube.

(Photo by Charles Thomas)

Unwinding in Hurley's with reporter David Diaz and deputy assignment editor Neal Rosen at the end of the day. *(Photo by Charles Thomas)*

"Going back to May eleventh," he said evenly, "I see that eighty percent of your stories have been under two minutes." I had to bite my lower lip to keep from saying, I told you so. Rosser's apology was oblique. "Pretty good, Bobby." I nodded and let it go at that.

When I reprised these minor triumphs to one of my colleagues, she regaled me with the tale of her successful encounter with an associate producer.

She had worked two whole days on a feature story—a real tough one to put together—and then they didn't bother to run it. That was Friday. The next Monday, she went to the producer and said it was still a good story, there were no time frames to worry about, everything that was true the previous Friday was still true. So why didn't he run it today?

The producer said he'd think about it. That's when she decided to use a little pressure. What she told him was, "Let's put it this way, honey. If you don't run it today, I'm going to spread it around that a certain associate producer has a small dick."

That may have gotten to him, because her story ran that day.

Newswriter Bernie Gavzer—after losing a big round to the 11:00 P.M. producer Sue Levine—said he was wondering if he should go into another line of work. "The bullshit around here is incredible."

Gavzer had been assigned to edit the videotape of Senator-elect Al D'Amato's news conference at Kennedy Airport upon his return from a trip to Italy, where many thousands of people had been killed or left homeless by an earthquake. When Gavzer finished, he dutifully notified the producer that the sound bite would run forty-two seconds.

"That's too long," Levine said flatly. "Cut it to twenty-two seconds."

"If I cut it that much," Gavzer protested, "what D'Amato says won't make sense."

"I don't care what he says," Levine explained, "so long as it fits."

Sometimes when you have managed to glide past the assignment desk, the associate producer, or the producer without any flack, you run up against an executive producer who wants to meddle with your story.

I had just returned to the newsroom after covering the last rites for Marine Corporal Steven Crowley, a national hero slain by a mob at the United States Embassy in Pakistan. During a news conference after the funeral in Port Jefferson, on Long Island, Crowley's mother had thanked the media—me in particular—for the sensitive, discreet manner in which she and her family had been treated throughout their ordeal over the previous three days of massive coverage. Her statement was on my tape. Carole Clancy got the word from my cameraman. She was ecstatic. Here was a chance to let an objective, unimpeachable source tell the world that Channel 4 reporters were good guys, the kind of sensitive and compassionate human beings who ought to be rewarded—preferably with a larger viewing audience.

"That statement by Mrs. Crowley praising you by name," Clancy said with a warm smile, "that has to go into your piece."

I was speechless for a moment. Whatever modicum of restraint and respect I might have shown the Crowleys would be wiped out by such a cheap self-pat on the back in my scenario. Hell, that woman had lost a son. "I can't see that on the air, Carole; not in my piece. If it has to be said, let the anchorman do it."

Clancy didn't answer. I walked away, and nothing more was said about my compliment, in the newsroom or on the air.

The conflicting priorities that so often compel television bird dogs to bark at their masters seem unavoidable—so long as assignment editors, producers, and news directors feel that the only way to stay on the payroll and someday become a vice-president or chief executive is to pull big numbers. Hence, they regularly clash with one another.

Let's start with the assignment editor. He or she constantly checks incoming wire copy and listens to radio newscasts, police and fire alarms—afraid of missing something big. He must also make phone calls to check out a rumor or set up shooting locations, while keeping in touch with reporters via phone and two-way radio. He has to know the geography, the politics, and problems of his broadcasting area; he has to anticipate what is likely to ensue tomorrow because of what did or didn't occur last week. He must know where to make arrangements to rent a helicopter, a jet, a power boat, or a LandRover; which private and public agencies deal with what. In other words, he is like a newspaper's city editor, responsible for the breadth and depth of news coverage. If another channel comes up with something hot or juicy that he failed to get, he is in big trouble. Therefore, in the process of deploying reporters, he is prone to overprogram them. "Be sure to ask people in the neighborhood about this angle. See if you can find somebody who will take the other side of the issue. Get pictures of this, that, and the other. Show us the scene and reenact the events that led to the showdown. We should also have some comment from the family—still pictures, too, if they have any, plus a strong sound bite from the FBI and a little reaction from the mayor."

In complying with those directions, the reporter comes back to the studio with more angles than his producer is willing to put on the air. "What? Three minutes?" he will scream. "No way. I've got a lot of other stuff to get on the show. Hold it down to a minute thirty."

Producers habitually think in terms of the pace and scope of their newscast. A little hit-em-in-the-guts here, a little soft-shoe there, a little sex, a little blood, a taste of something out of the ordinary. Above all, keep it moving. Work in a few freeze frames, wipes, and dissolves, with help from the graphics department. A live remote or two from the field—to hell with what it is about—would perhaps add some excitement to the middle section of the show to offset the dullness of a public hearing at City Hall.

In short, producers think in terms of production values. Reporters have to fight like hell to persuade them that a particular story deserves more time than has been arbitrarily allotted for it. Sadly, reporters tend to stop battling after losing four or five in a row. Consequently, the news show looks good from a production purist's point of view. Its news content, however, is diluted.

Ideally, the assignment editors and producers should agree on what to cover and how to cover it each day, so that reporters are not trapped in the middle of their conflicting goals. Normally, they do get together in the morning or early afternoon to discuss what is being covered or will be covered that day. Somehow, though, the assignment editor's broader concept of this or that story often is not communicated to the producer, or is ignored. As a rule, the producer does not want to hear about a story that runs more than two minutes, unless it is part of a series that is being hyped that week to boost The Ratings.

Periodically at the end of the work day, Channel 4 streetwalkers compare frustrations over a drink to find out which of us has survived the worst outing. A winning entry from Jim Ryan went like this.

"First thing this morning, the assignment desk sends me out with the Eddie Guilbaud crew to cover a news conference on the subway budget squeeze. We taped Dick Ravitch [then the newly appointed chairman of the Metropolitan Transportation Authority] telling us how the twelve-million-dollar deficit may force them to raise the subway fare. Before I have time to write a script, figure out a stand-upper, and package the story, my beeper goes off. Call the desk. Okay. 'There's a big explosion at Penn Station,' they tell me. 'Get right over there. Take the Ravitch tape with you; we'll send a courier to pick up both stories at Penn Station.'

"So we dash downstairs and jump into the car at Fifty-third and Broadway. Before we pull away from the curb, my beeper goes off again. Call the desk. Now the desk is saying there's no explosion, just a bomb scare. Don't go there. Hold off on that. 'Instead,' they say, 'head for the Brooklyn Bridge; there's a big riot going on down there.' Okay.

"This time we get as far as Forty-second Street and Third Avenue. The car radio comes on. 'Listen,' the desk says, 'forget about the riot at the Brooklyn Bridge; that was unfounded. Why

don't you try to get some reaction from subway workers to the statement Ravitch made. The AP quotes him as saying he would rather
see a subway strike than raise the fifty-cent fare.' I say okay. 'You
realize,' I tell the desk, 'the union headquarters is up around Sixty-
eighth and Broadway, and I'm down here on Forty-second at Third
Avenue in heavy traffic. Why don't you guys on the desk make a
phone call to see if we'll be able to get anything worthwhile up
there?' 'Okay,' the desk says, 'we'll get back to you on the radio.'

"A minute or so later, the radio comes on again. 'Give us a
land line,' they say. I get out of the car and find a phone. Now they
say I should leave the Guilbaud crew, take the Ravitch tape with
me, and wait where I am on the East Side for a courier. The Guilbaud crew is supposed to go to Penn Station to shoot the nonexplo-
sion. Another reporter is going to meet them there. So I stand on
the street corner for maybe twenty-five minutes waiting for the
courier. The only thing we finally get on the air out of all that stop-
and-go traffic, out of all those possible stories is a talking head of
Dick Ravitch saying he didn't know whether the subway fare was
going to go up or not."

Depending on who was top banana among the four or five people chained to the central news desk—dispatching and instructing
teams of grunts over our two-way radios—a day on the street could
be a pain in the arse or a pleasure, producing a good newscast or a
home movie.

Between and after Bob McCarthy (1963–69) and Roger Higle
(1973–76), we endured a series of assignment editors who failed to
fill the shoes of those two giants. There was only a single occasion
on which I beat one of them to the draw.

After driving around in circles through the streets of Elizabeth,
New Jersey, cameraman George Kamsler gave up in disgust.
"These directions you got from Higle are all fucked up," he
grumbled.

That couldn't be, the rest of us in the crew insisted, defending
our omniscient assignment editor. We were supposed to cover a protest rally by tenants at a low-income housing project called Pierce
Manor. The address in Roger's note was nonexistent, however.

"Wait a minute. There's a phone number written here," I said, "for the minister who organized the demo. Pull over to that telephone booth. I'll check it out."

As I was about to enter the sidewalk booth, a local fire department lieutenant emerged from a bright-red station wagon and approached me. Recognizing my face, he smiled. "I suppose you're here to cover the triple murder and suicide, right?"

I thought he might be pulling my leg, but something told me to play it straight. "What triple murder?"

"Oh, haven't you heard about it? A guy just killed his parents and his sister, then turned the shotgun on himself. It's right down the street from here. Follow my car. I'll take you there."

Less than ten minutes later, we were filming the four bodies being hauled from the house to the meat wagon. Only one other TV crew was on the scene, New Jersey's Channel 13. We double-teamed the homicide detective in charge and a couple of neighbors who had known the victims. What a coup; solid evidence to reinforce my position as the number-one bird dog in Kennel 4.

Our New York competitors still hadn't surfaced when I wrapped up the story with an on-camera closer in front of the death house. The cameraman canned the film.

As we returned to the car, our radio link with the assignment desk was practically smoking. "K-E-K three-two-two calling the Kamsler crew. Do you read? Over." Higle's voice was strained, exasperated.

My crew and I laughed out loud, guessing what was on his mind. "Can't you just see him?" Frank McBride, the lighting tech, asked rhetorically. "Chewing his nails and pulling out his hair."

"Let's have a little fun with him," I suggested, seeing a chance to go two up on our usually impeccable chief. "We were just about to call you, Roger," I said into the mike. "We got lost with those directions you gave us to the housing demo. Over."

"Never mind that. Forget the housing story. We've just got a tip on something really hot in the same town. If you give me a land line, I'll fill you in. Over." He was playing it close to the vest; no point in alerting a rival channel that monitored our radio transmissions from time to time, as we did theirs.

"Like I said, Roger, we are lost. No phones in sight. Just tell me the facts on the horn. Over."

"I'd rather not. This could be an exclusive. Do you copy? Over."

"Oooh," I said, as if finally seeing the light. "You mean the triple murder and suicide."

Higle gurgled, then lapsed into speechlessness.

"Don't worry, Chief," I assured him. "We've already filmed that exclusive. It's in the can."

Like McCarthy before him, Higle moved on to a better job in news biz. For reasons that none of us in the pits could fathom, the brass echelon seemed to hold that key position in low esteem, as if it could be handled by any college graduate with or without a solid background in wizardry.

Typically, when Higle told them of a tempting offer he had received from Channel 5, they made no effort to dissuade him. All they said was, "Don't forget to turn in your NBC credentials."

A year or so after Higle's departure, I got a brief glimpse of bird-dog paradise—not one but two assignment editors who apparently knew what they were doing. Bret Marcus and Sid Friedman, former associate producers, worked the desk in tandem.

Around midmorning, over the car radio, they told me they had come up with a better angle on the story I was covering in Manhattan's Diamond District. I told them that was fine since what I'd been getting from the cops was not too hot anyway and I had been struggling to jerry-build a second-day follow-up on the mysterious theft of millions in diamonds and the disappearance of the dealer who had owned them.

The Marcus-Friedman task force advised that the missing man's body had been discovered in East Stroudsburg, Pennsylvania. They had chartered a helicopter—at $285 an hour—to deliver me and my crew to the scene.

As Jerry Yarus parked our car at the Sixtieth Street heliport on the East River, we saw a whirlybird settling down on the concrete pad. Joe Gafa articulated the consensus. "Woof-and-dell.

What timing. Maybe Marcus and Friedman aren't like those other turkeys we've had."

"Right on," Yarus seconded. "And as they say back in the crew lounge, it's tough to soar like an eagle when you work with turkeys."

Three quarters of an hour later, as the helicopter descended at the airstrip on the outskirts of East Stroudsburg, we spotted a green and white taxi pulling up to the edge of the tarmac. Another point for Marcus and Friedman.

The taxi whisked us to the coroner's office in nothing flat. There, we taped the arrival of the dead man's family. We interviewed a brother, the coroner, and the Pennsylvania state trooper who had found the body on a lonely road outside of town.

"A very strong package," I informed the desk by telephone.

"We figured that," Marcus said matter-of-factly; a good imitation of Higle. "The producer plans to lead the six o'clock show with your package."

By prearrangement, the same taxi rushed us back to the airstrip. We were airborne within five minutes and back down to earth forty-eight minutes later at the heliport. The time was 4:50 P.M. My mental computer calculated my dwindling chances for leading the show. Our courier, certain to be standing by, could drive the tape cassette back to the studio within twenty minutes. I could supervise the editing of the piece in maybe thirty-five minutes, certainly by 5:55. It would be close, but I could make it.

However, there was one last detail that the dynamic duo on the desk had forgotten. No courier. Under the rules of the game, dictated by various unions, we were stymied. Only dues-paying Teamsters could bring film or tape from the field to the broadcasting base.

I phoned the desk. By the time Marcus and Friedman corrected their oversight, it was too late to make the top of the newscast. Once again, Gafa said it for all of us. "They're like the cow that gives lots of milk and then kicks over the pail."

You can't do it on-camera or show it on the tube without competent cooperation on many fronts: assignment editors, camera crews, couriers, writers, producers, editors, directors, studio technicians, and stagehands. None is more critical, however, than your primary source of information, drama, humor, and astonishment—ordinary people. Luckily, people are utterly fascinated by television, mesmerized. They allow you to invade their privacy, bare the secrets of their souls, and present them as "Loony Tunes" characters when you choose. Why do so many go along so willingly with almost any undignified game plan? Nobody has the complete answer. I gained a partial insight while covering a fire and three unrelated homicides years apart.

Cameraman Frank Follette parked the company sedan about a block and a half from a four-alarm disaster on the Lower East Side of Manhattan. As my film crew began unloading their tools from the trunk, a potbellied guy wearing rough work clothes waddled from a doorway, nursing a can of beer. "Hey, you guys are from television, right? How 'bout putting me on? I've always wanted to be interviewed."

Patiently, for the umpteenth time in my career, I explained that television didn't work that way, that the people we interview have to be involved in the story we're covering. Then I asked him if he knew anything about the fire.

"What fire?"

"There's a big one just around the corner from here."

"Oh. Anybody killed?"

"I don't know. That's one of the things we hope to find out when we get there."

The man was silent after that. He trailed us, at a respectful distance, to the scene. Ours was the only newsreel in sight.

I soon found a pair of survivors—two middle-aged women wrapped in blankets. Their grimy faces were strained and streaked with tears. As the potbellied man looked on from the background, they gave me the right words, the right grimaces. "The first thing I heard," one woman said, "was a big explosion. Ka-boom. It sounded like the end of the world. When I opened the door of my apartment, this huge ball of fire came roaring down the hallway straight at me. I ran the other way. I just barely got out the back window and onto the fire escape before the whole damn floor went up in flames."

105

A Red Cross van carried the survivors off to a temporary shelter in Upper Manhattan.

Several minutes later, after shooting more smoke-eaters in action and interviewing fire commissioner John O'Hagan, we started to leave. By now, other news teams were playing catch up. And there on the fringe of the crowd, we saw the potbellied guy in the glare of a Frezzi lamp, being interviewed by another channel. "The first thing I heard," he said dramatically, "was this big explosion. Ka-boom. It sounded like the end of the world. . . ."

I began to fully appreciate the lengths to which people would go to get on the air—a fleeting moment of glory, a chance to be somebody for a change.

Memories of that guy came back to me while covering a sixteen-year-old gunman accused of killing a New York cop. As detectives brought the young suspect out of the 104th Precinct station house to a waiting squad car, he looked squarely into the television cameras that would spread his fame. Even when they put him in the backseat of the car, he twisted around to keep his face in camera range. The kid, I sensed, had been living in a world in which nobody recognized his importance. And no matter what might happen to him later, being a homicide suspect had served an important purpose to him. I sensed, too, that there were many thousands more like him.

The second homicide story in this instructive trilogy expanded the knowledge gained from the first. An Associated Press bulletin informed the news desk that a woman, eight months pregnant, had been stabbed to death in her apartment on Central Park West. Police were looking for her husband.

It was a dreary, rainy morning on the Upper West Side of Manhattan. By the time I got there with a film crew, the trail was cold. The body and the homicide detectives had long since vanished. Two rival newsreels, led by Penny Crone of Channel 9 and Kristi Witker of Channel 11, were already there. Their cameramen were shooting exteriors of the apartment building. What else could anyone do?

"There's nobody around who knows a damn thing about it,"

Penny said dejectedly. "They've all gone to work. No neighbors who knew the woman, no witnesses, no nothing. How the hell are we going to make a story?"

Kristi had no answer. Neither did I. "I'm going to sit in the car and think about it," I said. "Maybe something will come to me."

Perhaps twenty minutes later, after Kristi and Penny had left, I got lucky. A tall, handsome man in a new trench coat went dashing through the rain toward the entrance of the building. He looked like a homicide cop. I ran to catch him at the door.

"No, I'm not a detective," he said. "I'm the husband."

Cooperative and anxious to please—saying in effect he had nothing to hide—the man led me and my crew into his apartment. He had been in Boston on business, he said, when it happened. He had just been released after hours of interrogation by detectives in the Fifth homicide squad.

Except for the body, which had been removed, the murder scene was still intact. A blood-soaked bed. Grisly stuff. Dick Lombard filmed it from several angles.

The dead woman's husband took us through the premises, showing no emotion, until he picked up a gold-framed color photograph of himself and his wife—their wedding picture. With the camera rolling, he clutched the picture and kissed it. Tears trickled down his handsome cheeks. "We were so happy together," he sobbed. "We were still in love."

He then moved to a baby carriage and picked up a blue wool blanket. Still weeping, he buried his face in it. "We bought this blanket together only a week ago for the baby. I'll never see my son," he moaned. "My baby, my wife . . . gone, gone, gone."

What a performance. Lombard caught it all on film.

Walking back to our car, we all agreed that the guy had been putting on a show. We were divided, however, on the question of motive. Had he posed for the camera to mask his guilt?

A few days later, after the husband had been cleared as a suspect, I replayed the scenario. It became clear then that he simply had not been able to pass up a once-in-a-lifetime opportunity to play Hamlet.

107

The third homicide told me more than the others. Witnesses on Bleecker Street in Greenwich Village reported that one building superintendent shot his next-door counterpart to death—the bloody climax of a long-running feud over who had been putting garbage in front of who's building on the sly. The dead man left a wife and two preteen children.

On this story, I vowed in advance, I was not going to be insensitive. Instead, I would show compassion by leaving the bereaved survivors alone. I would only use sound bites of neighbors and homicide detectives on the case. Which was exactly how I did it at first. I could afford to on this particular outing; no other newsreel was present to coerce me into typical gaucheries.

Jerry Yarus and Joe Gafa were packing their gear in the trunk, ready to leave Bleecker Street, when two urchins tugged my elbow. "Put us on TV, mister. We saw the whole thing."

I explained that I already had interviewed witnesses. I didn't need them.

"But it was our father who got killed," one of the boys pleaded.

My professional instincts got the better of me. Since they had volunteered, I could put them on-camera with a relatively clear conscience. And great God in the foothills! What terrific sound bites they gave me. In simple, dramatic sentences, they took turns telling what they heard, what they saw. Both were clinically perfect, as if sent from Central Casting in Hollywood. They could have been talking about the death of an alien from Mars. "And pow. He shot my father in the eye."

Again, my crew and I started to leave. An old guy wearing shabby, shapeless clothes tugged my elbow. "She's waiting for you," he announced. He pointed toward a frail young Puerto Rican woman in tears. She was wearing what had to be the prettiest dress she owned.

"The victim's wife?" I inquired.

The old man in the baggy suit nodded. "Yes, my granddaughter. She's waiting for you."

Reluctantly, I shoved the microphone under her quivering, freshly painted lips. She bewailed the loss of her husband, wept without embarrassment. Great TV. Some of her tears fell on my hand. That's when I got the message: she, as well as her kids, wanted the whole damn world to share their grief.

Experiences in that vein allowed me to feel more comfortable in my television role. There was a quid pro quo that mitigated my indiscretions to some degree. Just as I used people to suit my purposes, they used me. Why not? Television belonged to everybody.

Every year, more and more people seemed to have spotted our weaknesses in news biz and learned how to take advantage of them. I tutored a few aspirants off-camera.

My girl friend's next door neighbor asked apologetically whether I would consider giving TV coverage to a worthy cause in his school district. He was one of several counselors for roughly six hundred handicapped kids. "There are so many things we need in order to give these youngsters the kind of help they deserve. The Board of Ed just won't listen. We're planning a series of public panel discussions on it next week."

I was interested, eager to help the man to please my lady. In response to my questions, he said yes, a number of handicapped kids would be present at the discussions. Their parents and teachers had decided, however, that the kids should not be filmed or interviewed. No exploitation.

"With restrictions like that," I counseled, "there's no way to get on television. You have to understand that television is strictly amoral, as it exists right now. It doesn't give a damn one way or the other about politics, sin, or worthy causes. What news directors, assignment editors, producers, and vice-presidents care about are good pictures, action, sex, violence, confrontation, and controversy. It's a reaction medium, not an initiator. There are all kinds of people and organizations out there who are willing and anxious to play by our ground rules—politicians, professional image makers, flacks, promoters, and publicity hounds. They manufacture pathos, drama, sex appeal, and action on cue. If I tell the brass at NBC about your kind of panel discussions as a possible story, they'll want to know what kind of pictures, what kind of pizzazz I can get.

"Now if you guys decide to do a number on the Board of Ed—like a protest march or a school boycott, for example—something dramatic with a bunch of Tiny Tim Cratchits on crutches or in wheelchairs, ready to go on-camera—hell, you'll have every newsreel in town on your case."

He caught on. "In other words, you're telling me we have to put on a show."

"Exactly. News biz, I'm sorry to say, is eighty percent show biz."

4

Instant Foreplay

WHAT WERE YOU DOING on the afternoon of January 16, 1981? That's when an all-media blitz promised, erroneously, that the release of fifty-two American hostages in Iran was only a breath away.

I was locking my desk in the Channel 4 newsroom, getting ready to fly away to a Caribbean vacation. Assignment editor Bret Marcus and associate producer Ginny Russo stopped me at the door that led to paradise. "I hate to do this to you, Black Arrow," Marcus apologized. "I know you're going on vacation, but they're about to release the hostages."

"That's great," I said. "Glad to hear it, though I don't see what that has to do with my vacation plans."

Marcus said he needed a reporter for a special job, and mine was the only body available. David Diaz was tied up with *blah*. Heather Bernard was busy editing *blah blah*. Jim Ryan and Felipe Luciano were staked out on *blah blah blah*. "We're setting up a live remote in Times Square right now at Forty-fourth and Broadway."

I still didn't get it. "They're going to release the hostages at Forty-fourth and Broadway?"

"No, but if the release comes off, that big electric sign that carries new bulletins on the Allied Chemical Tower will flash the word. They want you to get live *vox pop*—reactions from people on the street."

"Okay. That makes sense," I conceded grudgingly, mentally revising my getaway plans. "But I don't want to jerk off in public. If they fail to let our people go this evening, I don't go on the air jerking off, right?"

Marcus and Russo looked at each other, embarrassed. "We agree with you," the associate producer consoled me. "But," she nodded toward the executive offices at the other end of the newsroom, "they want you to do a couple of live spots regardless."

"That's so dumb," I bawled. "If those people haven't been released by the time I go on the air, there's no fucking story in Times Square."

"You're probably right," Marcus said. "They want you to ask a bunch of people if, after all the ups and downs we've been through on this crisis in the past four-hundred forty days, they believe it's going to happen this time."

Having no choice, I did exactly as instructed; not a news story, just a smooth on-camera performance dispensing pap. When I wrapped it up, Russo informed me over the telex in my ear that everybody in the studio loved it.

A couple of days later when the hostages did leave Iran on a flight to Algeria, the Channel 2 assignment desk ordered Vic Miles and a Minicam unit to Liberty Park in New Jersey for two live spots during the early-evening show— *vox pop* reaction to the good news. Why that location? Because on the distant horizon, miles away, you could see the backside of the Statue of Liberty in New York harbor illuminated by floodlights.

New Jersey residents, however, had not been advised of the role they were supposed to play in Vic's reports. Liberty Park was empty.

Vic called in to tell the assignment editor he thought they should forget about any live pickups from the park that night. It was raining and there was nobody there.

The editor's response was, just interview two or three people, anybody at all—we want the spots.

Vic repeated that there was nobody out there except him and the crew in the van.

There was a pause at the other end of the radio link in Manhattan, followed by the suggestion that he just do a stand-upper with the Statue of Liberty.

Vic couldn't believe it. "From here I'm looking up her ass."

The studio assured him that was all right; it would make a nice picture with his stand-upper.

A stand-upper about the hostages or about the fact that there's nobody here, he wanted to know.

After another pause, Vic was told to stand by and they'd read him some copy on the history of the Statue of Liberty. Then he could ad-lib stuff about the statue being the symbol of the freedom the hostages are coming home to.

Vic wrote it down word for word and recited it live as instructed.

Had some important story been omitted from the newscast, he wondered, to make room for his fandangos?

The same questions had crossed my mind during those two live spots from Times Square. I knew that two live remotes of no consequence had been aired the day before, helping to squeeze a news story out of the picture. Mike Dreaden had killed a film report by Heather Bernard in which the president of the city policemen's union, the PBA, reacting to the death in the line of duty of a comrade, urged all cops to "shoot first and shoot to kill." Dreaden said he didn't have room for that local story, though he did find time to run videotape about the effect of cold weather on citrus crops over a thousand miles away in Florida.

The following morning, Dreaden decided that the "shoot to kill" story was a big one. Presently, Bernard was sent out with a camera crew to reshoot the interview the producer had eighty-sixed.

News judgment of that ilk had become rampant at all six TV stations in New York by that time. Part of the reason was the natural attrition of older news executives who had come to television from print. Some of their replacements could be described as technologically oriented young "messiahs" who had grown up with the tube. Under pressure from The Ratings, New York stations imported them from the hinterlands in bunches. For the most part, they had been trained to produce "infotainment" rather than straight news.

New technology also played a major role, affecting every station's basic news operation in the early seventies. Marvelous improvements in the portable Minicam, videotape, and tape-editing machines ushered in the era of instant replay, instant foreplay.

The $50,000 Minicam, weighing in at thirty-five pounds, could be plugged into a microwave dish atop a van to broadcast live from the field, bouncing signals off the powerful antenna that crowned the Empire State Building. It could also be tied into a $5,000 portable videotape recorder weighing fifty pounds. Videotape was superior to 16 mm film—sharper pictures, truer to life. No time lost in the developing room. Faster editing. A machine that looked like something in launch control at Cape Canaveral dubbed the scenes and sounds we needed from the field cassette to a blank tape cassette, the second generation to be played back on the air. Incredible new toys for grown-ups. The younger news directors, producers, and assignment editors could rarely resist any opportunity to show them off. Arbitrarily, they scheduled live remotes a day or two in advance regardless of whether anything newsworthy was expected to transpire at the time, regardless of whether the same information could be gathered early in the day, with better action pictures, and aired as a videotape package.

In a way, our young news messiahs—eager to play with their electronic toys—were like kids who couldn't wait for the Fourth of July to set off their accumulated fireworks.

As a reporter, I too appreciated the speed, clarity, and versatility of electronic journalism's hardware. However, my initial experience in the tape editing room left me with the impression that the brave new world of EJ was going to drive us all bananas.

In our semidark editing cubicle on the fourth floor, George White dubbed the opening five-second scene I had selected from the closed-circuit monitor on our left—the one that displayed my field cassette, sound as well as pictures, on command, which meant punching certain buttons on the editing console in a certain sequence. A second monitor on our right showed the same scene as it was reproduced on the blank cassette of three-quarter-inch tape. Quick and slick. No wonder our three-man film crews were being phased out in favor of two-man Minicam crews.

After dubbing that one scene, my editor shut down the machine. "I'll be back in fifteen minutes," he promised, getting up from his chair at launch control. "Time for my green dot."

What the hell was a green dot?

"It's a break they have to give us periodically during the day. It's in our contract."

No point in arguing about it. The EJ union (NABET) had enough clout to intimidate even management. Without technicians, there could be no such thing as a telecast. So for fifteen minutes I watched the second hand on the wall clock over my head as it sliced away some of the thin time cushion between my unfinished story and air time.

We laid down two more brief scenes over my prerecorded narration track before the next interruption. "Goddamn machine," George cursed. "It won't make this edit. I'll have to call the supervisor."

Bill Lockhart came in. George rolled the tape by punching assorted buttons on the console. The three of us gazed hopefully at the TV monitors in front of us. No go. Lockhart tried his hand on the buttons. Still no go. "Something's wrong with this editing machine," he cleverly deduced. "I'll move you guys to another room, if I can find one that's available."

That took another ten minutes. By now I was sweating the clock.

We got halfway through my piece when the second editing machine balked. It simply refused to respond to any signals George gave it. Lockhart figured this one out in a sawed-off jiffy. "Of course it won't work. I can feel the humidity in here."

"What has humidity got to do with it?" I asked.

"These are very sensitive machines. If the humidity goes above a certain point, they jam. The same thing can happen to the videotape recorders in extreme cold or heat out in the field. I'll have to call maintenance and have them give it a blow job."

I sat there, limp. A machine that wouldn't work unless you gave it a blow job?

Sure enough, a tall young man in coveralls arrived and plugged in a gadget that looked like a portable hair dryer. After removing the plastic cover from the editing machine, he sprayed cool air on the electronic circuits and the servos. Or so he said.

The machine went back to work with alacrity. Minutes later, with only my stand-up closer to be dubbed, another catastrophe: the metal clamps that held the original tape cassette in place bit down hard and stubbornly refused to let go. The tape reel was frozen.

Lockhart phoned maintenance again. A different guy in coveralls looked it over this time and concluded that he'd have to take the whole machine apart.

Staring at the clock, I pleaded with the EJ supervisor. "Could you please move us to another cubicle so we can finish this thing?"

"Sorry. We have only nine editing rooms. They're all tied up with other stories, local and network."

My deadline was so close the second hand on the clock looked like a machete slashing at my jugular.

When the machine had been reassembled, George dubbed the final segment while I aged ten years. We made air by the skin of our balls.

Some of the technical imperfections in EJ equipment were either overcome or minimized by further breakthroughs in electronic legerdemain. Ironically, as the hardware became more reliable, it was used more and more for entertainment purposes, less and less to cover real news.

It was the Minicam's live-remote capability, more than anything else, that distorted news values. News directors and producers seemed to experience what I called "executive orgasm" when they could superimpose the four-letter word "Live" on the screen. Never mind the content of the picture as long as they could show it live.

That's why TV bird dogs all over town began baring their teeth and snarling "S-L-R," complaining about one of the most detestable gimmicks in news biz—the silly live remote. You've seen it—a live spot from the field that shows nothing of significance: just a reporter, surrounded by gawkers and "Hi-Mom" wavers, talking about something that either happened three hours ago or might happen an hour later. My colleagues Anthony Prisendorf, Phil Barnow, Liz Trotta, Victor Madrid, and I all agreed that doing an SLR was akin to indecent exposure.

"It's a blatant insult to the viewer," Barnow fumed. "As if we're saying they're all a bunch of dummies out there on the other side of the screen; that they can't tell the difference or don't care—so long as we tell 'em it's live—that the content is strictly bullshit."

What infuriated us most about the SLR was the fact that in nine cases out of ten, the same story could have been covered much better earlier in the day. Management should have realized that, too. They simply could not resist the temptation to show off their new toys, even when it meant diminishing the quality of our newscast.

A case in point: At 11:00 A.M., while interviewing leaders of the striking New York Newspaper Guild, I learned that a massive demonstration was scheduled for 5:00 P.M. outside the offices of the *New York Post*. Their target would be Rupert Murdoch, the publisher. I telephoned the tip to the central news desk, pointing out that it would make a perfect live remote for the top of the five o'clock segment of our show. We couldn't have arranged it any better ourselves—about two thousand newspaper people with sympathizers from the building trades unions, screaming for Murdoch's head.

A deputy assignment editor informed me ruefully that the producer wanted me to tape the 5:00 P.M. demo instead. Only one live-remote unit was operational that day. Plans had already been made for it—a so-called health spot by Dr. Frank Field with doctors and medical gadgets at a clinic.

"That's crazy," I bellowed. "You're talking about live coverage of a setup, not a news event. Hell, Frank can do that stuff any old time on film or tape—right now, if he wanted to. What I'm offering live is a happening."

"I couldn't agree with you more," the assignment editor answered. "The trouble is, we announced on the show yesterday that Frank was going to do it live. We're locked in."

Some of the managerial goofs I've recounted sound unbelievable. Unhappily, the most frequently repeated phrase in news biz is, "I can't believe it." By the end of your first day on the job, you've either heard it from the old hands or said it yourself.

Jack Cafferty, newly arrived from station WHO-TV in Des Moines, barely had time to unpack his bags in New York before saying it. For his first live remote on Channel 4, Cafferty rode a taxi to Greenwich Village. He knew from his briefing that a couple of Students for a Democratic Society had blown themselves to bits on that site at West Eleventh Street several years ago. Now that one of their fugitive leaders, Mark Rudd, had resurfaced in New York after hiding underground for so long, the assignment desk found a typically flimsy excuse for revisiting the clandestine bomb factory.

Cafferty asked cameraman Jeff Scarborough, Chuck Scarborough's younger brother, if this was the right place. It was the right place but there was nothing there to shoot, as Cafferty pointed out.

Right again. The four-story brownstone where the SDS had set up its bomb factory had long since vanished, razed and hauled away. The entrance to the now-vacant lot was blocked by a weather-beaten plywood fence that was plastered with outdated political posters.

Knowing a deadbeat when he saw one, Cafferty called the desk on the two-way radio in the van to tell them that there was nothing at the location to justify a spot—nothing to shoot, no pictures, no building, only a plywood fence and a vacant lot.

After a pregnant pause, the desk responded that the producer wanted a live spot, so do it anyway, standing in front of the fence.

"I can't believe it," Cafferty confessed to the crew, officially becoming a member of the club.

Hearing about Cafferty's coverage of a nonevent, Heather Bernard reacted with irate empathy and chagrin. "Why do they keep doing that to us?"

During her videotape coverage of a hostage situation in a New York bank, Heather had taken full advantage of the police contacts she had cultivated over the years. As a result, she got better, closer pictures than any other news team on the scene. One segment showed the gunman reaching a hand through the bank's front door for a pack of cigarettes being offered by the wily chief of the NYPD hostage negotiating team, then pulling it back before the trap could be sprung. Dynamite stuff.

Hours later, after the gunman had been persuaded to surrender, Heather telephoned the newsroom to describe what she had on tape.

"Never mind the tape for now," she was told. "They want you to do a live spot within the next ten minutes. They're going to break into the afternoon soap opera for your report on how the cops finally freed the hostages."

Heather did the spot. Now she was anxious to rush back to the studio to edit her tape for the regular six o'clock news show, and said so on the phone. The news desk, under orders from higher-ups, ordered her to send the tape back by courier and stay on the scene. Somebody else would supervise the editing. "They want you to do a live wrap-around of your tape package."

Heather argued against it. She had four 20-minute tape cassettes—over an hour of pictures, sound bites, and on-camera bridges to be sorted out and condensed into a sensible package of two and a half minutes or so. It was an impossible task in the time span available unless the person guiding the videotape editor knew in advance where the best stuff was on which cassette. "Besides," the veteran reporter pointed out, "there's no reason to do anything live from this location at six o'clock. It's all over. No further developments are coming up. There won't be anything here to show except me standing in front of a bank that's been closed for hours. No cops, no hostages—none of the elements I've got on tape."

The desk refused to budge. Case closed. In desperation, Heather appealed directly to Ron Kershaw, the news director. Among other things, she told him the disastrous consequences, under comparable circumstances, on a previous assignment—the

Waldbaum's supermarket blaze in which six firemen perished when the roof collapsed. "Whoever edited my tapes not only did a lousy job of it, but also finished so late with so many complicated cues for the control room that the pictures I had of the fire never got on the air. It was mostly me standing there after the whole thing was over, talking about it and stumbling all over my words because I was so upset about not having pictures to lay over my narration. I think it would be a big mistake to risk having the same thing happen on this bank hostage story."

Kershaw upheld the assignment editor's decision. So Heather did the live spot—with no pictures whatsoever. As predicted, the newswriter they assigned to edit her tapes failed to finish by air time.

"What's the silliest live remote I've ever done?" Cliff Morrison of Channel 4 pondered. With Felipe Luciano, Robert Potts, and Will Spens, we were comparing outrages in the corner saloon. "That's easy. Hurricane David. Atlantic City.

"The desk had sent me down there to do live spots on something else—the Miss America Pageant. Okay, that made sense. But a few hours before air time, they read on the wires that Hurricane David was kicking up a storm in the Caribbean and heading up the Florida coastline. So they got me on the phone and said forget about the beauty pageant. Do the hurricane and Atlantic City's feverish preparations to weather it.

"I told them I had already checked it out with the weather bureau and civil-defense authorities down there. The storm was not coming our way. All we'd get down there was high winds, a little rain. Nothing heavy. They still wanted a spot. I said, 'Okay. Just remember what I said, though. It is not coming up this far. There's nothing to worry about in Atlantic City. So whatever you do back there in the studio, for God's sake, don't build it up.' They agreed.

"Then we come to show time. The first thing I hear over my telex is the anchorman saying a killer hurricane is roaring up out of the Caribbean and bearing down on Atlantic City; we switch now to Cliff Morrison for a live report on preparations for the storm.

"When they come to me, I'm standing there on this sunny

beach with the waves rolling in gently. I start by saying, 'Well, as you can see, it's a beautiful day in Atlantic City, and nobody here is really concerned about Hurricane David.'"

Felipe Luciano, who worked the street between weekend stints at the anchor desk, said his all-time worst remote had been inflicted on him during a PATH commuter train strike. "They sent me with the van to the Jersey end of the PATH line in Hoboken, where shuttle buses were bringing commuters back from Manhattan in the evening to make connections with another commuter railroad that was not on strike. Conrail. When we got there at the tailend of the rush hour, there were buses all over the place and wall to wall people. Thousands of them, confused and angry, anxious to get home. By the time the control room switched to me, however, it was all over. Nobody was there except me and the crew. Had I warned them over the radio? Of course. I said, 'Let's scrub this spot; the rush hour is over.' They insisted on coming to me anyway. All I could do was tell it like it was. I said, 'If you had switched to this location five minutes ago, you would have seen. . . .'"

News directors, producers, and assignment editors seemed to have one-track minds on live remotes. Once they had inked the spots into the show routine, that was it. Any effort you made to persuade them to cross it out was like trying to turn a freight train around. It was that kind of overcommitment that forced John Hambrick, sent out of town for a big story, to go through with a live remote that should have been delayed if not eighty-sixed.

A corporate jet plane carrying several executives of Texasgulf had crashed around 6:45 P.M. in rain and heavy fog during an instrument approach to Westchester County Airport. Hambrick was inked in to update the story at the top of the 11:00 P.M. newscast on Channel 4. Less than a minute after his car reached the location where the live unit had set up earlier, he saw anchorman Chuck Scarborough on the TV monitor near the camera. The show was on the air. Hambrick was still in the process of plugging the telex in his ear when Scarborough said, "A tragic plane disaster in Westchester County tonight. A private four-engine jet went down in fog and rain near the Westchester County Airport. Eight or nine executives of the Texasgulf Corporation are believed dead in the crash. John Hambrick is at the scene. We switch to him now for a live report. John?"

"Well, Chuck," Hambrick began uncertainly. "I'm not really at the scene. The plane went down in those woods you see behind me, about a mile from here. I arrived just moments ago, and I really haven't had time to find out what happened." He went on like that, telling what he didn't know as well as anyone could, for nearly four minutes.

Another critical factor rarely considered by aficionados of the live remote is the untenable conditions a bird dog can encounter in the field.

One Christmas Eve, they sent me to do a live remote at Macy's, the world's largest department store, featuring last-minute shoppers. On the preview screen I always carried in my head, it looked like a sugarplum assignment all the way. No sweat.

My Minicam crew and I had a miserable time, however, due to circumstances beyond our control. About thirty minutes before air time, cameraman Bob Friedman and audioman Nick Mayer told me they could not transmit a live signal to the studio from our location on Thirty-fourth Street at Sixth Avenue.

I wondered how the hell that could be. The microwave dish on top of our van was only a block and a half from the relay antenna at the tip of the Empire State Building. If the antenna collapsed, it would crash through the roof of our van.

Nick said something like, "The problem is in the giggahertz and the thermopolator connection to the frammis."

I took his word for it and asked if anything could be done to fix it.

Friedman said we could try backing the van a hundred yards closer to the Empire State Building. We did that and, sure enough, we bounced a picture to the studio in Rockefeller Center. However, about ten minutes before air time, a policeman said the end of our van was sticking out so far into Broadway it was creating traffic problems. He couldn't let us stay there.

I tried to reason with the man, explaining that this was the only spot on the block we could broadcast from. If we moved down the street, one of those tall buildings between us and the Empire State antenna would block our signal.

He was adamant. He understood the problem but he couldn't let us stay there. We'd have to move the van.

"Okay," I said. "If we do that, though, this telecast goes down the drain. My office will have to call your office and say it was you who fucked it up."

The policeman chewed on that one for a while, then brightened as he told me that, since he couldn't allow us to stay parked there illegally, he'd just leave.

Agreed, which proved to be a big mistake.

Five minutes to air, several hams among the Christmas shoppers clustered around our van—fully aware of our purpose—began jockeying for positions. Almost everybody wanted to be interviewed or at least get close enough to our camera to wave to mom. Arguments erupted. Some wiser heads in the crowd urged the hams to back off, to let us do our jobs. That led to insults, pushing, shoving, and finally fistfights; a full-scale donnybrook. Christmas packages were used as blunt instruments of vengeance. A few smart asses began grabbing packages and pocketbooks. Several noncombatants started snaffling electronic gear from our van.

Friedman, Mayer, and I fought our way to the van, salvaged what we could, and locked the doors. The melee around us was so close and thick we couldn't drive off. I called the news desk on the radio. "May Day, May Day. This is the Macy's unit calling. We're in the middle of a riot. Call nine-one-one and send the cops."

On another traumatic occasion, they sent me to the armpits of New York—the South Bronx—to do a live remote on complaints about the Sanitation Department's failure to clean the streets. The inevitable crowd convened as Fred Gutman and Gene Broda set up their hardware for my spot. The gawkers were relatively sedate until anchorwoman Pia Lindstrom, communicating over my telex, introduced me.

As I began my memorized commentary about dirty streets, my image could be seen on the miniature TV monitor my crew had placed on the sidewalk. A rowdy bunch of teenagers surged into the picture. They waved and shouted to the camera. At least two rambunctious girls grabbed my balls. At the same time, I could see some opportunists attacking our van, ripping off valuable equipment. Sheer chaos. I abbreviated my script without missing a beat and threw the ball back to Lindstrom in the studio.

In her comfortable, air-conditioned studio, she could not fully appreciate the contretemps at my location. In an effort to "relate" to me and further demonstrate that my spot was a live one— as our news directors constantly advised—Pia tossed a question at me.

"Sorry, Pia," I improvised, looking puzzled and disappointed. "I can tell from the TV monitor that you're trying to ask me something, but we've lost audio out here."

My favorite blonde on the tube, Mary Alice Williams, took a Minicam crew to Seventh Avenue at Thirty-third Street to do a live remote outside Madison Square Garden. An unprecedented disaster. Being a seasoned performer with an elephantine memory, MAW took appropriate steps to circumvent the kind of profanities and disruptions that had brought havoc to so many live spots in the field.

"First, I lined up three respectable-looking people to be interviewed—guys I knew were not the type to say four-letter words into the mike. They were waiting in a crowd to catch a bus at six-o-seven for the suburbs, which was okay since we were supposed to go on the air for only three minutes at six-o-two. The next thing I did was appeal to the crowd around our camera to cooperate—give us room to work in—and they did. About a dozen people formed a human chain that held the mob at bay. Perfect.

"At six-o-two, they told me over the telex that something had gone wrong in the control room. They couldn't come to me right then. We waited. We waited. We waited. Finally, the director said in my ear that they were switching to me in ten seconds. That's when four bad things happened all at once. Some guy broke through my human chain and tried to stick a knife in my cameraman. As the human chain regrouped and wrestled him down, the six-o-seven bus arrived. My three interviewees got on, leaving me standing there. Alone.

"The anchorman, Tom Snyder, said in my ear, 'Tell us about it, MAW.' At that point, a big black guy grabs the mike out of my hand and yells, 'Fuck you, white bitch.' Can you believe it?"

Channel 7 reporters have been equally miffed over the bastardly live remotes being forced on them. Peter Bannon was the first to fight back effectively. His weapon was later described by an admiring teammate as "almost passive resistance."

After his second live cut-in on the same nonstory during an hour-long "Eyewitness News" show, Bannon offered sound advice to the control room. Over the two-way radio, he candidly admitted to having exhausted his meager bag of relevant facts; nothing left to say. "So don't come back to me."

The director insisted on one more spot a few minutes later.

"If you come back to me," Bannon warned, "all I can do is tap-dance."

They came back to Bannon anyway. Humming a lively tune, he did a pretty good imitation of an inept tap dancer on "The Gong Show." The control room cut away from him, back to the anchor desk, after twenty embarrassing seconds.

No, he wasn't fired for his insolence. They simply warned him not to do it again. And the SLRs continued.

What could have been a respectable live remote from City Hall was downgraded to an SLR by the news decision makers at Channel 4. Jim Ryan was standing by in the Blue Room at City Hall with a hot Minicam. Mayor Koch was scheduled to enter shortly after 5:00 P.M. to announce details of his long-awaited six-point plan for combating subway crime.

About five minutes before air time, Ryan learned that Koch would be a few minutes late. He counseled the control room not to come to him at the top of the show. He'd give them ample warning when the mayor was ready.

Approximately one minute after five, they switched to Ryan as originally planned. He backed and filled two of the longest uninformative minutes in the annals of broadcast journalism.

Minutes later he alerted the control room that Koch would be walking into camera range momentarily so they could switch to him at any time and he'd vamp until the mayor started talking.

The mayor's news conference ran thirty-five minutes. When it ended, everybody except Channel 4's live unit packed up and skedaddled. That's when the control room finally came back to Ryan— in an otherwise empty Blue Room.

Slinking back into the newsroom from an SLR, Chauncey Howell was convicted on the spot by executive producer Hardie Mintzer, who told him that the live spot he'd just done made no sense at all. It wasn't interesting. It wasn't informative or even colorful.

Chauncey concurred, pointing out that he could have told Mintzer that in advance.

Then why had he done such a dumb story, Mintzer wanted to know.

Because that's where they'd sent him with the crew, Chauncey replied.

Acting on a telephone tip, the assignment desk dispatched one of my teammates, Robert Potts, and a crew to the Bay Ridge section of Brooklyn for a live remote on the evening show. Irate parents had disrupted traffic during the morning rush hour to dramatize demands that the bus stop at a dangerous intersection be moved down the block to cut the rate of accidents involving kids on their way to school.

It was all over when the Potts gang got there. No demonstrators in sight. The Transit Authority had capitulated and moved the bus stop to a safer location hours before.

Potts found a phone and informed the producer, Jeff Rosser.

"Maybe you can find somebody out there who can put you back in the picture," Rosser suggested, "somebody who was involved in the protest. They could tell you on-camera what happened earlier and how it was finally resolved."

Dubious but game, Potts gave it the old college try. He combed retail stores, coffee shops, taverns, and private residences in the neighborhood—a vain search for a suitable talking head. He called Rosser again. "There is nothing here. Nothing."

"I understand what you're saying," the producer said. "However, the show routine has you listed for a live spot near the top. I want at least forty seconds from you."

"Forty seconds of what?" Potts queried.

"Forty seconds of nothing."

For the better part of a year, Connie Collins was assigned to a weekly spot called "Speakout"—live *vox pop* at various locations in the city during the six o'clock newscast, allowing nondescript anybodies, uninformed or misinformed, to broadcast their opinions on the high cost of living, deteriorating subway service, or any other topic in the headlines.

With the exception of Collins, who loved the exposure she was getting, the rest of us grunts regarded "Speakout" as a trite and useless drill; bad journalism. Eventually, the news director came to the same conclusion and canceled that segment—not because we had told him ad nauseam, but mainly because one man on the street voiced an opinion on-camera that got through.

"Do you think the death penalty should be reinstated?" Collins asked person after person during her spot. As usual, some said yes, some said no or maybe. Then she held the mike under the chin of a well-dressed man who echoed her question and then responded, "I say yes, but only for the producers of this news show who would put something like this on television."

After an all-night vigil with a live unit outside New York Hospital, Chuck Scarborough had nothing of consequence to report the following morning. The deposed and ailing Shah of Iran was still inside, waiting to be granted sanctuary elsewhere. Nothing new had developed since Scarborough's 11:00 P.M. update. The *ayotollahs* of "Newscenter 4" were not deterred, however. If a live unit was out there in the field, by God, they used it no matter what.

Scarborough's spot during the local news cut-in on the "Today" show made me cringe with embarrassment for him and for our news team, which was still dead last in The Ratings.

127

He improvised professionally. Pointing to a bundle of newspapers on the sidewalk in front of the hospital entrance, he said the headlines in those copies of the *New York Times* backed up the previous night's reports that the shah's plane was standing by at LaGuardia Airport. Taking a few steps to his right, Scarborough squatted beside the papers, his news source.

"Great God in the foothills," I said aloud in the newsroom where a bunch of us were watching the TV monitor. "He's on location at the story, but he's not talking about what's going on there. He's telling what the goddamn newspaper says is happening miles away at the airport. Is that what they mean by live television coverage?"

Our assignment desk sent Jim Ryan with a live Minicam to Central Park's Tavern on the Green one evening. It sounded like a reasonable exercise at the outset: a star-spangled benefit party to mark the opening of the Alvin Ailey Dance Theater's season at Lincoln Center. The publicity handout, sent to all the media, had listed Harry Belafonte, Geoffrey Holder, and many other show-biz luminaries as guests—big names that everybody in New York would recognize.

"So they sent me to interview all the celebrities," Ryan said later. "But the closest thing to a celebrity that came to the party was me."

In that case, the live remote should have been scrubbed, right?

"So we did *two* live spots. In the first one, I started out by saying there was supposed to be a bunch of celebrities here. Harry Belafonte was supposed to be here, but Harry didn't show. Then I started making up names. I said Benzi Scopolino was supposed to be here, too. And for all you Jay Benson Fong fans, Jay Benson also failed to appear. I mean, I played it for laughs, and we got through the spot."

Meanwhile, back at the studio, the producer and director were extremely disappointed—though they had been given advance notice by the reporter that the party was a big fat bust. They decided that Ryan should do a second live spot, on the theory that maybe some of the missing celebrities would arrive by that time. None did. The desk was so advised. The official response, as usual, was do it anyway.

"The second time around there was still nobody there, absolutely no celebrities—just the usual bunch of freeloaders sopping up booze and munching hors d'oeuvres. Once again I ran down the list of big names that didn't show up. Then I said, 'Now a serious note. This is a benefit for Alvin Ailey, who certainly is one of the main cultural forces in New York City. And as an indication of that, he didn't show up either."

Next to the SLR, nothing raised my hackles more than banal chitchat among reporters and anchors on the studio set. Our executives, however, were hooked on the stuff, oblivious to rank-and-file reports that it was hazardous to the health of a news show.

In the tiny ready room adjacent to our new set in Studio 3-A, I sipped a free cup of tea while wishing I didn't have to be there. At the same time I was mentally editing the ad-libs I would use on the five o'clock segment of our two-hour show. David Diaz came in from the makeup room next door and asked about my mission. I told him I had prepared a videotape package of Brooklyn longshoremen reacting to the possibility of a shipping boycott against the Soviet Union in retaliation for the Russian invasion of Afghanistan. The tape would be shown on the second segment only. The five o'clock producer, Ricki Stofsky, wanted me to discuss the story with Pia Lindstrom and Melba Tolliver, live on the set. No pictures. This had become a rather common malpractice on the bifurcated newscast. "And right behind the SLR," I said, "it ranks second in my lexicon of how not to do a newscast—a bird dog barking in the studio with no film or videotape to back him up."

Diaz chuckled, hugely enjoying my discomfiture. "They got me into one of those live chitchat numbers last week," he said, "about the story I'd covered on unsafe conditions in public housing projects. A few days later, I got this letter from a fan saying, 'that was all very interesting, Mr. Diaz, but I thought you were a television reporter. If you are, you should have covered the story with a camera.' When I showed that letter to the producer, she said, 'I think I should show this to the executive producer.' And she did."

"What did the executive producer say?" I asked.

"I don't know," Diaz said, "but here we are again, right? With no pictures."

Number three on my list of how not to run a news operation was the heavy-handed art of beating a story to death—another habit picked up by our assignment editors from bad companions in the Golden Ghetto.

More than a week before Pope John Paul II's historic visit to New York, Operation Overkill was launched by all six television channels. Assignment desks began scrambling crews like straws thrown against the wind. No angle was too obtuse.

We saluted a high-school choir rehearsing popular melodies to be sung for the pope. ("Do you think he will like this music?") We practically canonized a blushing six-year-old chosen to hand flowers to the pope a week later. ("Are you the proudest little girl in your class?") We glorified the TWA pilot, who would be flying the pope around the States. ("Will you feel any safer with him aboard?") We deified the chef selected to cook for the pope. ("What are some of the Polish dishes he likes to eat?")

Like most of my colleagues, I suffered such foolishness—not gladly—until our news desk sank to what struck me as the depths of journalistic garbage. The assignment day book said one of us would have to do a piece at the bakery that was preparing thousands of communion wafers for a papal event at Yankee Stadium.

"Jesus," I groaned in the back of the newsroom, looking for a place to hide. "I hope I get a murder instead."

Film editor Hal Becker was amused by my chagrin. "If you think that's bad, I've seen worse around here."

Becker recalled the FBI's capture of a Russian master spy, Colonel Rudolph Abel, some years earlier in New York. "The network guys covered the main story. The local news desk had to find a local angle. So they sent Gabe Pressman out with a crew to interview Abel's butcher."

5

Brass Tactics

A BOAST I'VE OFTEN HEARD among reporters from rival TV stations goes like this: "I'll bet our management is more fucked up than your management. Let me tell you what they did today."

Then after another competitive catharsis, vilifying the brass, our chauvinism gives way to mutual sympathy. "Well, I guess it's the same all over," said J. J. Gonzalez of Channel 2. "They seem to be living in another world."

From Penny Crone of Channel 9: "Our management could fuck up a wet dream."

At Channel 5, reporters constantly gripe about a money-saving handicap inflicted upon them by management. On a typical day, five or six reporters will be sent into the field, juggling three camera crews among them. That means the reporter often goes to the scene alone by private car or taxi. By the time a crew becomes available for his gig, he has missed some elements of the story that cannot be recouped. The action is over. The principals have been removed by ambulances or police cars. The witnesses have dispersed. And the quality of Channel 5's news program is affected.

Such pennywise-pound-foolish practices are common in news-biz management. Aside from budget-cutting absurdities, there seems to be a lack of communication among the executives, and between executives and underlings. In that respect, news biz is probably no different from the rest of American business in the 1980s. Experts in the management field have published reports about this country's decline from world leadership in business management after World War II, now trailing Japan and West Germany. Maybe we should start sending our managers to Tokyo and Frankfurt to get their acts together. They could at least learn that the "quick-fix" approach to solving business problems is not always best, that sacrifices made for quick profits, at the expense of quality, productivity, confidence, and morale, can be self-destructive in the long run.

"You didn't say a word through the whole thing," Heather Bernard whispered accusingly.

I nudged her with my elbow, steering her away from the pack. We had just emerged from one of our periodic free-for-all staff meetings in the fifteenth-floor conference room in the RCA Building after working hours. Bird dogs versus bosses—low-keyed but hostile as usual.

Casually, we headed around a corner toward a different bank of elevators, avoiding our peers. Only when we were alone, descending, did I begin to satisfy her curiosity. "You have to understand that even though you've been here four or five years, you are more or less a virgin in this cathouse. I've been going to these pep talks since nineteen sixty-three, every time The Ratings take a turn for the worse and every time we change news directors. This is seventy-nine. I see no change. The news director always starts by telling us grunts how bad The Ratings are and it's all our faults, implying quite bluntly that if any of us holdovers from the old regime really knew our jobs, the Nielsen numbers would be higher. Then he usually mouths something my company commander was fond of saying when I was in the army. Like, 'You can tell me your problems, fellas. I used to be an enlisted man myself. Just tell me how we can help you do your job better so we can all pull together.' When the troops sounded off, however, the brass hat didn't want to hear it."

Heather was skeptical, saying that she had the impression that they did want to hear from us, and pointing out that the news director, the executive producer, and the producer were all taking notes on what everybody said.

My answer was, "Sure, they take notes, pages of them. As a rule, though, that's about all that ever comes out of those pep rallies, then or later."

By that time we were walking along Sixth Avenue toward Fiftieth Street, deliberately shunning the group post mortem at Hurley's bar in the opposite direction. "You remember what Kershaw said when Bill Ryan suggested spending a few bucks on print ads and air spots," I resumed, "to publicize the talents of our reporters on the show?"

Ryan had said Channel 7 and Channel 2 were getting a lot of mileage out of their promotional ads. Kershaw replied that he didn't think publicity was the answer to our problems. He wanted us to do a better job, show more enthusiasm on the air.

I mentioned that I thought it was Phil Barnow or Liz Trotta who raised the same point with news director Dick Graf when our ratings started slipping in the late sixties. I'm not saying publicity would solve all our problems, but it certainly would help. The point is, the leading stations were doing it and our chiefs wouldn't even try it. Graf's response back then was exactly like Kershaw's a decade later. I also reminded her that somebody at our meeting had complained about coming back from the field with a real heavy story and then being told that the producer had decided in advance that it could only run a minute thirty, a minute forty-five. That problem had been raised by Norma Quarrels and Robert Potts when Bernie Shussman ran the show. Tonight, someone else had asked if we could have wireless mikes issued to all film and tape crews as standard equipment. It's a pain in the arse to have to make special requests for the RFM mikes when you want to do walking stand-uppers, re-creations, or demonstrations with your hands—as if we could always predict when we'll need to have our hands free in the field.

Heather defended the news director, reminding me that Kershaw had said he would talk with the producers and the engineering brass to see what could be done about those problems.

133

"Uh-huh," I grunted. "The same answers I got from Dick Graf over ten years ago. Which was the last time I voiced a complaint at a pep rally."

(By the spring of 1981—a year and a half after my conversation with Heather—a publicity campaign extolling the virtues of Channel 4 reporters had been run in print and on radio and TV. Abetted by other factors of undetermined impact, The Ratings improved dramatically. The wireless mike problem persisted, however. So did the silly live remotes.)

Playing the elder statesman, I tried to condense the impressions I had picked up in a decade and a half in news biz. The overriding reality, I said to Heather, was that television was such a new medium that nobody had learned all the answers, especially the brass. They were flying by the seats of their pants, reacting and adjusting to phenomena they didn't fully understand, blaming somebody else whenever possible for whatever might have gone wrong, taking credit for what went right.

A definitive word on that had come to me from Bob Micus, one of the few chaps in middle management who was highly respected by us grunts. Following his promotion from the junior executive ranks to newsfilm coordinator, I asked Micus what it was like being a heavy-hitter. He shook his head, a look of disenchantment in his eyes. "You wouldn't believe it. At this level . . ." He searched for words. "The higher up you go in this company, the harder it is to get any work done. You spend only ten percent of your time actually doing your job. You have to back and fill the other ninety percent to cover your ass."

Some of the ass-covering tactics I had witnessed over the years were mind boggling—like the time Norman Fein gave us grunts a lesson in executive math, refuting the pedestrian notion that one plus one equals two.

During an after-hours pep rally on the fifteenth floor, Fein diagramed his equation for succeeding in The Ratings where his predecessor had failed. He was not going to build a new studio set or change the name of the show, rejecting some of the standard gambits we had come to expect from fledgling news directors. Instead, Fein said he planned to enliven "Newscenter 4" and attract new viewers by increasing consumer-oriented features, reorganizing the format, and reshuffling the anchor personnel.

Viewer surveys in the metropolitan area, Fein announced, had proved quite conclusively that our anchorman on the 5:00–6:00 P.M. segment, Jack Cafferty, was very strong. The same was true of the 6:00–7:00 P.M. anchorman, Chuck Scarborough. "Let's say each of them gets a very strong one in The Ratings; call it one-plus, for each of them. So what we're going to do is put together a totally new anchor team for the five o'clock show. Cafferty and Scarborough will be teamed at six. That way—since they're both so strong individually—one plus one, in their case, equals three."

P.S. It didn't work.

Fein was subsequently moved upstairs as director of special projects and shortly after left to go to Channel 7.

Fein's successor in the hot seat at Channel 4, Ron Kershaw, also failed to perform an overnight miracle. In the fall of 1980, about fifteen months into his reign, he summoned the hired hands to another after-hours pep rally, presumably to boost our sagging morales. First of all, he accepted none of the onus for our plight— third in The Ratings. What the hell, he had resurrected the local news operation at WBAL-TV in Baltimore in a span of three years. Coming to Channel 4, he said, had not been the wisest move for his personal career because, "I stepped into a pile of shit."

You can imagine what that did for morale.

Kershaw and his co-host at the meeting, general manager Al Jerome, insisted nevertheless that "Newscenter 4" was on the upswing, making respectable progress in The Ratings. All we had to do was try a little harder to be the best. Again and again both executives referred to our improving numbers in the Arbitron surveys. Every listener in the conference room wondered why nothing was being said about the Nielsen numbers, which were paramount—the ones used by television-time salesmen and by sponsors looking to puff their whatnots on the tube.

Connie Collins asked the uncomfortable question, "Why don't you guys tell us about the Nielsen ratings?"

Jerome's answer was, "Because Arbitron works better for us."

The news manager, Kershaw's chief deputy, was another

highly touted messiah who was supposed to help lead our wayward congregation to the promised land. One of his early sermons seemed to point us in the wrong direction, however.

The night assignment editor, Jeff Green, wanted to send Heather Bernard and a Minicam crew to the Bronx where the cops had captured a gang of kidnappers. It was a front-page story that every reel in town would be pursuing.

The news manager canceled that assignment on the grounds that the only Minicam crew available at that late hour had been on duty so long that this story would put them into overtime. He was sorry about that. An edict had come down from the cost-accounting boys saying in effect that local news had been spending too much money for overtime.

Since the man had been obeying orders on that occasion, I reserved judgment. Some weeks later, while rummaging through the voucher bin in the newsroom, I found that four of my weekly expense accounts had not been processed by the brass, which meant I could not be reimbursed. "This is ridiculous," I bitched to the news manager. "These vouchers have been sitting here for weeks."

"Vouchers have always been slow at NBC," he said matter-of-factly.

"I know, I know. But why can't something be done to speed them up?"

"Well, first you have to make me aware of the problem," he replied.

Several weeks afterward—the vouchers, by the way, were still just as tardy—I approached the news manager with a serious problem that could have affected the fortunes of our team as a whole. Channel 7 was trying to steal our courtroom artist, Ida Dengrove, the fastest draw in the territory. Cameras were not permitted in New York courtrooms; only artists with sketchpads were allowed to make pictures at arraignments, hearings, or trials.

"As you know," I reminded him, "Ida is the best. She says Channel Seven is offering her more of everything than she's getting here, including money. We can't afford to lose her."

"You're right," he agreed. "She's the best. I certainly hope she makes us aware of those other offers."

A firm determination to do absolutely nothing unless forced to—that was the hallmark of successful Empty Suits. Clearly, that news manager had a bright future in news biz.

A classic example of executive inaction occurred one night around nine o'clock. About a dozen of us professionals in the newsroom—studio talents, writers, associate producers, and managers—were at the peak of the evening's activity, getting ready for the "Eleventh Hour News." We were pounding typewriters, revising wire copy, taking notes, gabbing on the phones.

Bing! Bing! Bing! An urgent bulletin was moving on the AP Teletype machine: a major earthquake in Alaska; many killed, many hurt or unaccounted for. One hell of a story in the forty-ninth state.

Producer Henrik Krogius and anchorman Frank McGee began rearranging the unfinished script. The earthquake, of course, would lead the show. By telephone, Krogius cranked up the graphics department and the researchers in the NBC library. He wanted maps, file film, facts, and figures on Alaska.

"Great. But what are we gonna do for on-the-spot pictures?" somebody wanted to know. After all, that's what television was all about.

We gathered around the central news desk, which was manned at that hour by Bob Matthews and Jim Doherty. The upshot of our discussion with them was there seemed to be no chance at all of getting pictures out of Alaska in time for our broadcast. However, we certainly would set things in motion for getting film for the next day's newscasts. Reporters and crews would have to be roused from their beds. Airline and hotel reservations would have to be made for them. Expense money would have to be obtained, thousands of dollars.

Matthews and Doherty admitted with regret that on their own they could not authorize such a huge and costly undertaking. The slide-rule boys in the Golden Ghetto had been complaining in recent weeks about operational costs that exceeded the local news budget.

At that time of night, the only news executive in the RCA Building with that kind of power was the vice-president on our floor.

A split second later, the door to the vice-president's office, a few paces off the newsroom, slammed and locked.

The news managers knocked on his door. No response. They tried calling him on the telephone. No response.

Somebody suggested that maybe the guy had collapsed. We never found out. He remained incommunicado. Matthews and Doherty had to call a less Empty Suit at home to get the authorization they needed.

The news staff was stunned by the startling scuttlebut that the new executive producer, Robert Lissit, had eighty-sixed our PROBE unit.

Lissit had done a superb job at a Philadelphia station before coming to Channel 4. Maybe he wasn't aware that PROBE had recently aired two dynamite series on our six o'clock newscast. One showed corrupt cops buying and selling drugs on the street; the other showed how the Port of New York Authority was cheating the public.

Alvord, Trotta, Norma Quarrels, and I were not directly affected by Lissit's decision. Field producer Selwyn Raab was. He had built PROBE into the best investigative reporting unit in New York. We were standing at the bar mourning his demotion to the writers' pool when Raab came in. Under questioning, he reprised Lissit's rationale.

"Lissit said they've decided to improve our ratings by going after a different audience, a younger crowd. They feel that this younger audience is more interested in softer stuff—consumer affairs, health, entertainment, and changing lifestyles for example. So investigative reporting is *kaput*."

"I can't believe it," Alvord and Quarrels said in chorus.

"You haven't heard the punch line," Raab continued with an impish grin. "The PROBE unit has just been named the winner of three important prizes for investigative reporting—two Emmys and the Sigma Delta Chi [professional journalism fraternity] Deadline

Club Award. I can't wait to see the look on Lissit's face a couple of weeks from now at the awards dinner. As executive producer, he'll have to be there when we pick up our marbles."

A similar shock wave jarred the newsroom when Fred Feretti, promoted from the ranks to producer a year earlier, stepped down voluntarily. Under his aegis, our "Eleventh Hour News" show with Jim Hartz had climbed back to the top of The Ratings. Oddly, Feretti was walking away in a huff, returning to the pool of newswriters and part-time streetwalkers.

How come?

"It was the stupid, frigging memos from the Empty Suits upstairs," Feretti fumed. "As you know, the "Eleventh Hour" was dead last in the numbers when Reuven Frank [NBC News president] put me in charge. He swore I would have a free hand. In something like four months, we were number one. That's when the memos started flying, mostly from Russ Tornabene, Bill Corrigan, and Ray Hasson. They would ask me things like why did I play Story X in the latter part of the show while Channel Two or Channel Seven played it up higher. I'd tell them that's where I thought Story X belonged in the overall context of the show.

"When something went haywire on the air—you know, the wrong tape coming up because the technical director pushed the wrong button—I'd get memos asking why it happened. I'd write back saying it happens on everybody's show now and then because the TD pushes the wrong button.

"Then they wanted weekly reports on everybody's job performance, which I refused to do until they forced me to. I'd write back saying each guy connected with the show was fantastic, best week he's ever had. They soon got the message and gave up on that one. They still kept sniping, though. They never came in for any discussion on the concept or content of the show; always this piss-pot stuff. I just can't take it any more."

Weeks later, the ex-producer walked again. I had thought he was content as a newswriter and part-time reporter.

"There's just too much bullshit around here," he complained. "I'm going back to print; got a job reporting for the *Times*."

Since most print jobs paid considerably less than television, I had to wonder what final indignity had compelled Feretti to lower his standard of living.

"Like I said, too much bullshit. Let me tell you about the turd they dropped on me the other day. First, you have to know the background. I did a freelance piece for *New York* magazine last week on the public school system—the integration mess in Brooklyn. It was a controversial piece because I described the situation as a classic case of racism. Okay. Now we flash forward to the day Dick Graf sent for me. He didn't say a word about my magazine piece, though I'm sure that's just what was bugging him. Anyway, he talked instead about a news story I had covered on-camera that day. He said, 'I have to let you go. You're too wooden on the air.' All of a sudden I'm a piece of wood.

"I told Graf he couldn't fire me without going through a grievance procedure. I've never joined AFTRA [the union that represents air talent]. I'm still a member of the Writers Guild. And there are rules about that in the contract, rules AFTRA doesn't have to protect its people. Graf said he'd get back to me.

"The very next day he called me to his office again. This time he said, 'Reuven Frank and I had a talk. We really think you ought to stay.'

"So help me, he started praising my work on the air. All of a sudden I wasn't a piece of wood any more. I asked him to put those compliments in writing, and he did. I've still got the letter. I am leaving anyway. I don't feel comfortable around Empty Suits."

Bernie Shussman, who followed Graf as news director, was a lot like his predecessor. I got a close-up of Shussman's approach in his third week at WNBC-TV.

My agent had arranged a voice-over-film gig for Mobil Oil. I would have to go to Philadelphia to record it. I went to Shussman's office to ask for time off the following Thursday.

The news director gave me a flat no, citing NBC's policy that doesn't allow news correspondents or anchors to do commercials.

Of course. I knew all about it and explained that it wasn't a commercial I was talking about. It was an industrial film, never to be shown on television or in public theaters, just to Mobil Oil personnel, stockholders, and potential customers.

Shussman looked dubious.

I said if he checked with the big wheels upstairs, he'd find that there are precedents, including a film I had voiced-over for Coca-Cola the previous year.

The man behind the desk suddenly changed the ground rules, explaining to me that he couldn't let me go because I was too valuable to the team. "Come on, Bernie," I said. "I've got a chance to make big bucks on this thing in Philadelphia. I'm paying a grand a month in alimony. I need the dough." My inflection, I hoped, made it obvious that I knew my rights and intended to go regardless.

Shussman advised me to come back later. He wanted to discuss it with Reuven Frank and others.

When I kept that appointment, he leaned across his desk, as earnest as a scoutmaster. Looking me straight in the eye, he told me that he'd gone in there and fought for me. "They raised a lot of objections, but I beat them down. You can go."

Serially, Lissit, Graf, and Shussman were moved upstairs. Each had left us worse off than we had been when they came to the rescue. Without them, morale in the trenches surged upward. According to scuttlebut, our next news director, Earl "The Pearl" Ubell, would be different. He had earned our respect in recent years as an on-camera science reporter for WCBS-TV. He seemed to be one of us.

Ubell's first moves were typical, however. He ordered the construction of a new $350,000 set, hired a few, fired a few, changed the name and format of our news show. I disagreed with other survivors in the newsroom who questioned the changes, wondering whether Ubell knew what he was doing. My attitude was, what the hell, the survivors at Channel 7 undoubtedly had pissed and moaned in the late sixties when Al Primo scrapped the old studio set, fired a few, hired a few, changed the name and format of the show and replaced a competent anchorman, John Shubek, with the team of Roger Grimsby and Bill Beutel. But those changes catapulted

Channel 7's "Eyewitness News" team ahead of everybody else.

Who could tell? Maybe Ubell had conjured up a winning formula.

My tentative confidence in Ubell eroded swiftly during a getting-to-know-you chat in his office.

"Glad to see you again," he said with the hearty enthusiasm of a chamber of commerce spokesman. We had bumped into each other many times on common assignments in the field. "Sit down, relax. As you know, I'm seeing everybody on the staff, one on one, informally. What I'd like to do is get ideas from each of you as to what's wrong here—what we can do to turn things around, make this the best news operation in New York."

Precisely what I had in mind, too. "Well, Earl, I've been thinking . . ."

That was as far as I got. "Of course, you understand that I know all about what's involved in TV reporting. I know what you're up against out there. I did it for eight years at CBS."

My own career on the tube, at that point in time, dwarfed Ubell's in longevity. I said, "As a matter of fact, Earl . . ."

He kept talking as if I hadn't opened my mouth, giving a rundown on the big stories he had covered for Channel 2. "I've also written a couple of books," he added.

Maybe, I thought, he would be interested to know that I had written three books myself. "Speaking of books, Earl . . ."

The news director cut me off. He was off and running on another tangent, telling me how he wanted to see his reporters getting personally involved in their stories, walking around on-camera and picking up objects that dramatized what we were talking about. "And when you're interviewing somebody, make sure your cameraman zooms in real tight on the face. Let us see the emotion in their eyes."

The next thing I knew, Ubell was on his feet ushering me toward the door. "It's been great getting your slant on things," he said. "I'm sure we're going to work well together."

Almost daily, air talents and technicians working together played a cathartic game of Can You Top This, exchanging ribald tales starring the rascals who ran news biz. In the spirit of negative chauvinism, film crews and film editors claimed that no matter what absurdities various news directors inflicted on reporters, we were lucky because we had no direct dealings with Sig Bejak, director of newsfilm operations.

At one point, with the air date approaching for a three-hour documentary on crime in America, Bejak assigned film editor Darold Murray to work overtime to put it all together. The raw footage ran into the thousands. To beat the deadline, Darold had to hump about twenty-five hours straight.

He was wrapping it up early the next morning when Bejak came into the cutting room, smiling uncharacteristically. "All finished? Great. It was really swell of you to work around the clock like this, Darold. You saved our ass. Were you able to get any rest at all?"

"A little, this morning," the weary film editor replied. "I laid down on the couch in your office for maybe an hour."

Bejak's smile faded instantly. "Well, you know I can't pay you for that."

Bejak further deflated his suit when sent to the NBC bureau in Rome to supervise film coverage of the latest Arab-Israeli war. The bureau there had the best communications system in that quadrant of the globe: European and American wire-service Teletypes receiving news around the clock from the Middle East and elsewhere, plus technical facilities for transmitting words and pictures back to New York via satellite.

Bejak's principal contribution, his underlings said, was tantamount to sabotage. At the end of his first evening in the Rome bureau, he found a way to save a few dollars on the company's electric bill. He turned off all the Teletype machines overnight.

Returning from Brooklyn late one afternoon with the hottest local story of the day, I gave a copy of my scenario to producer Mike Dreaden in the newsroom. "It's one of the best stories I've covered this year," I told him. "A seventeen-year-old Hispanic kid in a stolen car, shot to death by two white cops in front of witnesses. One of the cops got plugged in the arm, but the bystanders claim he was shot by his own partner, that the dead kid didn't have a gun. And so far no third gun has been found."

"That sounds great," Dreaden enthused. "We're getting close to airtime, though. When can you have it ready?"

I glanced at the clock on the wall—5:20. "The lab says my film will be out of the soup at five fifty-five. I can have it ready by six thirty at the latest. No sweat."

In the cutting room at 6:10 P.M.—the show was on the air—I got a call from the producer in the studio control room. "I don't think we'll be able to run your shooting story. We're very tight today."

"You've got to be kidding," I said tentatively, half expecting him to finish a joke. "You can't kill a story like this."

Dreaden said he was sorry, but the way things looked at the moment, he might have to. "As you know, we're in the middle of the February sweeps. I have to fit in those long features we've been advertising. I'm locked in. But keep working on your package, and we'll see."

Associate producers Henrik Krogius and Ginny Russo, standing nearby in the film editing complex, couldn't believe it. They checked their Xeroxed copies of the six o'clock show routine to see what the hell was so important in the second half of the hour-long newscast that could possibly warrant killing my controversial homicide. Among other things, they found three minutes reserved for the weather, five minutes for sports, and over two minutes for a feature about toys to be be sold by the Parker Brothers Corporation next Christmas, ten months away. Both associate producers called the producer on the studio line and leaned on him.

Dreaden told them to ask me how long the piece would run.

I'd just finished cutting it, and it ran two minutes and fourteen seconds.

Dreaden didn't like that answer and wanted me to cut it down to a minute thirty.

"No way," I bellowed. "I've got three conflicting versions of this homicide to tell and nobody knows which one will prove to be the right one by the time this whole thing is sorted out. It's got to run two fourteen."

In the end, Dreaden ran the story my way. The Christmas toys, too. Nonetheless, I felt foolish and angry. Why should a veteran reporter have to fight to get the top local story of the day on the air?

Jim Ryan had an equally infuriating experience in which Christmas preparations took precedence over hard news. While awaiting an assignment in the "News 4 New York" bullpen one morning in November 1981, Ryan overheard a conversation that, hours later, mutilated his morale. The news manager, Bob Davis, was saying to the assignment editor that he would like to see a story that day on the early Christmas rush. It wasn't yet Thanksgiving, but a lot of places were gearing up for Christmas already—decorations were going up all over.

Later that morning Jim was sent to City Hall to cover two stories. One was about the City Council being in chaos over alleged discriminatory redistricting. A federal court ruling maintained that the ten at-large City Council seats, which were created almost two decades ago to insure minority representation in city government, were unconstitutional: a violation of the one-man-one-vote rule.

The second story he did was on a decision coming down as to which of the many bidding companies would soon get cable TV franchises in the four boroughs of New York outside Manhattan. It wasn't a final decision but one that was certain to become final with a few variations—a very important story because at stake were billions of dollars, so far the largest cable TV market in the country.

But before he went inside City Hall to cover those two stories, he spotted workmen outside putting up the City Hall Christmas tree. He had his cameraman shoot the scene, thinking it would make a good picture to go into whatever package somebody else might do on the story Bob Davis had envisioned. When the newscast went on the air that night, the only one of his stories to make air was the City Hall Christmas tree.

Lest you suppose for a moment that saner conditions prevailed at the network level of news gathering, I hasten to point out that local grunts who had been borrowed by that echelon usually came back mumbling about "the nutwork."

The last time I played hardball with the big guys was a year or so after the bloody rebellion in Attica State Prison in 1971. The network set me up there with field producer Jerry Rosholt and a film crew. I interviewed prison guards, inmates, and townspeople. The scenario I put together would show how conditions, regulations, and the mood of Attica had changed for the better in the wake of reforms motivated by the massacre.

By 2:00 P.M. I was ready to record my off-camera voice track and on-camera closer outside the prison gate. Until then, the scholarly field producer had allowed me to do things my way. Now he advised me that I had to call the "Nightly News" "committee" in New York to get final approval of my script.

I objected.

Rosholt explained apologetically that it was a new rule. All the network correspondents had to do it—Fred Briggs, Richard Valeriani, Herb Kaplow. Everybody.

Grudgingly, I read my script in a conference call with Gilbert Millstein, Joe Angotti, Bob McFarland, and a fourth associate producer whose name I didn't catch. Millstein did most of the editing: don't say that, say this. Kill your third sentence. Move your last paragraph up to where paragraph two is. Add this line.

"That is not the story I covered," I protested. "That's not telling it like it is. If you don't trust my judgment, why didn't you send somebody you do trust?"

Millstein et al were not moved. They wanted their "Nightly News" productions to have a certain tone—a uniform style. They knew best.

"Now let me get this straight," I said almost evenly, struggling to control my temper. "I'm up here covering the story. You guys are back there four hundred miles away, reading wire copy. And you're telling *me* what the story is?"

Indeed they were.

"Okay. Let's make a deal. I'll change this script to fit your specifications. But from now on, don't call me. I promise I won't call you."

Larry Spivak, then producer of the network's "Meet the Press" public affairs show, once called me from Washington. He wanted to borrow me for one of his upcoming inquisitions. "Our guest next Sunday will be James Farmer, the black civil rights leader. I've already cleared it with your station for you to be on the panel asking questions if you're interested."

I said fine, on one condition. "Invite me back for another shot three or four weeks later to question a senator or a cabinet secretary when the subject is not civil rights. I don't want to get stereotyped or boxed in as a one-dimensional reporter. Okay?"

Spivak's disbelief came through clearly. "What else do you know anything about?"

"Come on, Larry. Are you trying to tell me you never heard of a black general-assignment reporter? You don't think I can do my homework the same as anybody else, including you, to get ready for a particular assignment? Hell, I often serve as the moderator of our local public affairs shows—'Direct Line' and 'Searchlight.' "

Spivak hemmed and hawed, saying he would think it over and get back to me on the phone. He never did.

Happily, Spivak's racial blind spot was not typical of NBC management. Sure, there was racism in broadcasting almost everywhere, but no more so than any other segment of American society. From my point of view, the most blatant failings among television news executives had more to do with bullshit than bigotry.

"This network hasn't got the common sense God gave a meatball sandwich." Anchorman Lew Wood handed up that indictment. "No wonder we're slipping in The Ratings." He had just trudged into Hurley's bar from a network assignment in the field, playing a relatively minor role in NBC's live coverage of Op Sail in New York harbor.

"I couldn't believe it," Lew said grumpily. "There we were— me, David Brinkley, and John Chancellor with a live Minicam crew—on top of the south tower of the World Trade Center overlooking the greatest spectacle ever seen. The network president, Herb Schlosser, was also up there with his wife and kids just watching. Brinkley and Chancellor were on the air live at the time I'm talking about: two or three minutes before noon. They're vamping about the main event of the Op Sail festival, which was coming up precisely at noon.

147

"In just a few minutes, they told God knows how many viewers, church bells would start ringing in the five boroughs of New York; the parade of tall ships would begin in the harbor; city fireboats would paint the air with spumes of water dyed red and blue; several warships would fire their big guns—a dramatic, colorful salute to this country's bicentennial, with tens of thousands of spectators lined up on the shore and thousands more on pleasure boats and sightseeing craft on the Hudson, waving American flags and patriotic banners.

"Then exactly at noon, before any of these wonders could be aired, the NBC network cut away from our live Minicam that was focused on the harbor and went to Dullsville—the 'Meet the Press' show in Washington. Brinkley and Chancellor were pissed.

"When Herb Schlosser saw it happen on the TV monitor near our camera, his face turned all sorts of colors. He whispered to me, 'Lew, do you think that's a good idea?' I felt like screaming to the world that it was the all-time fuck-up I've ever seen. But I couldn't say that to the network president, could I? What I said, very quietly, was 'No sir; I don't think it's a very good idea.' Schlosser didn't say anything after that. He just stood there. The network stayed with 'Meet the Press'—a special, expanded edition that ran a whole goddamn hour. By that time, the greatest Fourth of July celebration, the greatest picture story in New York's history, was over."

An unforgettable memo from network brass advised the newsfilm department that the common practice of renting chauffeured limousines to carry news crews and their bulky paraphernalia to the airport for out-of-town assignments was henceforth *verboten*. Instead, the traveling crew should borrow one of the chauffeured limousines rented by the company for top executives. Most of those cars, the memo said, usually sat on the street in Rockefeller Center all day after bringing the brass to work, waiting to take them home.

The supervisor in charge of film crews, Bill Kelley, made a gallant effort to comply. He was about to send a crew to cover the bloodshed in Honduras. Upon learning that an NBC News executive had a rented limousine parked near the entrance to the RCA Building, Kelley called the great man's office. The man's secretary was rather shocked by the supervisor's request. Kelly read a pertinent passage from the memo. She promised to call him back.

Fifteen minutes later, the executive himself was on the phone. "You mean you want to send a film crew with all their personal baggage and equipment trunks to the airport in *my* car?"

"Yes, sir."

"I can't let you do that. I have an important meeting to go to—way downtown."

A network executive—in a moment of candor at the annual NBC Christmas party—disclosed a few suppressed details of an infamous corporate fiasco: the tortuous birth of the modernistic red and blue N as the network logo.

"It was a Rube Goldberg invention all the way. The peacock had been retired, right? The NBC snake that took its place was dying. Now the big boys are going to come up with a different logo. So what do you do at NBC with a problem like this? Do you go to the artists in our graphics department and ask them to draw some possible logos, if we don't like that one, give us another one? No. They create a whole new division of the company—the Division of Corporate Identification, with a vice-president in charge. Under the vice-president, we get the directors, the managers, the administrators, the secretary, the paper, the office space—hundreds of thousands of dollars' worth.

"Eventually, with the help of some very expensive consultants, they come up with this N. You know, the N, which looks just like the one that's been in existence for years at this little dipship educational TV network in Nebraska. All right. So there's a big court fight. This little network sues the big giant. They settle for something like seven-hundred-fifty thousand dollars plus a lot of NBC video equipment. It was like giving away a part of the store—cameras, videotape recorders, cables, all sorts of expensive gear. Of course, it was old equipment that we were going to replace anyway. Tons of it.

"So now we've got the rights to the N. Okay. But you would think that the Division of Corporate Identification would be in contact with other branches of the company, right? Wrong. They go ahead and print up new, expensive stationery and calling cards with the N on it for every executive in the company. The new calling cards are very fancy. You know, raised and elegant printing, with a telephone number on it. Circle-seven–eight-three-hundred.

"About three weeks later, NBC decides to put the whole complex here on the Centrex telephone system. Now all the fancy cards and the brand new stationery with the N on it are obsolete. Every executive in the company, every reporter, producer, and manager has the wrong telephone number."

NBC's flagship station did not have a monopoly on brass boggles. Gloria Rojas told of a dumfounding decision by the Channel 7 assignment desk.

"I was covering a story way down the road in South Jersey with a two-man Minicam crew when we got a message from the desk. The courier they had sent by car to pick up our tape had been forced off the highway. A mechanical breakdown. Well, since this is an emergency situation, I told the desk, we can bring back the tape ourselves. I said the crew was willing, even though it would mean going without a lunch break.

"The desk wouldn't hear of it, saying the brass had put out a memo insisting that crews be sent to lunch on time. Otherwise, the company has to pay them a penalty—something like thirty dollars a man. So to avoid that, the desk said, 'We'll send a helicopter to pick up the tape.' "

All of us at the third-ranked station were taken aback by confirmed reports that news director Ron Tindiglia of Channel 7 had been fired by ABC vice-president Bill Fyffe. What the hell, the "Eyewitness News" team was still number one.

"Why would they dump a guy who's on top?" I asked Milton Lewis of Channel 7 on the street.

"I got it from a very high source," Milton answered. "They told him he was too humane."

The possibility of inhumane firings on a massive scale sent waves of panic through the NBC complex in the spring of seventy-eight. A memo from the top informed all hands that a new messiah would soon appear—the great Fred Silverman, who already had brought salvation to CBS and ABC. Of course, we wanted to be saved. The question was, how many of us might be sacrificed in the rites of purification. According to sympathetic colleagues at ABC, one of the first things Silverman had said when he showed up there was, "I'm not here to fire people. I'm here to fire departments."

The day he joined us began with disarming innocence. Assignment editor Fred Ferrer was scanning a fat sheaf of wire copy, looking for suitable examples of the human comedy that ought to be chronicled on our show. His early-morning bird dogs—Heather Bernard, Robert Potts, David Diaz, and I—hovered around his desk, eager to pick up the scent.

Fred sat back, pushed his glasses up on his forehead, sighed, and told us there wasn't a hell of a lot on the wires. Then he looked at me with a mischievous smile and said that, nevertheless, he had a terrific little story for me.

Ugh. That preamble was familiar. It usually meant covering a dull public hearing at City Hall or a ground-breaking ceremony in the Bronx. "No thonx." A seasoned bird dog lusted for blood and disaster.

"This is June ninth, nineteen seventy-eight—the great Fred Silverman's first day here. You will have the honor of interviewing Mr. Silverman as soon as he arrives, about forty minutes from now."

Potts and Diaz looked at each other, relieved. The short straw had been planted in my hand arbitrarily.

Like a felon going to the gallows, I was allowed a last request. The desk man gave me my favorite Minicam crew, Jerry Yarus and Joe Gafa. When we hooked up in the ground-floor lobby, their lack of enthusiasm for this gig matched my own.

Yarus surmised gloomily that the desk must have figured I was expendable. Gafa agreed.

I shrugged. "I don't have any choice, though, do I?"

We approached the special bank of elevators that would take us up to the executive suites on the tenth floor. We were joined by a couple of rival newsreels, three print women, and a couple of radio guys with tape recorders.

On the tenth floor, waiting in the corridor, we taped a parade of NBC messengers delivering flowers, bottles of booze, and other gifts to Silverman's office. A pair of nervous network flacks emerged from the inner sanctum. "Mr. Silverman will be along in a few minutes. You can take pictures, but no interviews."

My teammates looked at me with raised eyebrows. Silently, I mouthed the answer they expected. "Bullshit."

The new president of NBC appeared without fanfare—a well-tailored guy with a diffident smile. The cameras rolled in dead silence for perhaps half a minute. "Sir, if we're to do this story right for Channel Four," I began, "we need some comment from you."

Silverman nodded to me in agreement. I moved in close with a mike, followed by others. "To begin with, you must have been watching NBC in recent weeks. What's your impression of the network as it is right now?"

"The network is in very good shape."

I had to struggle to keep from gasping. Hell, we were number three. That's why he had been hired for a million bucks a year. "In very good shape," I echoed dumbly. "Then why do we need you?"

From the background came strangled objections from the flacks. "That's all, Bob. Thank you, Bob."

Silverman was amused, only slightly ill at ease. He laughed. "Well, I hope it's going to be in even better shape with my help."

Again the flacks tried to cut off the interview.

"Just one more question, sir," I continued. "A lot of people here at NBC have been shaking in their boots waiting for you to arrive. Do they have reason to fear for their jobs?"

"Not at all."

"Then you don't plan any wholesale housecleaning?"

"No, I don't."

"Thank you. Thank you very much."

An hour or so later, as I finished cutting the tape with an editor on the fourth floor, the desk called me. The brass had heard about my interview with Silverman. They had serious doubts as to whether they should air it.

"Fuck it," I said. "I did my job. If Silverman knows his job, he knows I did what had to be done."

I learned later that, after screening my edited tape, management decided to air it, on the grounds that to kill it would have made them look like wimps when the word got out, as it surely would, to the *Daily News,* the *Times* and the *Post.*

Next morning, the news director told me that Silverman had liked it and they were giving him a copy of the tape for his personal library.

Silverman's departure from ABC had been masterminded by a personable but tough businesswoman named Jane Cahill Pfeiffer. As a consultant to RCA, she had approached him at the other network with an offer he couldn't refuse: the NBC presidency. Once aboard, Silverman engineered her elevation to the NBC chairmanship and the RCA Board of Directors with an annual income well above $400,000.

However, Pfeiffer soon became embroiled in a series of corporate clashes, she acknowledged later, with RCA chairman Edgar Griffiths. When Griffiths tried to force her out, Silverman defended her, assuring her that she would remain at NBC as long as he did.

Then, as NBC's Nielsen numbers continued to skid in 1980, Silverman's own position became shaky. Griffiths wanted his scalp. Silverman bought time for himself by throwing Pfeiffer to the wolves.

During the same era, an angry tribunal of nonair grunts convened one night after working hours to voice their complaints against local news managers. The consensus was that management simply was "not managing."

An associate producer summed up the situation. "Basically, we're pissed because there is absolutely no direction from the top. No communication, except for nit-picking. We have no idea what kind of show they want us to put on—no specifics, that is. The only word we've heard from the news director is that he wants an upbeat show. Now, who the hell knows what that means? He never comes to us to say, 'Hey, this is what I want.' The people directly under him in the chain of command may or may not reflect Kershaw's policies. Sometimes, in fact, when we do specific things that Clancy has asked for, it turns out to be something Kershaw doesn't like. So apparently they don't even communicate with each other. When something goes wrong on the show, however, they come down hard on us; like it's all our fault."

A junior assistant on the assignment desk said the incident that had galvanized the NABET shop steward to call this formal bitching session was a recent monumental fuck-up. "By the time the brass decided we should have a big year-end-review segment on our New Year's Eve show, it was Friday, December twenty-eighth. They should have decided three or four days earlier and assigned a team to put it all together. It's like they let nineteen eighty sneak up on them. You know, reviewing a whole goddamn year means checking hundreds of pages of the show logs, screening hundreds of stories on film and videotape to select the clips you need. A big job like that just can't be done on the spur of the moment.

"Even after they decided on Friday that we should do it on Monday, they did nothing about revising the work schedule to put a team on the case over the weekend. There were no film or tape editors available to screen all that stuff for David Diaz until eight o'clock Monday morning [December 31, 1979], the day the year-ender was supposed to air.

"Diaz did one hell of a job. He made air with a damn good package, all things considered. But he tied up so many editors and machines all day long we had the devil of a time getting the regular news stories edited in time for the show. I mean, it was a hairy situation for everybody."

A disgruntled newswriter picked up the story from there. "After the year-end show, [producer] Hank Krogius went to see the news director. He had to explain why the credit crawl at the end had been too slow. Krogius blamed the brass for lack of planning, saying that under the circumstances they were lucky a hell of a lot of other things hadn't gone wrong. Krogius said the brass had a habit of bucking every problem downward instead of handling it.

"It got wild in there. We could hear them screaming at each other out here in the newsroom. Kershaw fired Krogius on the spot. When Hank came out of the office Kershaw called him back and fired him again."

Krogius carried a NABET card in his pocket, however. The

firing didn't stick. Only talents—members of AFTRA—could be liquidated that easily.

NABET's militant watchdog in the newsroom, Lorrin Anderson, filed a formal notice of grievances, on behalf of his associates, with the labor relations department. He charged, among other things, that our news-show formats "are not being designed to present the news most effectively; rather, the news has become the servant of the format—news stories chosen not for their significance or freshness but for the way they will fit into the show routine, a journalistic corruption that cannot be camouflaged by optional gimmicks, dubious 'exclusive' supers, or remotes ordered for no apparent reason beyond the opportunity to slash the word 'Live' on the screen. And more and more, we see the local news operation of NBC's flagship station treated as a commodity with no inherent integrity, to be hyped and trivialized, peddled like a cross between the 'Dukes of Hazzard' and 'The Dating Game.'

"A television station is more than a private money machine. It is a public resource and a social responsibility, with an important role to play in the welfare and self-understanding of the city. When half its news staff is systematically undercut, antagonized, attacked, ignored, or constantly, arbitrarily reshuffled, it is not only the individuals who suffer but the news programs themselves, to the detriment of the audience we are serving—or once served."

A few months after Anderson's memo made the rounds, some significant changes did occur in our news operation, under the aegis of Al Jerome. His commitment to solid news coverage reminded old bird dogs like me of the late William McAndrew. It was Jerome who lured Gabe Pressman back to Channel 4 after eight years at Channel 5. Although our 5:00–6:00 P.M. show, "Live at Five," continued as an "infotainment" vehicle, our six and eleven o'clock newscasts deemphasized frivolity. Both shows remained flawed, however, by inane wisecracks in the studio and silly live remotes.

There was also an indication, in the summer of 1981, that SLR's might soon be eighty-sixed by Kershaw. He was conferring with Mike Dreaden and Bret Marcus in the newsroom one day when I arrived from the field to fight against a scheduled live remote from Kennedy Airport. After calmly pointing out that I had covered the airport story on tape and nothing relevant would be happening there at 6:00 P.M., I lost my temper. "We're working against ourselves with these silly live shots," I shouted. "When are we going to cut out this bullshit?"

Marcus and Dreaden argued that my being there on-camera would lend a certain "immediacy" to the story. I said bullshit three more times. Kershaw said nothing.

I stalked back to my newsroom cubicle, having lost again. Minutes later, however, Marcus came to and said, "Not because you were right, but for other reasons, you don't have to do that live remote. We found something better for that slot."

Exactly two weeks after that incident, Kershaw beckoned me into his office off the newsroom. I expected to be chewed out. Instead, the news director said, "I just want to let you know that when you were shouting in the newsroom the other day, I agreed with you. I didn't say anything then because . . . well, those two guys are responsible for putting the show together. But you were absolutely right. We've got to stop doing those things. We did it again just the other day when we had David Diaz on the Brooklyn Bridge live instead of covering the story itself. I think there are only three reasons to use live remotes: one, obviously, is when something is going on; two, when we can't get anything else on the story, it can at least give us a presence at the scene; and three, just for fun—like sending a live unit out to the park on a beautiful day."

I felt like hugging the man around the knees.

At the same time, however, I wondered why he didn't tell Dreaden and Marcus in private what he had told me. And so the SLR's continued.

6

The Farce Is with You

*I*F TRAUMATIC SKIRMISHES with management in the broadcasting complex and with disruptive meddlers elsewhere comprised the whole mosaic of news biz, no one could stand being part of it. Fortunately, there is a mitigating element: if you work at the grunt level, the farce is nearly always with you. Every day you laugh a great deal—at your adversaries, at yourself, and at the ineluctable happenstances of a peripatetic profession that tickle and astound you. That is the stuff that talents and technicians from all six New York stations bitch, brag, or joke about during long stakeouts in gang pursuit of a story: waiting for the cops to bring out what they describe as "the alleged perpetrator"; waiting for the mayor to come into the Blue Room at City Hall to make a statement; waiting for fire marshals to emerge from a burned-out tenement to tell us whether they have found evidence of arson; waiting for VIPs to land at Kennedy Airport; waiting for the jury to come in with a verdict; waiting for the tensions of a typical day to dissolve in the drinks we consume at Hurley's after working hours.

One fertile source of risibility is executive guesswork, off-target in so many instances.

Pat Trese, a former NBC network correspondent turned associate producer, recalled the uncertain creation of the most fabulous anchor team ever to hit the tube—Chet Huntley and David Brinkley. "This was back in the mid-fifties when our top news producer was Reuven Frank. Just like that we got a new talent from the West Coast. Huntley. Nobody had asked for him. The brass upstairs simply dumped him in our laps. Reuven and the rest of us on the network staff were trying to figure out what to do with Chet.

"Reuven finally decided to build the network's evening newscast around him; a half-hour news-in-depth sort of thing. For the pilot kinescope recording—which was supposed to sell the idea to the brass—Reuven included Brinkley doing a short, biting essay on cocktail parties in Washington.

"The deep thinkers in the network sales department—the guys who dealt with sponsors—looked at the kinescope with a big-name consultant, Herbert Bayard Swope. In his eyes, it was thumbs down all the way. Based on Swope's negative reaction, they told Reuven he had better go back to the drawing board. Huntley, they said, was much too serious on-camera. Brinkley, on the other hand, was not serious enough. That combination was absolutely hopeless. It would never sell."

So much for the perceptive powers of those deep thinkers in the Golden Ghetto!

WNBC-TV was the first station in New York to assign a female to interview heroic jocks and read sports copy on the air. In 1978 Sandra Deitz came to "Newscenter 4" with impeccable credentials. Her résumé indicated that she was a seasoned business-news specialist from a station in Cleveland, a competent young woman who had paid her dues in a smaller market and was ready for a shot in the Big Apple.

After screening Sandra's audition reel, however, news director Norman Fein, assistant news director Jerry Moring, and other star-makers developed a bad case of the doubts about her credibility as a business reporter. Their solution was to let her do sports. That

158

decision only widened her credibility gap, however, and roughly six months later she vanished in it.

Another executive guess resulted in the creation of a profitable private enterprise called the Grinsberg Film Library.

Sherman Grinsberg had worked for years in NBC's voluminous newsfilm storage facility in the wilds of New Jersey. Since current events often required the resurrection of yesteryear's footage to tell today's big story in perspective, couriers were frequently dispatched to the storage vault to bring back snippets of history.

One day the heavy-hitters decided that many old reels in the archives would probably never be useful again, a notion inspired by dwindling storage space. Building more vaults would cost a lot of money. Cutting down the inventory would be cheaper. That's when Grinsberg volunteered to save the company the added expense of hauling away and destroying all that trash. With a couple of rented trucks, he carried tens of thousands of feet of celluloid gold from the premises.

A few weeks later, the Grinsberg Film Library began renting old film to NBC at thirty dollars a foot.

A mental typographical error by news manager Buck Prince wasted hundreds of NBC dollars and made him famous.

It all began with a memo from an NBC local news producer.

To Buck Prince
Please send film crew to cover Cleveland Amory news conference at 11:00 A.M. tomorrow.

The local news manager followed through forthwith, but the film crew wound up on the wildest goose chase in the annals of New York journalism. After flying hundreds of miles to the Midwest, they found nothing to shoot at the Cleveland Armory.

Another false start of histrionic proportions cost the company even bigger bucks.

Network executives got excited when an intriguing story came in on the AP wire from Toronto. A little-known Canadian-born industrial psychologist, in a telephone interview with a Toronto newsman, had boasted of perfecting a new technique to prevent shoplifting in department stores—subliminal I-won't-steal messages on audio tape, to be inserted during routine announcements over the store's public-address system.

In the RCA Building at 30 Rockefeller Plaza, the network assignment desk cranked up for a maximum effort. After several phone calls, the desk obtained the psychologist's home address in the Toronto suburbs. Field producer Ted Elbert, reporter Georgette Bennett, and a two-man Minicam crew flew to Toronto through a frightening snowstorm.

When they finally reached the man's home by taxi, his wife answered the doorbell. "He's not here. He's at his office."

"Where is his office?" Elbert asked.

"In New York. The RCA Building at Thirty Rockefeller Plaza."

Fred Freed's memory lapse resulted in a classic out-of-town *gaffe*. He and his documentary unit had gone to Boston to film a major segment of his "Urban Crisis" opus. On the final day of the shooting schedule, Freed was buttonholed in the lobby of the elegant Copley-Plaza Hotel by a former Boston bureaucrat. The stranger claimed to have solid information, chapter and verse, about graft and corruption in high places. After questioning the man briefly, Freed decided it was dynamite stuff. He'd put it all on film, and to protect the man from reprisals, show him only in silhouette, under the alias of Marvin X. He'd have to do it later, however, after a shooting date across town.

Before departing, the producer arranged for Marvin X to stay at the Copley-Plaza, at NBC's expense.

A full month went by. At his office in New York, after the documentary had aired, Freed got a hostile call from the Copley-Plaza. The manager demanded payment of an overdue bill for lodging, food, drinks, laundry, and dry-cleaning service.

Freed insisted that the bill had been paid before he left. He had the receipt.

The Copley-Plaza informed him that Marvin X was still on the premises, living very high on the hog.

Freed groaned, remembering for the first time that he had forgotten to interview Marvin X.

No harm was done, no money lost. Assignment editor Bob McCarthy simply massaged a lot of funny bones in the newsroom with his approach to covering a predicted eclipse of the sun. His last-minute instructions to cameraman Art Goldman went like this: "Pick up a long lens from the equipment room upstairs. Then rush down to Thirty-fourth and Fifth Avenue as fast as you can. I want you to shoot this thing from the top of the Empire State Building."

Goldman blinked. Since the sun would disappear over the whole eastern seaboard at that hour, he wondered why he had to shoot from that particular location.

"Because," McCarthy explained, "up there you'll be closer."

Last-minute instructions to Ludovic Geiskop brought unforeseen, apoplectic results. Before making his exit, en route to covering a pro football game—New York Giants versus Baltimore Colts— at Yankee Stadium, the cameraman was admonished by the weekend news producer, "Whatever you do, for God's sake, don't overshoot. If you come back with a thousand feet of film, like some guys I could name, you'll give the editors a headache trying to weed out the action we want. So just shoot the scoring plays—touchdowns, extra points, and field goals."

Geiskop offered assurances that, though born and raised in France, he had since become a knowledgeable football fan. He picked up his Auricon camera and departed.

Geiskop returned with less than six hundred feet of film. Bravo.

An hour later in the cutting room, the producer screamed in disbelief. "It can't be. You've got everything except the record-breaking field goal that won the game for the Colts. Fifty-three yards. How the hell could you miss that?"

Live and Off-Color: News Biz

Geiskop shrugged with Gallic aplomb. "You told me to shoot only the scoring plays. I didn't think he would make it."

Mike Dreaden, an expatriate from Indianapolis, Indiana, had not yet become a knowledgeable New Yorker when he made his debut as a stand-up comic in the Channel 4 newsroom.

Bing, bing, bing! An "urgent" came clattering into the wire room on the AP Teletype machine shortly after 8:00 P.M.

HASSID RABBI KILLED IN CROWN HEIGHTS
STICK-UP. NO DETAILS.

A young desk assistant ripped it off the machine and rushed to Tom Medarasz. The night assignment editor announced to the newsroom that a big story had come in—a new lead for the late show. He quickly roused a dozing bird dog and a Minicam crew, launching them toward the badlands of Brooklyn.

Dreaden, in charge of the 11:00 P.M. edition of "Newscenter 4," looked on in bewilderment. When he asked what the big flap was all about, somebody showed him the AP bulletin. Dreaden frowned and asked, "Who is this guy Hassid Rabbi? What's so important about him?"

The best comedy routines are often improvised in the field rather than the newsroom.

Impatient to get going one morning, I rode the elevator from the seventh floor up to the ninth to flog my film crew into action. They were standing there, equipment in hand, when the doors slid open.

"Give me one more minute," begged cameraman Frank Follette, turning back toward the crew lounge. "I've got to tap a kidney. I'll meet you guys at the car."

I swallowed my impatience. What the hell, Frank was pushing seventy. His kidneys were not what they used to be when he was shooting silent flicks in Hollywood.

162

He soon took his place in the driver's seat of the company car. We were on our way to a cross-burning story in Brooklyn.

When the four of us piled out of the car and opened the trunk, Frank discovered that he had forgotten his camera. What to do? If he called the assignment desk on the radio and explained, the bosses might interpret his lapse as proof positive that old Frank was over the hill.

After weighing the truth against alternatives, Follette said brightly, "I have it. We'll finesse 'em." He called the assignment desk on the radio. "We've got a camera malfunction out here in Brooklyn; too serious to fix in the field. Would you please ask the equipment room to send a replacement by courier? Over."

The desk promised to get back to him after checking with the equipment people upstairs.

The desk reported back that there were no spares available— not a working Auricon in the house.

"Yes there is," Follette replied with confidence. "Tell 'em to look in the john in the crew lounge."

Newsreel cameramen from around the globe converged on New York harbor to shoot Op Sail seventy-six. From their point of view, this was the kind of assignment that made them drool—a gaudy, exciting, maritime extravaganza, an ideal opportunity to display their full talents as cinematographers. No "talking heads" for a change. Instead, they shot continuous daylong action involving perfect specimens of everything sleek and beautiful, past and present, that could float—from Chinese junks and nineteenth-century schooners to modern ships of war—animated poetry in buttery sunshine on the Fourth of July.

Aboard the press boat, no one zoomed, panned, and tilted his Minicam with more relish than Herbie Schwartz of WCBS-TV— a middle-aged veteran behaving like a kid with a Christmas toy. Too bad his stuff never got on the air.

Toward the end of the day, with deadlines approaching, the press boat raced back to the pier on the Hudson. About twenty-five feet from shore, as the boat slowly maneuvered for docking, Schwartz spotted the Channel 2 courier. By making faces and pointing at his watch, the courier signaled that he wanted Herbie's tape casette—ten minutes ago if not sooner.

Knowing that every second counted now, Herbie yelled, "I'll toss it to you." And he did. Splash. His toss fell five feet short.

Dave Gilbert (now at Channel 4 in New York) made quite a splash himself in the course of doing an unforgettable feature on boating safety for KSTP-TV in Minneapolis. "It was a two-man crew, me and my cameraman in separate canoes five or six feet apart on this lagoon near a school that taught the kids how to stay afloat and stay alive. Everything went fine until I got to my on-camera closer—the last shot in the story. In the middle of the closer, kneeling in my canoe, I turned to point to something or other. Inadvertently, I shifted my weight and the canoe tipped over. Big splash. I'm in the water, completely submerged. A goddamn army of leeches comes up from the mud and starts latching onto me—all over my body. I panic, naturally. When I come up to the surface, I'm turned around and disoriented. I reach for the first solid thing I see, thinking it's my canoe. Actually, it's my cameraman's canoe. I grab, trying to pull myself up. It tips over. The cameraman and his camera go flying into the lagoon. He screams at me, 'You motherfucker.' Another big splash. Luckily, the water was only four feet deep. I somehow had the presence of mind to snatch the camera before it went under completely and saved the film magazine. I got the story on the air all right, but I never lived it down in Minneapolis."

"Being a courier can be fatal," said Joe Gafa. One chilling near-miss, he amplified, had spurred him to abandon the corps of couriers in order to gather news in the safety of a group instead of alone.

The film traffic coordinator sent Gafa to make a pickup in Newark, New Jersey's black and volatile Central Ward one night. He neglected to warn the courier that racial violence had erupted there earlier in the evening, simply scrawling a note giving road directions and a street address where Gafa would meet the crew.

Cruising slowly through the outskirts of the ghetto on his

motorcycle, Gafa couldn't understand the hostile black faces he saw or the gratuitous insults yelled at him.

"Luckily, I was still several blocks away from the real trouble zone when the crew I was looking for piped up on the radio. They said, 'Joey, if you're riding a bike, don't come any closer. Just give us your present location; we'll come to you.' Then they told me that the blacks in their area were really up in arms over the incident the crew had come to cover: four black homes had been firebombed a few hours earlier by a gang of white guys on motorcycles."

Black violence was the catalyst that did in fact kill a white broadcaster's budding career. With all of our seasoned bird dogs either off for the night or sniffing elsewhere in the jungles of New York, the assignment desk pressed one of the newswriters into service to do a live remote from Harlem. Scattered outbreaks of vandalism and looting had occurred up there the night before.

Like practically everybody else in the writers' pool, the guy had been dreaming of a break like this.

Holding a notepad in one hand and a microphone in the other, he opened the spot like a pro. Then, distracted by a noisy commotion nearby, he followed with, "Wait a minute. Something's happening now . . . there goes a bunch of cops chasing a bunch of niggers down the street."

Experienced TV reporters, as a rule, are wary enough to censor their first thoughts while ad-libbing on-camera. Off-camera anything goes.

One of my infamous shots from the lip came while covering the last rites for a New York cop gunned down in the line of duty. Newsreel teams in cold-weather garb waited impatiently outside the church during the mass of the Resurrection; no cameras were allowed. We had to hang in there for one more shot—the flag-draped coffin and the mourners filing out for the trip to the cemetery.

Nearly an hour went by. All of us were chilled to the bone. A few more minutes in that February freezer might finish our frigid digits.

"Jesus H. Christ," I whined. "What's taking them so long in there? I'm beginning to wish this guy had never got killed."

Reluctantly, I reigned as the king of gaucherie until the throne was usurped by a queen-jester—a reporter from Channel 7. At least thirty news scavengers—TV, print, and radio—were hovering at the entrance to a luxury apartment building on Fifth Avenue. Mrs. Vernon Jordan, a wheelchair invalid, would soon be coming out to catch a plane for Fort Wayne, Indiana. Her husband, executive director of the Urban League, had been critically wounded by a sniper in a motel parking lot. Hungry for salacious tidbits, we were primed with loaded questions about the attractive blonde who had been his companion at the time.

As our vigil dragged on into its third hour, the grousing among us took a typical turn toward macabre speculation. The Channel 7 reporter's punch line was the topper. "If Mrs. Jordan really loved him, she'd be coming out by now. After all, how long does it take to get into a wheelchair?"

Some of the funny surprises we encountered in the field made us rant and curse. The laughter came much later, in retrospect. Like the time I didn't do a live remote from Hoboken, New Jersey.

Long before daybreak, my crew began setting up our gear at a busy railroad terminal. Thousands of harried commuters were making connections there with shuttle buses that would take them through the tunnels under the Hudson River into Manhattan. Their underwater rail link had been shut down by a strike.

Working with defective equipment, Yarus and Gafa had to drag cables, splice this and patch that, devising electronic miracles to send a live signal back to Rockefeller Center. By radio, they kept the assignment desk apprised of their progress.

At 6:52 A.M., three minutes before the first morning newscast would go on the air, we were ready. I took my place in front of the hot Minicam with my back to the swarming commuters. Gafa raised the Studio 3-K control room on the radio. Director Paul Freeman, an urbane transplant from London, wanted to know where we were and what we wanted. Gafa told him we were scheduled to do a live spot for Jane Hanson's newscast in less than three minutes.

"A live spot?" Freeman exclaimed. "You chaps have got to be pulling my leg. We're not set up for that. Nobody in the news department told us anything about it."

Nearly a week went by before Jeff Scarborough could see the humor in the wildest live remote of his career. Working without a reporter, he and audioman Nick Mayer drove their van to the eastern shore of Staten Island. Hurricane Donna was coming their way. Their mission was to provide "bumper shots"—live inserts of a continuing scene—between commercials on the evening newscast.

A cold rain was falling when they started setting up on the beach. The director in the Studio 6-B control room spoke into Scarborough's headphone, telling him to get as close as he could to the water. They wanted shots of the surf pounding in and breaking on the rocks.

Jeff advanced his Minicam to within ten feet of the surf. The control room, reacting to the picture coming in on the studio monitors, said it was great and told him to lock it right there.

A few minutes later, the rain grew colder and heavier, riding winds of ever increasing fury.

Since the camera was locked in place on its tripod, they left it there, still transmitting pictures, and went inside the van. By then Hurricane Donna was lashing the shoreline with her watery windblown skirts. Suddenly Jeff and Nick heard a tremendous roar. Peering through the window, they saw an enormous water monster rising up on its hind legs—a mini-tidal wave that came crashing down on the beach. The $50,000 Minicam toppled and rode the crest.

"This is Studio Six-B calling the Staten Island crew. We've just lost your picture. What's going on out there?"

Jeff began his explanation with the standard preface, "Six-B, you are not going to believe this . . ."

The same crew lost another expensive piece of hardware during preparations for a live broadcast from Times Square. While Jeff mounted his camera on a tripod atop the van, Nick sat in the van adjusting the sound apparatus and a small TV monitor that was tuned to the early-evening news show.

When everything was set, Connie Collins briefed the cameraman on the shooting sequence her scenario would require in the spot coming up in five minutes. Jeff suddenly lost the program audio being fed into his headphone. "Hey, Nick. How come I can't hear program anymore?"

"You're not going to believe this," the audioman replied laconically. "A big black hand just reached inside the van and stole the monitor."

It was a different kind of ripoff that infuriated Heather Bernard. Shooting a videotape package in Alexander's department store, she decided to emphasize the ruses and distractions being employed by pickpockets. A store detective, assigned as her personal escort, provided relevant tips on what Christmas shoppers should do to protect their wallets from professional hands known to be quicker than the eye.

Those tips would be the basis of her stand-up closer holding a wallet stuffed with cash as a prop. Having very little money in her own wallet, Heather borrowed sixty-eight dollars from members of her crew.

With the store detective standing close by, keeping curious spectators off her back, Heather faced the camera in a narrow aisle between display counters. She was about to start talking into the mike when she noticed that somebody in her entourage had dumped her new winter coat on the counter across the aisle, touching a tray of open lipsticks that could smudge it. Placing the stuffed wallet on the counter at her hip, she leaned across the aisle to move her coat, an action that lasted five seconds. When she turned back to pick up the wallet, it was gone.

One of my exasperating comedies in the field starred a zealous member of my film crew.

Supersonic Concorde jets had been disrupting the suburban tranquility of the Howard Beach community in Queens at the edge of Kennedy Airport. I went out there, and I simply held the microphone under the angry masks of housewives and senior citizens, letting them bitch.

Then I got the kind of break I hadn't dared to hope for: as an irate young mother of three articulated personal woes created by the thundering jets, I heard the unmistakable roar of a Concorde taking off in the distance. "My nerves are frazzled," the woman wailed. "My kids can't sleep because of the noise. It's even interfering with my sex life." The Concorde was zooming closer and louder. In just a little while, it would drown her out—dramatically making the central point of the story, better than words.

Five or six seconds before the decibels reached that level, however, my audioman shook his head in disgust and turned off his amplifier. "Cut. Sorry, Bob. That goddamn jet is making too much noise."

Our on-camera science and weather reporter, Dr. Frank Field, persuaded a handsome young couple to let him witness and videotape the birth of their first child.

When the woman went into labor, her husband telephoned Frank, who practically sprinted to the hospital with a Minicam crew. The nurses helped them scrub and cover themselves with surgical masks and gowns.

The delivery went smoothly. Frank had it all on tape. *Cinema verité*. A hell of a spot for tomorrow's evening newscast.

However, when Frank went downstairs to the EJ complex to edit the piece, the supervisor gave him the news. "There's been an accident. We don't know how it happened. Your casette got mixed in with some other tapes that one of the editors had been told to erase."

Was it always somebody else—rather than the reporters themselves—who loused up a story or otherwise failed to be completely professional? Don't ask me. I'm prejudiced. I will confess, though, to having become quite adept at dodging lousy stories, especially on those cold gray mornings after a big night out.

Dozing at my desk, feet propped up, I was awakened gently by

Bret Marcus. My eyelid moved; nothing else. It was 7:15 A.M. I was in no mood to cover anything less important than the outbreak of World War III.

"Sorry to disturb you, Black Arrow," Marcus said sympathetically. "We've been thinking of having you do a story about the American journalists being kicked out of Iran and Afghanistan."

Whatever consciousness I could muster organized itself into an impregnable defensive crouch. "Yeah. Well, you realize of course that nobody out there gives a damn about newsmen overseas unless they manage to get themselves killed or captured, right? Secondly, the only people worth interviewing about it are TV news executives—at ABC, CBS, and here. It's my guess that what we would learn would embarrass us. ABC and CBS have probably made intelligent arrangements to get some coverage over there anyway while our Empty Suits have been playing grab-ass in the locker room."

The assignment editor turned and walked away.

My second claim to fame was being the only bird dog in our kennel who was not required to wear a beeper.

Robert Potts approached my cubicle with a company memo in hand, a pipe between his teeth, and question marks in his eyes. "Are you a privileged character around here or something?"

I admitted hankering to be one, but hadn't been able to sell the idea to the brass.

Potts unfolded the memo from the news director. "It says here the rest of us are supposed to pick up our new, improved beepers from the assignment desk—the rest of us, that is, except you."

"Oh, that's great," I reacted cheerfully. "I've always hated to wear the damn things anyway. It's like having Big Brother watching me. Besides, they say if it's hooked to your belt and you don't respond when it beeps, it explodes and shatters your hip."

"I can understand that," Potts allowed, "although I do know people who wear them as a status symbol; makes 'em feel they're impressing strangers when they're paged."

"Not me. A beeper is an invasion of what little privacy I've managed to keep in this business. We live in a goldfish bowl as it is."

Potts was amazed. "You mean they actually accepted that explanation and exempted you?"

"No, nothing like that. The news director is just trying to save money. Those beepers cost about three hundred bucks apiece. In the past year or so, I've lost five."

Correspondents Lloyd Dobbins and Robert Hager were among the first to beat the onerous system in the network news division, finessing their way past the "Nightly News" committee that was forever tampering with everybody's script.

In the EJ complex, editor Ed Smith chastised Hager for consistently bringing his field tapes in at 6:05 P.M., facing a deadline at 6:30. "You put me through this sweat every time, just like Dobbins. Why can't you guys get your stuff in here early?"

Hager was not contrite. "Would you rather we gave it to you at five-oh-five so you could keep making the changes phoned down by the committee until six twenty-five?"

Smith conceded with gratitude.

In an effort to circumvent censors in the local news department, Anthony Prisendorf put his tail in a sling.

"Is There Sex after Death?" That question in a *Daily News* headline sent Prisendorf and a Minicam crew to the city morgue. Several meat-wagon drivers and body handlers on the overnight shift, the newspaper said, had been enjoying themselves among the stiffs—wild parties between midnight and dawn with booze, drugs, and prostitutes.

Back in the studio, writing his script for a live wrap-around in the studio, Prisendorf came up with an idea he thought was funny. He tried it out on Bret Marcus, then an associate producer for the six o'clock show. "I was thinking maybe I could throw in a gag, like, 'This story adds a new dimension to the age-old question, Is there sex after death?' What do you think?"

"I don't think you should say that," Marcus answered.

Prisendorf accepted the veto. However, at the end of his live wrap-around on the set, he was asked spontaneously by anchorman Tony Guida what he thought of the sex scandal. Prisendorf ad-libbed the first thought that came to mind. "Well, Tony, you might say this story adds a new dimension to the age-old question, Is there sex after death?"

Witnesses in the newsroom said Ubell, watching the show on the monitor, damn-near climbed the wall. Earl the Pearl was livid. He summoned the blasphemer to his office, chewed him out, and suspended him from live broadcasts for a month.

Several days after their confrontation, subsequent developments in the morgue scandal required a videotape follow-up by Prisendorf. This time, off-camera at the morgue, he told the city's chief medical examiner, Dr. Dominic DiMaio, the circumstances that led to his banishment from the studio. DiMaio was amused. His interview with Prisendorf, aired that evening, included a familiar line that drove Ubell even farther up the wall. "Doctor, what do you make of all this after-hours activity in the morgue?" Prisendorf asked in a tone that advertised his innocence. "Well, Tony," DiMaio responded affably, "you might say it adds a new dimension to the age-old question, Is there sex after death?"

Although news-biz executives would encourage you now and then to incorporate more sex and blood in your scenarios, you had to assay each situation carefully to decide just how far you should go.

When I reached the scene on West Twenty-Third Street, where a taxi driver had been robbed and shot to death, his brains were splattered all over the front seat of the wrecked Yellow Cab. A gory mess.

"Hold it, Jerry," I cautioned my Minicam man. "We'll never get away with a shot like that on the air. Let's wait until the cops cover it up with something." They always did eventually.

Dave Monsees of Channel 2, taking the same tack, added a pertinent footnote. "If this were California, where I used to work, we could get it on the air just like that. They really go wild out there." Monsees went on to tell us about a KGO-TV newscast he had watched in San Francisco.

"At the very top of the show, they ran this film clip of a detective using a pair of tweezers to pick up a bloody, severed penis and put it into one of those plastic evidence bags. At the same time, Van Amberg, the anchorman, was reading the headline: "Today's top story—Male Member Found on Railroad Track in Oakland. Stay tuned for details."

Itinerant newshounds, either job hunting or chasing front-page follies in New York, brought equally fractious fables from California. One concerned the famous "Eye in the Sky" news chopper sent up daily by a station in San Francisco.

As police boats maneuvered to recover the body of a suicide jumper in the Bay, the Minicam crew aboard the whirlybird directed their pilot to descend for close-ups. He did. And the downdraft from the rotor blades sank the body.

The crusty local assignment editor for Channel 5 in San Francisco was widely known for his curt, intimidating dialogues. Responding to an anonymous telephone caller who warned that a bomb had been planted in the Channel 5 building, he growled, "I got no time for that shit. Call Channel Four."

As chairman of NBC, Robert Sarnoff—the son of our founding father, General David Sarnoff—commanded fear and respect. During a rare descent into the pits, Chairman Sarnoff mentioned to his minions in the newsroom that he planned to watch the upcoming America's Cup yacht races off Newport, Rhode Island, aboard the NBC boat. He was assuming, incorrectly, that a vessel had been chartered for our news team as usual.

"By the way, what's the name of our boat?" the chairman asked.

No one knew. Everybody quivered in his private crucible of insecurity.

"I'll find out, sir," an Empty Suit volunteered, "and let you know."

Now the truth was, the slide-rule boys upstairs had decided not to charter a boat that year; too costly. In fact, no arrangements had been made to cover the races. Same reason. Yet nobody dared to tell the emperor he had no yacht. So they scrambled, consulted, telegraphed, and telephoned until they found a yacht for hire—an expensive fifty-footer with luxurious accommodations and a crew of five.

To rationalize this outlay of megabucks, a nervous Empty Suit summoned cameraman Bob Donohue to his office. "We want you to go up to Newport with your camera; just you. All you have to do is enjoy yourself on the NBC yacht and pretend to be covering the races. We really don't want any film on them. What we want to do is impress Mr. Sarnoff. He's going to be on the boat. So just go through the motions and look professional."

Donohue went, alone, with an Arriflex silent camera. "Aside from the captain and the deckhands," he said later, "I was the only one aboard. I didn't have to shoot a single frame. At the last minute, Sarnoff got an invitation to watch the races on the committee boat with all the other big shots."

With the deadline approaching for the 6:00 P.M. edition of "Newscenter 4," half a dozen of us bird dogs, back from the boondocks, were working feverishly with videotape editors in our respective automated cubicles. I was putting the finishing touches on the lead story, a double homicide in Brooklyn, gangland style. Chauncey Howell was struggling with what eventually would be one of his typically irreverent whimsies, this one about the final dress rehearsal for the following night's grand opening of the Bolshoi Ballet.

"A call for you, Chauncey, from the desk," somebody yelled in the corridor. "Extension thirty-one."

When he picked up the phone, Chauncey was informed by the assignment editor that NBC News president Les Crystal had called a few seconds ago and wanted to see him. Chauncey was worried. Management almost never wanted to see you about anything good.

As Chauncey went flying out of the editing cubicle, Pete Gilmore tried to stop him, warning him that they might not make air if they didn't keep at it. The rules prohibited an editor from making a move on the machine unless the reporter was physically there to pick the scenes.

Chauncey paused, but only for a micro-jiffy, just long enough to tell Pete that it was Les Crystal he had to see and if he were in some kind of trouble, keeping him waiting would only make it worse. Off he went.

He returned from the executive suite upstairs several minutes later with smoke flaring from his nostrils.

"What happened?" I asked apprehensively.

"You wouldn't believe it. Crystal said, 'Could you get me three tickets for the ballet tomorrow night? If you can't get three, I'll take two.' "

Yes, Empty Suits inadvertently played straight men in some of our burlesque routines. They seldom heard the closing boffo line or saw the comical slow burns we emoted as the curtain came down on our skits. On the other hand, there was one player in our repertory company at Channel 4 who deliberately provoked consternation and embarrassment—a grunt who specialized in stealing scenes.

This audioman in our pool of film crews had earned the sobriquet "Captain Class" because after nearly fifty years of ingracious living, he had developed absolutely none.

One of the first scenes he stole, to my knowledge, was played during an out-of-town assignment covering Senator Hubert Humphrey's presidential campaign. After the candidate's final speech in Los Angeles, the film crews from all three networks traveling with him reassembled at the airport for the flight back to New York. Captain Class arrived by taxi with five huge cardboard boxes. "Hey, guys," he yelled to the other technicians. "Anybody want to buy a new bike for your kids? Only five bucks apiece."

To those who expressed interest, he explained archly that he had "made a good contact" in the Watts ghetto. Five unassembled bicycles. Finding no takers, Captain Class hired a skycap to load the boxes on the plane with the rest of NBC's equipment. "I can

175

sell 'em for fifteen or twenty bucks apiece back home."

Everybody wondered what Senator Humphrey would have said had he known that his plane was used to carry hot bikes out of California.

In Hurley's bar one evening, Captain Class boasted of his latest coup.

"We were covering one of them big exhibits they're always having at the Coliseum. This redneck dude was showing us how to work a new fishing rod he'd invented—slick and fancy with all kinds of shit you could attach to it—looked pretty damn good to me. So when the interview was over, I said, 'Hey, pal. I like to fish. Let me have one of them fancy rods.' That sucker wasn't expecting nothing like that. He says to me, 'Gee, I'm sorry, but the main shipment for the exhibition hasn't arrived from the factory yet. This is all I've got right now; just one.'

"I picked it up off the table and walked away. I said, 'That's all I want, pal. Just one.' And I had me a new fishing rod."

Happily, the most regrettable character I had ever met in news biz made fewer and fewer personal appearances in my field assignments as videotape gradually superseded film as television's primary medium. One day, when all the tape crews were tied up elsewhere, I had to take him with me to cover the only egg farm in the city. A group of enterprising teenagers at a high school in Queens was running a hatchery on their campus, and selling the hen fruit to their neighbors. Solid human interest stuff.

The cameraman shot the laying brood, the egg-crating process, and the young student-farmers in the barnyard. While we were packing up our gear, one of the kids said, gratefully, that the publicity was certain to help their business, and asked if we'd like a few eggs to take home as a token of their appreciation.

Captain Class—who had been hinting rather bluntly along that line since we arrived—spoke up first, loud and clear. "Yeah, pal. I got a big family. I'll take four dozen."

The two other members of the crew and I couldn't bring ourselves to accept even a single egg.

The captain strolled back to the company car humming a happy tune; with the exact amount he had demanded.

Aside from glomming souvenirs on the con, Captain Class loved to dump on big shots, completely oblivious to the shame he painted on the faces of his teammates. He did it again as part of the film crew assigned to interview former-Mayor John Lindsay. Channel 4 had just hired Lindsay as an in-studio analyst for our election coverage the following week. Carl Stokes, the former Cleveland mayor turned newsman, would be doing a similar job in the same studio that evening.

As the Lindsay interview ended, Captain Class removed the lavaliere mike he had clipped to Big John's necktie. "I can't understand why they're putting you and Stokes on the air together," he said through a mixture of gravel and scorn. "You two guys have fucked up two cities between you."

Lindsay, ever the politician, tried to ride it out with a good-natured chuckle.

"I can see the ads now," the captain expanded. He gazed into the middle distance over Lindsay's handsome blond head. "Be sure to watch Channel Four on election night, folks. We'll have assholes back to back."

Only strangers, never teammates, lodged official complaints against Captain Class, but there was not stipulation in his union's contract that allowed dismissal for exacerbated churlishness, so long as his technical expertise was up to par. There was a chorus of hallelujahs throughout the news complex when the newsfilm fadeout finally pushed him into retirement.

One of the unwritten rules of news biz is that talents and technicians cover for one another when somebody goofs—provided the error in question does not prevent completion of the mission in time to make air.

Between 1963 and 1982, I blew the whistle on only one team-

177

mate, a cameraman. I had no choice.

After loading his gear in the trunk of the company car early in the morning, the cameraman said he had to go back to his locker for a minute. He'd forgotten something. He soon returned with a black attaché case in hand. The rest of us in the crew assumed he had picked up some important personal papers or his lunch.

Much later, en route to our third assignment of the day, we discovered the truth quite by accident. The car shuddered, reacting to punishment from a New York pothole. The attaché case on the front seat fell to the floor and popped open. A quart bottle of Russian vodka, three-fourths empty, rolled out.

We kidded the cameraman about it, appreciating his ruse. He laughed, too, apparently unaffected by the booze. Everybody knew he liked to drink. We had never seen him bagged on the job, however. His camera work was always A-OK.

An NBC courier picked up our third story outside the criminal courthouse in Brooklyn. We had shot an exclusive with the Reverend Mr. Milton Galamison, a militant civil rights activist who had been appointed only hours before to the Central Board of Education. No other bird dog had been able to track him down. Ironically, Galamison had been in court that day to face an old charge stemming from a half-forgotten act of civil disobedience against the Central Board of Ed a year earlier. His reaction to my questions about possibly being "bought off" by the establishment made damn good television fodder.

Heading back to the studio in Manhattan, we felt like heroes. Then we got a radio call from the assignment desk. Our first story had eighty-sixed—out of focus. The desk man thought that our lens adjuster might be out of sync. Then he reported that our second story was overexposed—also unusable—and wondered if the camera had a light leak somewhere.

The cameraman said it was an old Auricon. He would bring it up to the equipment room for inspection.

The whole crew felt rotten. All of that work for nothing. We realized then that it was the man behind the camera who had been out of focus and out of sync. I prayed that nothing had gone wrong with my exclusive.

I was in the editing room when the Galamison film came out of the soup—completely blank from end to end.

I didn't want to believe it. "How the hell could that happen?"

The editor surmised that our cameraman must have forgotten to take the dust cap off his lens.

The cameraman was sent away for the cure. He never came back.

7

Going Steady With Eighty-Six

*I*N A WAY, it seemed to me, being a news-biz star was something like mountain climbing in the Alps. When teammates close to you were deliberately cut loose to plunge into the murky abyss of expendability, you became quite paranoid, acutely aware of your own precarious foothold on the slippery crags of stardom. The cutters-in-chief—incoming executives at this station or that one—invariably subscribed to a Spartan philosophy that was difficult to refute: if the sacrificees had been pulling their weight, this team would have reached the summit long ago.

Understanding that pragmatic philosophy, superstar Tom Snyder, then host of NBC's "Tomorrow," made a dire prediction in the winter of 1980 as Fred Silverman's regime continued pasting "expendable" labels on a multitude of veterans. "I think anybody who was already here when this new bunch came in is a dead fish."

Snyder was not reading tea leaves. By the time he made that observation, more than seventy NBC vice-presidents—not to mention talents and managers—had been eighty-sixed, frightened into early retirement or forced to jump ship. Survivors trembled, with good reason. (By the end of 1981, Snyder was no longer with NBC.)

Concurrently, seismic shock waves were rocking the news team at our sister station, WRC-TV, in Washington, D.C., as David Newell took over as news director. Within fifteen minutes after Newell's coronation, reporter Robert Endicott was fired. The fact that he was competent, handsome, mellifluous, and dedicated, with over ten years of hard work behind him, was irrelevant. Newell was the messiah. He said he simply didn't like Endicott on the air.

Knowing that such judgments were beyond appeal, Endicott went peaceably. He left a classic memo on the WRC newsroom's bulletin board that newshounds throughout the sprawling NBC network applauded as copies of it made the rounds:

> Plans for my first day following dismissal from NBC.
> 10:00 A.M.—Start book about news directors I have known and respected.
> 10:01 A.M.—Finish book. Robert Endicott.

Logically, you could extrapolate from Endicott's execution that if management liked you on the air, you were safe, right? Not necessarily. At WCBS-TV not long ago, Michele Marsh—beautiful and competent, with a high Q rating—was downgraded from anchorwoman on the 11:00 P.M. newscast to "special correspondent." It happened less than two months after the show she had co-anchored with Rolland Smith won the February sweeps and an Emmy award as the best local newscast in New York. Why did they replace her? Because months before those coveted accolades had been bestowed on her, the executives at Channel 2, worried about The Ratings, had committed themselves in writing to giving her berth, plus $400,000, to Dave Marash to lure him back into the fold from the ABC network's "20/20" news program.

Of course I was shocked by what happened to Michele, even though I had witnessed similar cataclysms before.

My first shocker involved the departure of New York's number-one weatherman in the mid-sixties, Tex Antoine, from Channel 4 (his tasteless crack about rape on Channel 7 came several years later).

For well over a year, I had the fun of working closely with Tex on the "Eleventh Hour News" five nights a week. He and I were studio talents, second and third bananas under anchorman Frank McGee. Tex was a witty, red-haired leprechaun of a guy who drew appropriate cartoons on cardboard while telling viewers whether it would rain or shine the following day. After getting word one night that Tex would not be with us any more, I called his home. The deposed weatherman told me cheerfully not to worry about him. He had something good cooking over at Channel 7.

"That's great, Tex. Good news for a change. I hope you beat our brains out over there. We deserve it. But what the hell happened? I thought you were an institution around here."

It was all about bullshit, Tex told me. In negotiating a new contract, he had easily obtained a fat pay increase and a very comfortable package of fringe benefits. No sweat. But then he asked if they would reimburse him for his drawing materials—crayons and cardboard. Fifteen dollars a week. They said no, absolutely not. He got angry, saying he thought they were being pretty goddamn petty. They got angry. So they huffed and puffed at each other. And that was that.

An even more curious ideological conflict resulted in the departure of Sherman Jackson—Channel 4's first Puerto Rican reporter—from our ranks. His sin had not been divulged by either side when we read in the gossip columns that Jackson had filed a hefty human rights suit against the station. This struck everybody as mighty peculiar since it was common knowledge that his Latin heritage had been the decisive factor when they hired him more than a year before, to ethnically balance the staff. So where did human rights or racial discrimination come into the picture?

We got the answer a week or so later when a forlorn figure came trudging into the newsroom—a modern brown-skinned Diogenes in search of a TV talent who was honest and courageous enough to be a witness in his lawsuit. Jackson swore that news director Bernie Shussman had fired him unjustly at the insistence of vice-president Irv Margolis.

As usual, no volunteers stepped forward to defend the outcast. Jackson had been around long enough to understand why. "Look. I don't want to put any of you guys under the gun, but I'm desperate. They're saying the reason they fired me was poor reporting. You've all seen my work. You know that isn't true. The real reason was something else. They told me that even though I look Puerto Rican, I don't sound like a Puerto Rican. No accent. And a reporter who signs off his pieces as Sherman Jackson, they said, doesn't advertise the fact that they have a Puerto Rican on the show. They gave me the sack when I refused to change my name to something that sounded Hispanic."

Jackson failed in his legal battle for reinstatement. After protracted litigation, he settled for a bundle of cash, getting a job in the meantime in public relations.

Reporter Victor Gil de la Madrid had a name that was ethnically correct. He didn't last much longer than Jackson, however.

As I arrived in the newsroom several minutes later than usual one day, four teammates—Ken Alvord, Heather Bernard, Robert Potts, and Mary Alice Williams—were visibly in mourning.

Recognizing the syndrome, I surveyed the starboard quadrant of the pits. Uh-huh. One of the partitioned cubicles had been stripped of the flotsam that usually littered a grunt's natural habitat—no recent scripts, reference books, note pads, souvenirs, or snapshots—as if Victor Gil de la Madrid had never existed.

Although it happened every six months or so—a respected talent suddenly becoming an unperson—we survivors were nonetheless traumatized. Every time.

Why had they eighty-sixed Victor, we asked one another. Officially, nothing had been announced or leaked to the papers. He had seemed to be the ideal Puerto Rican air man the Empty Suits had been looking for.

"Right. He didn't have the wrong name or the wrong accent,"

Potts reminded. "He looked and sounded Hispanic—a really authentic accent."

"Handsome, too," one of the women added. "A Tyrone Power look-alike."

Then why had they done the man in?

Alvord rubbed his chin thoughtfully, speaking very carefully as he made a guess. "Well, I'm not sure that this is the reason. I suspect that it is, however. The last time I saw Victor a couple of days ago, he was coming out of Earl Ubell's office. He looked like a man who had just read his name on a tombstone. When I asked what the problem was, he said, 'They're getting on me again about my heavy accent.' "

We were gratified to learn months later that Victor was alive and well, doing daily broadcasts for a Spanish-speaking station in Puerto Rico.

Victor might have found small consolation in the parallel misfortune of a white female reporter at Channel 7, Penny Crone. Her downfall was an intermittent lisp, which did not prevent her from later becoming a news-biz star on Channel 9 in New York.

After a year of news broadcasting on the ABC radio network, Penny told me, she made a videotape audition reel for the flagship TV station. The "Eyewitness News" director, Ron Tindiglia, hired her on the basis of it.

"Everybody at Channel Seven thought I was just perfect for the first couple of days. Roger Grimsby said, 'Don't change a thing, honey. You're terrific just the way you are.'

"A day or two after that, the news director called me into his office. 'My God,' he says, 'you've got a lisp.' He sent me to the ABC speech therapist, Lillian Wilder, for lessons. Naturally, the lisp got worse. I was so self-conscious it made me nervous. In a few weeks, though, my lisp just about disappeared—except for those times when I had to do something on the air under tremendous pressure.

"Then all of a sudden they started telling me my hair was wrong. They brought this beauty parlor guy into the studio every day to paint my face and fix my hair before I went on the show for live wrap-arounds with my tape. Grimsby said, 'Jesus Christ, what have they done to you? You're not the same Penny Crone.' What could I say?

"Finally, about fourteen months after they hired me, Tindiglia called me in again, told me I was fired. I could keep on working for six more months, he said, but after that I'd have to go. I said, 'I suppose you're telling me there is nothing I can do to change your mind in the next six months—even if I walk on the East River.' Tindiglia said he was sorry, but that's how it was. Then he sent me over to the Burlington Building to see one of the ABC vice-presidents, Bill Fyffe. When I got there, he said to me, 'I think you're entitled to know why we're letting you go in six months. You have a lisp.'

"I said Barbara Walters also has a lisp. Fyffe said, 'Yes, but yours is different. Why don't you go out and take some more speech lessons: Come back in six months and we'll talk about it.'

"I threw up both hands. 'Thay no more. I quith.' And that was that."

In an act of self-liberation from Channel 4, Jimmy Breslin eighty-sixed himself. His verbal swats had proved ineffective as they buzzed around his ears for several weeks. The syndicated newspaper columnist was not slick and svelte on the tube. He usually looked and sounded like a disgruntled grizzly bear awakened prematurely from hibernation. No matter. He was one of the best tellers of New York stories since Damon Runyon.

One afternoon while pounding out his column for our TV show, he was stung once too often by a kibitzer. Manager Shelly Hoffman volunteered criticism and suggestions that sounded like censorship. Breslin's style was too abrasive for Hoffman's sensibilities.

The grizzly bear bristled. With several books and thousands of columns behind him, he was deluded by the notion that he was a better judge of his prose than Hoffman. Rising from his desk, leaving the unfinished script in the typewriter, Breslin composed a gruff exit line: "Okay, you write it."

When next seen on television, he was doing commercials for what he described as "a good drinking beer."

When word filtered down from the newsroom to Hurley's bar that Liz Trotta had been sacked, my mind boggled. "Not Liz. What the hell are they trying to do, break up the team?"

God knows I hated to see her go, though I was confident that she would soon be picked up by another network (as she was). She was tough, persistent, skeptical, and intelligent. I had shown her the ropes on the very first morning she arrived from the Long Island paper *Newsday* back in 1965.

Normally, when a raw recruit came aboard, he or she was assigned to tag along with Gabe Pressman or me for a week to learn how to do it on the street. When Betty Rollins came over from the expiring *Look* magazine, vice-president Lee Hanna put her on my coattails for three weeks, getting her ready for instant stardom on the network show. With Liz, the orientation took exactly one day. She asked only relevant questions about my *modus operandi*. When we came back to the newsroom late that afternoon, I told the news director, "Don't waste the lady's time. Give her a crew." He did.

Liz was one of the first females to cover combat action in the Vietnam War. Okay, maybe she was sassy and brassy to the point of insubordination now and then. What the hell, she had to be. As the first female to join our team, she had to be tough. First, she had to fight her way out of the powder-puff corner—proving beyond executive doubts that she could handle any assignment as well as any man. She forced politicians and rival reporters to take her seriously as well.

What I loved most about Liz Trotta was her flaming wrath. It came boiling to the surface whenever she felt that management or anyone else had failed to show the proper respect for her talents as a serious journalist. There had been a time in the middle of her NBC career when she set her heart on getting the Paris bureau assignment. Bernard Frizell had left that beat. Liz promptly applied for the job. Upon hearing through the grapevine weeks later that they had given that plum to Aline Saarinen, Liz was furious. Having paid more dues than the other woman, she stormed into the executive suite with eyes that burned like brimstone. Bearding the first Empty Suit she encountered, Liz demanded, "Who do I have to screw to get a good job around here? The problem is," she added later, "even if I wanted to go that route, there's nobody around here who appeals to me."

Almost everybody would go along with President John F. Kennedy's wry observation, "Life is not fair." In news biz, you learned all about that. As a rule, there was nothing you could do about it. In 1977, however, a women's committee for equal opportunity at NBC, having sued the company for sex discrimination, won a $2 million out-of-court settlement. Over two thousand female employees shared the back pay awarded by that agreement. It also stipulated minimum goals for hiring and promoting women in the future, covering job categories seldom open to them—camerapersons, producers, directors, and managers.

Encouraged by the feminist triumph, cameraman Mike ("Fellini") Calvacca sued the company for a million dollars. He thereby earned respect and plaudits from other grunts—from a safe distance of course.

"I sued," Calvacca said, "because I got sick and tired of being passed over while they upgraded guys and women who haven't been here as long as me." Managers had refused to give him the rating of newsreel-documentary cameraman, which he clearly deserved after ten years at Channel 4. Without that rating, he was being paid about thirty dollars a week less than his peers.

His silent fans in the newsroom felt from the beginning of the lawsuit that Mike was right; he had been getting a raw deal. Robert Potts was one of the very few who had the guts to testify to that effect at the trial. Scuttlebutt had it that Calvacca couldn't lose. NBC's lawyers would have to prove that this stout-hearted veteran was incompetent behind a camera. No way.

"My lawyer and I knew they couldn't prove that. You should have seen the trial, though. Unbelievable. When they put Bill Kelly [the film crew supervisor] on the witness stand, he told them I was the world's worst cameraman. Under oath, he said that—the world's worst. They had gotten Kelly out of a sick bed to testify against me. God only knows who wrote his script. He said nobody ever requests Calvacca for a film job, that I'm only good for covering fires."

Another key witness for the company, Mike went on, was Geoff Pond, director of the network's Northeast bureau in Rockefeller Center. "Pond also said I was terrible, but he couldn't think of any specific stories I had shot that would show how bad I was. Then my lawyer asked Pond if he could look at a piece of film shot by me and film shot by camermen he considers good and tell which was which. Pond admitted that he couldn't."

Neither could anyone else.

Nevertheless, NBC won the case. Calvacca was later lopped off the payroll.

Was that the end of the "world's worst" cameraman in news biz? Nope. Calvacca worked for nearly two more years as a freelance news cameraman at Channel 4, under Bill Kelly's supervision, then joined the staff of Channel 7.

After seventeen years as "Mr. Street Reporter" at Channel 4, Gabe Pressman defected to Channel 5. Losing him from our team also cast a funeral pall over the newsroom. Gabe had been an indefatigable pioneer in news biz—the second streetwalker in New York, starting in 1953, after John Tillman of Channel 11.

This was not exactly a firing. Management spelled out new ground rules that made the old pro feel unwanted. First, they revised the format of our six o'clock show and expanded the reporting staff. The idea, they said, was to air a broader range of talents, more consumer-oriented features, more entertainment, less hard news. Second, since Gabe's role would be diminished, they argued, his six-figure salary should be cut by 25 percent. Bye-bye, Pressman.

In justifying his switch to Channel 5 (at six figures), Gabe told TV gossip columnists: "NBC is no longer the milieu for in-depth hard-nosed reporting." Not the whole truth, but dignified.

In the station's official response to the traitor's broadside—also chronicled in print—NBC News President Reuven Frank fired what many of us grunts regarded as a childish volley, saying in effect that losing Pressman was no big deal. In Frank's words, "Actually, Gabe never really lived up to our expectations."

Predictably, there was the vindictive hope in the newsroom that Gabe would finally live up to the president's expectations by breaking a lot of big stories and boosting The Ratings at Channel 5. Gabe did not disappoint us.

Although the Metromedia station boasted a solid news operation, and although Gabe was allowed to concentrate on hard news and human-interest features, he never was really happy over there. It was a smaller operation with inadequate facilities, fewer camera crews, and less prestige. He came back to WNBC eight years later in 1980. Everyone in the Channel 4 newsroom applauded. Unlike the rest of us docile malcontents, he did not live in the shadow of eighty-six. Feeling secure in his legend, Gabe openly challenged the Empty Suits as he always had. He didn't like what had happened to the news programs at Channels 2, 4, and 7 during his exile and said so to the *Daily News*. The Big Three, he complained, were now engaged in "cosmetic journalism" and he intended to fight it.

When asked about the growing tendency of anchors and reporters to sit there on the studio set chatting about the day's events and nonevents, Gabe spat angrily, "It's a kaffeeklatsch. I've made no secret of how repugnant I find the bouffant-hairdo, laugh-'em-up school of journalism. It started with "Eyewitness News" at WABC in the late sixties and has infected television news across the country. There should be more attention to the basic principles of journalism—the adversary relationship, toughness, human interest. I do not think journalists should be personalities. It's the substance that counts."

Gabe was able, more often than not, to inject those principles into his own reports. Our newscasts on the whole, however, continued to emphasize studio chitchat, entertainment, and silly live remotes. Virtually alone, the veteran fought a losing battle. Sheer cowardice in the pits prevented bold expressions of support. Only when the executives were out of sight did we dare to snarl our resentments.

Around 4:40 one afternoon, twenty minutes before our two-hour newscast would hit the air, David Diaz and I ambled into Studio 6-B, heading for the makeup room on the far side of that semidark cavern. One at a time, we were scheduled to go "live at five" near the top of the show; that is, each of us would chat with Melba Tolliver and Pia Lindstrom. Except for four camerapersons and a couple of idle stagehands, the studio seemed deserted, safe for off-the-record observations.

"You know, this live-at-five business is bullshit," I grumbled. "It ain't news."

Diaz disagreed. "Oh, I think it's a good idea."

"You only say that," I accused, "because you're only two years old in this business. You've never had an anchor slot, and you think being in the studio is where it's at. Maybe it is where it's at as far as making big bucks is concerned, but not where the news is covered." I went on to tell him what Walter Cronkite had said in that context. In a *Daily News* interview toward the end of his illustrious career with CBS "Evening News," he had said, "I'm afraid an awful lot of young people are coming into television journalism because they're more motivated to be stars then they are motivated to be journalists. I think a person who wants to be a newsman or a newswoman should concentrate on reporting, learning sources, where to find them, how to deal with them, and then to organize and write what they've acquired. And the presentation of that information by any means of television should be the last consideration. I think that, unfortunately, the priorities are reversed by too many young people today coming into broadcasting. This is partly promoted by the television stations and to some degree by the networks."

Diaz did not back off. "I can't argue with what Cronkite said, but I still think having reporters live in the studio is good television. It helps our viewers relate to us better than they can when they only see us in the field on videotape or film. I also think they like seeing us relating to the studio anchors, like they do it on Channel Seven."

I pounced on the man. "That's another boo-boo, David—'just like they do it on Channel Seven.' Don't you see? We're imitating the opposition. I know; they're number one. But I feel in my bones you don't beat number one by imitating it. You can only come off as a pale carbon copy. What we should do is get our own *schtick* together and beat them over the head with it: a straight news show, for example. That's how we could become number one; by doing our own kind of show, not theirs."

At that point in my angry dissertation, news director Ron Kershaw and Bucky Gunts, his control room director, stepped out from behind a make-believe wall in Studio 6-B. From the expressions on their faces, I knew they had overheard me.

I made a half-hearted effort to weasel out of it. "Of course, I could be wrong. I hope I'm wrong, but that's the way I see it. Good evening, gentlemen."

Kershaw and Gunts responded in neutral shades of civility. Diaz and I continued to the makeup room. I wondered whether I had just nominated myself for eighty-six.

Now before you render a final judgment on the gutless grunt who copped out so shamefully in Studio 6-B, walk for a moment in the shoes of a news-biz talent, going steady with eighty-six. How much true grit could you maintain if your union (the American Federation of Radio and Television Artists) had failed to win a reasonable job-security clause in its contract negotiations with TV stations? Unlike TV technicians, represented by NABET, talents can be demoted or fired for the flimsiest of reasons, and nothing can be done by AFTRA to protect us from such whims. AFTRA negotiates minimum pay scales, working conditions, and fringe benefits, period. Management's right to demote and dismiss without cause is spelled out in "personal services contracts" signed by each talent. In effect, the personal contract says management can terminate your services if it chooses at the end of each cycle in the contract. The standard cycles run thirteen weeks for neophytes, six months for veterans, one year for old reliable retainers with eight or ten years in the trenches. Would it ease your general anxiety to know that when they did eighty-six you, they would have to pay you for one more cycle whether you worked or not? Personally, I would feel better if AFTRA had the power to bring such firings without cause to arbitration—compel management to prove incompetence or dereliction of duty.

As it stands now, all management has to say is something like, "You just don't fit in with the image we want to project on this station." And there is no appeal.

The point is, Empty Suits are forever looking over their shoulders at The Ratings, at your Q numbers, and a hell of a lot of other variables beyond your control while deciding whether to renew their option on your services for another cycle. This tacit intimidation inhibits the kind of dialogue that is sorely needed in news biz— naked challenges by grunts against management's *modus operandi*. In short, all of us could perhaps contribute more in the way of upgrading news biz if we felt more secure.

Suppose you were working at Metromedia's Channel 5 and just happened to read the little item I spotted one day in the *New York Post*. It said Channel 5, though preeminent among news shows on the three independent stations in New York, faced an uncertain future. Its audience was growing older and therefore less attractive to advertisers. Market researchers had persuaded TV sponsors years ago that the potential customers they must reach were women between the ages of eighteen and thirty-four. Channel 5, the article said, was drawing only twenty-seven thousand female viewers in that category.

This meant that even though Channel 5 had a larger audience for its 10:00 P.M. newscast than "Action News," its competitor on Channel 11, it was the wrong audience. Channel 11's audience, though numerically smaller, included thirty-four thousand of those desirable young women.

Can you imagine how much panic that little news item—true or false—might have generated in the Channel 5 newsroom? It was like having an elephant dumped in your lap out of the blue. Some damn good reporters and anchors over there began gnawing their fingernails—seasoned professionals like Bill McCreary, John Miller, Judy Licht, Anthony Prisendorf, and Marvin Scott. Never mind that those market researchers probably didn't know what the hell they were talking about. They had spoken. The question was, how had those faceless nonentities become so critically involved in so many innocent lives in the first place? And what could be done? Where could they find those missing females and how could they woo them back to Channel 5?

No one could say. I was certain, however, that a lot of mortgage installments, alimony payments, orthodontist bills, and tuition fees were inexorably linked to those anonymous fugitive females.

Jim VanSickle's three-year contract was running its final cycle at Channel 4 when, typically, he became infected with a virulent strain of "worryitis." A new deal would have to be negotiated; that is, unless Fred Silverman or any one of several other executives developed the notion that Jim did not fit their image of the "mediagenic" newscaster. That adjective had been added to newsroom jargon during Kershaw's regime. The new talents he had imported— Jane Hanson, Dave Gilbert, and Roberto Tschudin Lucheme— were effervescent personalities with lots of curly hair, and were approximately twenty-five years younger than VanSickle.

Being a team player, however, VanSickle was bold enough to confront the news director with a suggestion for lifting morale in the pits. "We've got many dedicated people here doing a great job for this company, and they never get any credit. I'm not talking about reporters or anchors so much. I mean the guys and girls behind the scenes—the camera crews in particular. Some of those guys really break their humps in the field to give us that special shot that tells the story, or send back a live picture when conditions out there are impossible. I think it would help if when you see something on the show that's out of the ordinary, you take the time to drop a note to those guys; let them know they're appreciated."

Kershaw nodded. He said he might get around to doing that in time; right now he rarely had a chance to watch our show, spending most of his time "looking at audition tapes."

VanSickle dropped it right there, wondering whether his mediagenic replacements might be on one of those tapes.

It was generally understood that flagship stations were inundated with new audition tapes every week, from job hunters, talent agencies, and TV consulting firms such as the Media Associates based in Dallas and a New York outfit called Television News Research. Both employ batteries of TV news watchers who use video recorders in their homes to tape news flesh on every channel in their locales. The result is copious libraries of videotape cassettes displaying hundreds of talents who may or may not be eager to switch channels. If a network is looking for new sex symbols, Television News Research charges $35,000 for a package of 150 cassettes that show over fifteen hundred personalities in action. Independent stations can buy the same package for less, around $20,000, or 5 cassettes showing perhaps 180 talents for $500.

Jim VanSickle had been aware of all that when he went to the bargaining table at Channel 4. His face, emerging from the first round, looked like ten miles of bad road. "They've got me in a catch twenty-two," he confided glumly. "When I first came to work here a few years ago, they criticized me for being on-camera too much in my film pieces. Give us pictures and action, they told me. So I took the hint. I stopped putting myself on-camera unless absolutely necessary; when I had no pictures worth showing.

"Now I go into contract negotiations and they indicate to me they don't think I'm worth the money they're paying me, to say nothing of the raise I'm asking for. They say I have a low Q rating—no recognition factor among viewers."

I could not contain my laughter. "It's a dance, Jim," I assured the worried man. "They're just trying to soften you up. Hang in there. When I went in for my second contract here, in nineteen sixty-seven, their first offer was a ten percent paycut. I didn't accept it, of course, and eventually got more than I had asked for. Did you notice that they didn't show you the list of Q ratings for the station's talents? Of course they didn't. It's a dance."

VanSickle thought about it. "Is that why you're always so cool—because you've learned all the tricks they pull?"

I confessed to being as afraid as anyone else, but since there was nothing I could do about the uncertainties of our business, I simply made up my mind to do the best job I could day by day and try not to think about all the things I couldn't control.

VanSickle and I had work to do. There was no time then to tell him the rest of it. My apparent fortitude in the face of frightening probabilities had been strengthened at a City Hall news conference. When Mayor Koch unveiled his budget for the coming fiscal year, one of the print bird dogs challenged His Honor's arithmetic. Koch was balancing his $13 billion budget on a very shaky presumption: generous aid from Washington at a time when the feds—according to Senator Howard Baker of Tennessee—had "eight hundred fifty billion dollars less than no money at all."

The mayor's equanimity was undisturbed. "You may be right," he admitted quite blandly. "The feds may very well tell us to go slash our wrists. But we don't have to slash them in advance."

My fear of eighty-six not only began to subside but was partially displaced by sympathy as I learned to appreciate that the Empty Suits were trembling at the far end of the same boat. I still distrusted them, but I also admired their courage against difficult odds and extraordinary pressures. Ron Kershaw was the seventh news director I had served under at Channel 4. His predecessors had averaged only two and a half years at the helm. So had the managers and producers they appointed to oversee the grunts.

Despite the short life spans of our news directors, however, there were two occasions when I—encouraged by disgruntled comrades in the pits—applied for a shot at the catbird seat.

"It's true," Joe Gafa assured me. "They're going to eighty-six Norman Fein." We were riding with Jerry Yarus to the scene of a major narcotics raid on Long Island. "I got it from a guy who dates a secretary in the Golden Ghetto; what you would call an unimpeachable source. Jerry and I were saying this morning before you came down to the car, why don't you go after the job? You'd make a helluva news director."

Yarus backed him up. "Yeah. You know this business. You could eliminate the bullshit around here, bring us back to number one."

Though flattered, I brushed their suggestion aside. I chewed on it, though, for two or three weeks as the rumors of Fein's imminent departure continued. Eventually, I decided to put in a bid.

196

The WNBC-TV station manager, Ann Berk, was surprised. "I had no idea you'd be interested in switching to management." Like everybody else at Channel 4, she knew I was committed to the cowboy's life. "The fact is, the rumors are not true, Bob. We are planning no change at this time."

I was not convinced, having heard that tape before. I told her that roughly two years before—when the scuttlebutt was that Earl Ubell was under the ax—I had gone to see vice-president Joe Bartelme and applied for the job. "Bartelme also told me the rumors weren't true. Maybe two months after that interview, Fein replaced Ubell."

Her backbone stiffened momentarily, reacting to my oblique insult. Then she smiled. "And they never gave you a chance to compete for the job. Well, I promise to let you know if and when the rumors about Fein become true. I repeat, they are not true now. If we decide to make a change, you will have a chance this time to present your ideas, tell us what you would do to bring a turnaround."

Ann Berk probably intended to keep that promise. The next thing I knew, however, she was no longer there. Neither was Fein. Kershaw appeared out of nowhere.

"You're lucky they didn't make you news director." These words of consolation from Jim Ryan were delivered without a trace of humor. Ryan should know. The "Silver Fox" had spent his first year at Channel 4, after arriving from the *Daily News,* in management during the Fein administration. He swore to being much happier as a grunt.

Even so, I felt miffed over being denied a fair shot. "As a matter of fact, Jim, I've been thinking that if I did become news director, you might consider being my assistant. We'd make one helluva team."

Ryan shook his head emphatically. "Never, not even if they offered to double my salary. I was close enough, when I worked as executive producer, to see what it's like. You have no idea how much time a news director has to spend answering memos and phone calls from the big boys upstairs, and having meetings with

197

them. The subject is always the same: you have to explain why The Ratings aren't any better than they are. No matter what you tell them, they're never satisfied, always on your back, until you come up with the numbers they want to hear."

Jim Ryan's sobering evaluation was still reverberating in my mind when I bumped into a former Channel 4 news director on Madison Avenue one Saturday. Over a long cup of coffee, he candidly reviewed the vicissitudes of his reign, having extracted my solemn promise to forget his name and any other names he would mention. Still gainfully employed in news biz, he didn't want to antagonize old enemies who someday might be in positions to help or hurt his career. "It's a small club here in New York, you know. We go from channel to channel and sometimes back again."

Okay. Let's call him Jack.

"The bullshit quotient at my level," Jack said, "was even higher than it was at yours. I'm aware that reporters think of the news director as a god. Sure, I could hire and fire; but even that power was not entirely in my hands. I felt like the creature you guys called me behind my back, an Empty Suit. Responsibility without authority. It was like trying to fight my way out of a dark labyrinth with one hand tied to my balls. The important decisions were made much higher up. Government by committee. They didn't do anything about running the local news operation; no help whatsoever in solving problems. When The Ratings went up, it was because of their good judgment. When The Ratings went down, it was my fault. It's a slice of hell, that job.

"You are never comfortable in the news director's chair. Every day you get the overnight ratings. You see that your show is pulling only a twelve percent share of the audience. You know that your professional future, your family's future are riding on those numbers. You sweat. Believe me, you sweat a lot. And you don't have the power to do the things you'd like to do to bring a turnaround. It's out of your hands. Generally, they give you two years—time enough to try your luck with two new sets in the studio, costing three or four hundred thousand dollars each, and two sets of anchors. I repeat, however, that personnel choices are not solely within your jurisdiction.

"Like the very first day I took the job at NBC. The president of the news division calls me in and says, 'Jack, I want you to do something for me. Fire the six o'clock anchorman.' I didn't see any reason to do that. The guy's rating was only a point or so behind Channel Seven at the time. He was doing a good job. Nevertheless, the president says, 'I don't like him. Make up any excuse you have to; just get rid of him.'

"So I called the anchorman in and did it. What choice did I have? I said, 'We keep getting these phone calls and letters from your ex-wife and your creditors. It's a hassle that we just can't deal with any more. You have to go.'

"In my opinion, that's when Channel Four started sliding down into the crapper. After I fired that anchorman, we went into a period where we had to bring in a new anchor team every six months. The Ratings kept going down. And no wonder. We had no identity, stability, or continuity. What could I do about it?

"The committee upstairs hired a big ad agency—the same one that had done such a great job selling the WABC "Eyewitness News" team. These guys, I thought, had the right approach to helping us. While WABC was making points with the happy-talk format, they figured on doing a big promotion campaign for us that would emphasize a no-nonsense, hard-nosed approach to covering the news. But the committee—about ten big wheels altogether: the president and various vice-presidents and managers—couldn't make up its mind. Over a period of six months, they rejected five different promotion campaigns proposed by the ad agency. Finally, the agency guys said, 'Okay, we've had it. Don't pay us anything. We're through with this account.'

"Yes, I attended all those meetings during that crazy period, but I was the lowest ranking executive in the room. The truth is, the news director has very little input up there. He's the errand boy. The committee sat up there over my head—like mystery guests on a game show—and pontificated about local news policy. They didn't know what the fuck they were talking about. You may have noticed, for example, that you never see them down in the newsroom.

"It was damn frustrating. I wanted to be directly involved in running the shop; seeing to it that we covered what ought to be covered; seeing that the right people would be covering it. The reality was something else. I spent only twenty percent of my time worrying about the news. Fifty percent of the time I had to deal with personnel problems. There were always banks, creditors, department stores, ex-wives, and lawyers threatening to sue or garnishee somebody on the staff. The other thirty percent of my time was spent taking flak from the committee."

An executive at the "nutwork" level—also insisting on anonymity—furthered my education in *gonsamacherology*. Let's call him Mack. We had been good friends during his three years as a powerless drone in local news. Over drinks after working hours, he brought me up to date on my seventh news director's tribulations. Kershaw, Mack declared, was in big trouble after less than a year in the hot seat.

"As you probably know, Kershaw used to work for ABC. Well, the other day he had lunch with some of his old cronies over there. They made jokes at his expense, crowing over The Ratings. They're number one. He is still where he was when he came here—in the crapper. Kershaw was embarrassed, naturally. He defended his position by saying that Channel Four's eleven P.M. show would be doing a hell of a lot better in The Ratings if the network's prime-time lead-ins—the entertainment that comes before the local newscast—weren't so dull and dreadful—a bunch of garbage, in his opinion.

"Well, you know how it is in this business. It's impossible to keep anything secret. Naturally, Kershaw's comments somehow made the rounds, eventually winding up back here. Fred Silverman heard the story. Man, was he pissed. He got hold of Bob Howard [Ann Berk's successor as the station's general manager] and raised holy hell. Like, who is this guy Kershaw to question Silverman's decisions about prime-time shows? What had Kershaw done to get local news out of the shithouse? Fred was so pissed, he told Howard he wanted Kershaw out of here by the end of the week.

"Now Howard has to feel that if Kershaw gets eighty-sixed, he himself might get damaged. After all, he had a lot to do with hiring Kershaw to replace Norm Fein. Anyway, Howard and Kershaw went to Silverman's office the next day. Kershaw apologized all over the place. Silverman said, 'Okay, forget it; no harm done.'

"Hah. In a pig's ass he forgot it. He called Bob Howard later. 'Kershaw still has to go,' Fred said, 'not by the end of the week, but six months from now—unless, of course, he brings up The Ratings.' "

That kind of pressure, I surmised, had to push Kershaw to the edge of panic, which probably contributed to his decision to launch "Newschopper 4" with virtually no planning ahead.

If you know anything at all about telecasting live from the wild blue yonder, you have to know that it is a very tricky proposition. Special video cable, transmitter, and antenna; complicated engineering equations; and lots of luck are required. In midmorning, the Kershaw regime ordered our facilities and equipment manager, Joe Saraceni, to accomplish the impossible on short notice. They wanted a Minicam crew to transmit live aerial views of the city during our regular evening newscast. Saraceni began making phone calls and sweating. He obviously was under pressure from above. "You've got to save my job," he pleaded with Chuck Zanlungi, who regularly rented choppers to Channel 4.

WCBS-TV had put up its own "Eye in the Sky" about two weeks earlier. Not that it showed any news events or interesting happenings, just pictures of Manhattan after dark. Beautiful pictures. Since then, the Channel 2 chopper had been featured in TV and newspaper ads as a new dimension in news coverage—a bid to raise The Ratings. What raised indignation in our newsroom was the knowledge that Zanlungi had been begging management for the past five years or so to beat the opposition to the punch. Instead of renting one of his whirlybirds on a catch-as-catch-can basis for videotape assignments, he had argued, they should sign a contract with him that would keep one of his choppers at the ready with the special electronic hardware required for live transmissions from the sky. Sure, it would cost big bucks, Zanlungi agreed. The results would certainly be worth it, as already proved by TV stations in California. No deal.

So starting from scratch, Zanlungi and a Minicam crew had to jerry-build a chopper for the job. Saraceni had not been able to

round up every piece of special equipment they needed. Consequently, the first live telecast from "Newschopper 4" was something
less than successful. Each picture they transmitted during the show
turned to hash within five or six seconds.

Channel 2 had not been plagued by that problem because over
the previous few months—before its "Eye in the Sky" left the
ground on its first assignment—WCBS had spent about a million
bucks on equipment and tests to do it right.

One of Kershaw's former colleagues at ABC defended him,
facing less-informed critics, at a media cocktail party. Call him
Zack.

"I accept your criticism that Kershaw is not a good administrator. Ron himself would give you no quarrel on that score. But I
have known this man over the years, seen him closeup at his best.
He thinks, eats, and breathes news. That's all he talks about around
the clock. It's his life.

"In Baltimore, he built one of the finest—maybe *the* finest—
local news operations I have ever seen in my twenty years in broadcasting. He brought WBAL up from number three to number one
in three years. He was able to accomplish that despite the fact of
not being a great administrator, or a guy who knew his way around
the devious politics of this business. He did it because the general
manager down there at the time, a fellow named Beauchamp, gave
Ron a free hand to do it his way; to create what Kershaw called a
theater of facts.

"After they reached the top, the success Ron had knitted
began to unravel, as it always does at any station, usually for the
same reasons. His best anchorman got a terrific offer from a TV
station in Phoenix. Beauchamp went to Phoenix, too. You know
how it is: everybody wants a messiah.

"When Beauchamp left, a new GM came in from Detroit with
a bundle of strange ideas. Kershaw couldn't play politics well
enough to cut him off at the pass. The Ratings went down. Pretty
soon, WBAL slid back down to third place. Ron quit in frustration.

"For the next six months—I'd say the better part of a year—
he isolated himself from almost everything and everybody. At first,
he lived with close friends of his and mine, saying very little, trying

to get his head together. He spent five months like that, later going back to North Carolina, where he had come from originally. Down there, he isolated himself even more, up in the mountains. Completely alone. He must have spent months up there in the hills, like a yogi, contemplating whether he should ever come back to news biz. In the end, of course, he decided to give it another shot—just one. He came to NBC and—to use his phrase—he stepped into a bigger pile of shit. Hell, I feel sorry for the man."

Prior to Zack's revelations, the hard-news facet of Kershaw's kaleidoscopic commitments had not been detected in our newsroom. We may have been too busy worrying about eighty-six to notice it. Whatever the case, my teammates and I got a brief glimpse of it at our next staff meeting over coffee and Danish pastry in the fifteenth-floor conference room—reporters, anchors, and executives only; no producers, writers, assignment editors, desk assistants, EJ editors, or camera crews.

"We need your help in running this shop," Kershaw said. "After all, it's your shop too." He urged us, in a passionate monologue that must have run ten minutes, to assert ourselves in the newsroom and anywhere else—to challenge and protest any unprofessional conduct by writers who butchered our scenarios, by assignment editors who wanted to send us to nonstories, by desk assistants who failed to look up addresses or make phone calls that would help us, by producers who failed to respect our judgment on the merits of the story we had covered, by anyone and everyone who threatened our efforts to become the number-one news team in the business. "Don't go off in a corner and gripe among yourselves, as you usually do, after the fact. I want you to yell, raise hell, and kick ass on the spot."

Amen and hallelujah. Could this mild-mannered news director be the common-sense messiah we had all been waiting for? Chauncey Howell voiced the delight common among us. "That's great. How violent can we be?"

Kershaw said we could go as far as we felt we had to, "and *we* will back you up," indicating himself, news manager Bob Davis, and executive producer Carole Clancy, seated at the oblong conference table. He also committed himself to putting more news on the air, more original stories initiated by reporters. The time had come to wean ourselves as much as possible from the wire services, newspaper headlines, and publicity handouts. "I'd like to see each reporter ask for a day off now and then to develop an original story to be taped the following day. I would expect you to drill dry holes sometimes, but don't worry about it. You will not be criticized for that. You have to drill dry holes here and there. But on those days when one of you is taking time off to work up a story, we'll be a reporter light, which means the rest of you will have to hustle to make up for it, doing two stories that day instead of one."

Exactly three days after that pep talk, giving Kershaw the benefit of my doubts, I tried to implement his first edict: protest bullshit on the spot.

After taping a story about a possible increase in the subway fare from sixty to seventy-five cents three months hence, I telephoned the news desk, as I normally did, to outline the elements of the mission just accomplished. The assignment editor acknowledged that I had covered all bases, "but the producer wants you to do a live remote on this story for the six o'clock show."

A live remote? Nonsense. The whole story was on tape. Nothing was going to happen between noon and 6:00 P.M. to change it. I told him that this was one time I was not going to let them do it to me. I was going to fight this thing all the way up to Kershaw if I had to.

During the drive from City Hall in Lower Manhattan back to Rockefeller Center, I bitched and moaned to my crew. Wisely, they cautioned me to enter the arena like a patient matador, not like a raging bull. "I know," I muttered angrily. "Nine times out of ten it's the bull who gets eighty-sixed."

Carole Clancy and Mike Dreaden were huddled at his desk when I stalked in. "First of all, I'd like to remind you of what Kershaw said at our meeting the other night. He said we should protest nonsense on the spot, not after the fact, and that's what I intend to do here and now. I hope we can settle this quietly without making a big thing out of it, but I'll go all the way to Kershaw with this if I have to." So far so good; quiet, controlled, and confidently firm.

Clancy and Dreaden watched and waited noncommittally.

"I am protesting the live remote you guys have ordered from a subway stop tonight. I think it's bullshit." Here, in spite of myself, my voice began to rise and harden. "I don't want to do it. There is absolutely no reason to do a live remote on my story. It's all on tape—subway trains, turnstiles, straphangers sounding off, buses and bus riders bitching. I have covered the facts as well as they can be covered." By then I was shouting at them in a newsroom that had suddenly hushed.

"Well, we don't think it's a bullshit remote," Clancy said with perfect aplomb. "You can still use your tape as part of a live wrap-around."

I felt like strangling the woman. "Don't you see? There is nothing I can get in the subway live at six o'clock that I haven't got on tape—except for a bunch of weirdos waving 'Hi, Mom' to the camera and shouting four-letter words into the mike."

Dreaden cleared his throat in preamble. "We realize that there's always a chance of having people saying dirty words on the air in a spot like this, but we're thinking in terms of enhancing the story. I mean, your presence in the subway would underscore . . ."

I couldn't stand it any more. "Bullshit. Don't you understand? People out there are laughing at us for doing these silly remotes. They know when we've got nothing to show and nothing to say— that we're just jerking off in public."

Both of them said they didn't believe viewers were laughing. And they still wanted me to do the spot.

I was not getting through. Something deep inside me calmed itself, retreated, then counterattacked with a soft finesse. "By the way, I should also add that I'm still having trouble with my voice from the flu bug that knocked me out of the lineup a couple of weeks ago. You probably can hear it in my voice right now."

Clancy admitted that I did sound a bit scratchy.

"To my way of thinking, it's not worth standing around in the cold on a remote like this—a legitimate big story, yes—and risk having a relapse that would knock me out again."

"Well, that's different," Clancy conceded gracefully. "If you've got a medical problem . . ."

Seeing an opening, I couldn't resist a final thrust. "Look. You

pick the reason, medical or otherwise. Just so I don't have to do it."
Exit the winner.

I reached my apartment that evening in time to witness the
denouement. My subway story led the six o'clock show. Chuck
Scarborough, in the studio, immediately introduced co-anchor John
Hambrick "who is standing-by now with a live Minicam in the subway. John?"

Hambrick, standing in front of a busy subway turnstile, said
it was probably going to cost seventy-five cents to go through that
turnstile ninety days from then, vamping in that vein, with no other
facts whatsoever, for maybe fifteen seconds. I felt sorry for the man.
Then he said what Scarborough should have said in the first place:
"Bob Teague has details on that story."

My tape package ran. My way.

Back in the newsroom the following morning, I asked the
assignment editor if he had seen the Hambrick remote, "and did
you notice how dumb it was?"

"It seemed all right to me," he said with a perfectly straight
face. "I thought it was sexy television."

So much for Kershaw's good intentions.

There was little opportunity or inclination down in the pits to
fret about Kershaw's game plan. A more ominous threat to our
peace of mind was looming at a much higher level. Silverman and
Salant were bringing in executives they had worked with at CBS—
Bill Small, Lee Currlin, Irwin Segelstein, Perry Lafferty, and Les
Midgley.

The most paranoid grunt among us was Gerald Harrington, a
sturdy network correspondent. Bill Small had fired him from CBS
about three years before. "It was a mindblower," Harrington told
a knot of us in Hurley's. We were going steady with strong libations
that evening. His face was grimly bemused, reflecting the smouldering anger that kept him ever ready to tackle Empty Suits on prin-
ciple. "You know me. I want to do it my way. When they tried to
tell me how to do a particular story at CBS, I couldn't help myself.
I fought them. You know, like what I should say in my voice-over
track; what I shouldn't say in my stand-upper. My attitude was,
what the hell, I was there. It's my interpretation, my voice, and my

face that are going on the goddamn tube. So I fought the bastards; not that it's any different at NBC. Same shit."

Had there been any specific act of rebellion that put him in the eighty-six column?

Harrington shook his head and took another sip of his scotch on the rocks. "No. As a matter of fact, about six months had passed since the last really nasty confrontation. I thought the whole thing had blown over. Then it happened, exactly two weeks before Christmas. I had just come back from the field that day, rushing to get a script together for the story I'd covered that morning. One of Small's hatchet men came up to my desk with a shit-eating grin on his face. I forget the bastard's name. Anyway, he said, 'Gerald, I don't know how to tell you this. As you know, your option comes up a few days from now. Mr. Small has decided that CBS should not renew it.'

"I got up from my desk and walked out, leaving the unfinished script in the typewriter. All I said to the hatchet man was, 'That's a hell of a Christmas present.'"

A meddlesome communiqué from the executive suite, relayed to Chauncey Howell, had the immediate effect of robbing Channel 4's funnyman of his genial bonhomie in the newsroom. Kershaw warned him that one of Silverman's trusted confidants, Irwin Segelstein, didn't like his style.

"He said Segelstein thinks I'm not dignified enough on the air."

What a dilemma. Being undignified in his sassy putdowns of high fashion, fads, and human follies had propelled Chauncey to stardom. Kershaw had encouraged his outrageous behavior, until hearing Segelstein's critique. Now he had a second master and perhaps a third to please. "They're trying to drive us all crazy," he wailed.

"A few of us can say we are as good as Robert Potts. None of us would dare to say we are better." Those words were mine, reacting to the veteran reporter's sudden disappearance through the trapdoor. The news director or one of his overseers had decided that

Potts—bespectacled and gray at forty-nine—did not fit the image to be projected on Channel 4.

In the newsroom, Chauncey Howell wept. Jim Ryan, Mary Alice Williams, David Diaz, and Carol Jenkins all said the equivalent of "I can't believe it. If they're stupid enough to eighty-six a guy like Potts, there's no hope for any of us. We're all dead ducks."

Clearly, a big wind was blowing. It was time to grab a strong tree and hang on.

Several of us called Potts at his home in Brooklyn Heights to commiserate. There was nothing we could do, however. Like the gentleman he had always been, Potts was taking it in stride. "Don't worry about me," he said over the phone, not a trace of self-pity in his voice. "Just keep your head down, big fella. You're dealing with some really nasty people up there."

His advice already was being followed instinctively. The trapdoor loomed large in everybody's nightmare.

In a stealthy, ineffective act of retaliation, somebody papered every bulletin board in the NBC complex with Xerox copies of a *Newsday* column by TV critic Marvin Kitman. He deplored "one of the more bizarre incidents heard of in some time. . . . The firing of Robert Potts reflects badly on the judgment of the new hotshot news director, Ron Kershaw." Citing specific news features that Potts had aired with wit, sensitivity, and imagination, Kitman also wrote a line that all of us survivors felt should be said to Kershaw in particular and to Empty Suits at large: "He [Kershaw] doesn't even know he did anything wrong."

Eventually, Potts found a broadcasting job with the National Public Radio network. In his spare time, he began work on an autobiographical treatise that "will expose what those pricks are doing to television news. I'm going to call it 'Forty Seconds of Nothing.'"

Before anybody had time to fully absorb the shock of the Potts affair, Kershaw jolted us again. My Saturday off was ruined by an 11:00 A.M. phone call from the newsroom. The weekend news producer, Art Bonner, awakened me. Had I seen the morning edition of the *Daily News?* I had not.

208

"It says they've done it to Mary Alice," Bonner said angrily. "They're not going to pick up her option."

My skepticism circuits dismissed Bonner's report as a practical joke. MAW was a television sex symbol as well as a terrific reporter. It couldn't happen to her.

Bonner agreed with my evaluation, but insisted that he had read it in the *News*.

I dialed MAW's apartment in Greenwich Village, having no idea of what to say. Somehow, though, I had to reach out to her— to offer whatever lame comfort I could muster.

There was a brave smile in her voice, and gratitude. "I was hoping you would call. I couldn't bring myself to tell you yesterday. I knew it was my last day, and I was almost in tears. I just wanted to get out as quietly as I could without saying anything to anybody. The maintenance people cleaned out my desk and sent all my stuff down here by messenger just this morning."

My indignation quotient rose to anger. "I can't believe it, MAW. How? Why? It doesn't make any sense. Did they give you any reason? What did they say?"

"No, they didn't give me any reason—not at first. They had a desk assistant call me last week when I was on vacation out in Minneapolis for my sister's wedding. The desk assistant called me at my mother's home. My husband answered the phone and said I wasn't in, thinking it had to be something I wouldn't want to hear. He was right. The desk assistant said Mr. Kershaw had something important to tell me. I called Kershaw a few minutes later, knowing that I was probably fired. He said he was sorry, but that was it.

"When I got back from vacation, Kershaw said, 'Like, you're beautiful, you're wonderful, you're a good reporter, and everybody likes you on the air. But you will never be a star, baby.' "

Both of us worried momentarily about me. My option was coming up in less than two months.

"I think what they're doing," MAW guessed, "is breaking up the family. And what a scummy way to do it—a phone call from a desk assistant."

MAW went on to reassure me—yes, she was comforting me— that she would be okay. "Don't worry about me. I've already got offers. In fact, one news director paraded me around yesterday afternoon. That's how word reached the *Daily News.* I might be switching to another channel."

Thank God for another channel. "Look, MAW. When I talked with Art Bonner, he was saying your husband is out of town for UPI this weekend and maybe a bunch of us should come down to your place this evening. Unless you'd rather be alone."

"No, I don't want to be alone," she said. "I'd love to see you and the gang. Please come."

Late in the day, after my phone confabs with MAW and other members of our decimated team, I went out for a copy of the *News.* The headline read:

CH. 4 SHOWS MARY ALICE THE DOOR

The report, under George Maksian's byline, gave no details as to why. It did confirm a rumor on a second front, however. Will Spens, a short-term weekend co-anchor, had also been given his "walking papers." (Felipe Luciano had resigned earlier to seek a new career in show biz.) Kershaw, the *News* disclosed, was bringing in a new anchor from San Francisco to join Carol Jenkins on the Saturday- and Sunday-night newscasts.

When Kershaw was asked if any other changes were in the offing, the newspaper added, he answered, "In any reorganization, you must make changes. We're not doing a Broadway show. We're doing news."

I also bought a copy of the *Post,* which quoted Kershaw as follows: "There'll be some people going and some people staying. When you're number three, you gotta go through some changes."

One of Kershaw's old chums from his halcyon days at WBAL-TV in Baltimore confided later, "Ron admits to having made a mistake in firing Mary Alice. After thinking about it, he planned to bring her back at some point, but things just didn't work out to make that possible. He got distracted, I gathered, by other problems. He still regrets it."

By the time that secondhand confession was on the record, Mary Alice had been happily employed for months. Cable Network

News, just getting off the drawing board, hired her as its first New York bureau chief and anchorwoman, with the power to hire and fire.

As the Silverman gang at NBC continued harassing Kershaw's tender flanks, guess who had the *chutzpah* to make a plaintive appeal to CNN's New York bureau chief for a job that would be commensurate with his experience as a news director?

Guess what Mary Alice told him?

The Missionary Position

8

I FORGET THE GUY who said it first: you hang around, you learn.

During nearly two decades in broadcast journalism, I have come to understand some of the main reasons why news biz has less integrity than it ought to, and to appreciate with gratitude and surprise that it isn't any worse than it is. In a society marred by rampant corruptions, self-interest, hype, and deceit, how could news biz be expected to stand apart, pristine and untainted? The whole damn country is coming apart at the seams. Almost nothing works the way it is supposed to, including the American Dream and the government.

Okay. I have criticized and complained. Now I will sing a song of specific remedies. First, however, I should bring you up to date on how television works; where it is at present; and where it is logically, inexorably heading in the sociological, economic, and technological theaters.

News biz, like the government and other institutions, requires many different people with a wide variety of skills to execute many different exercises exactly right to make a single one-minute TV spot come off like magic, conveying a certain amount of information and reality. Scores of men, women, and machines, scientific principles, physical and electronic processes have to be completed within tight parameters in a controlled time frame. Which means that virtually every endeavor for the tube gets on and off the screen against astronomical improbabilities. If one link in the chain of necessary events happens to weaken—if one technician forgets to punch a particular button—it is all for naught, like not quite flying to the moon.

Then, too, you have to give weight to the fact that television is very young, less than half a century old. (NBC went on the air in 1941.) Nobody has had time to figure out what makes good television all the time, or what is going to please the audience more often than not. Audiences and their tastes are in a permanent state of flux—forever becoming something else.

If you perform on the tube, you gradually come to understand that no matter what you do or how you do it, a certain number of people within your own organization and a certain number out there in "Watchville" are going to love/hate it and you. Everybody brings his/her whole bag to the tube. By sheer luck, you stumble upon a repertoire of techniques that sort of work—for a while. Television is so pervasive and relentless that sooner or later it overexposes everything to the point of weary redundancy.

If you play this game at the executive level, you are tormented by the unreliable history of the tube: what worked for Channel A, when duplicated by Channel B or improved upon by Channel C, may not necessarily produce the same response, the same ratings. There is no handbook you can consult to save you from egregious, costly blunders. You yearn for the simplistic guidelines an auto mechanic can find in his manual on how to fix a busted transmission. You have to fly by the seat of your pants. No wonder then that TV executives often shrink from the challenges—shrink into Empty Suits. Any decision they make could literally cost or earn millions of dollars.

All of this is buried in the equation that translates into the power and responsibility one has as a broadcaster. At intermittent, incandescent moments of my career, I have held the eyes and ears

214

of maybe twenty million Americans at the same time with a single network spot—billions of viewers over the years if you count Channel 4's local news audience day by day. With all the power, prestige, and paraphernalia of a TV station or a whole network behind me, I am automatically accorded a certain amount of credibility and respect. They know I wouldn't dare say it or show it on the air if I knew it wasn't true.

If you can dig that, you can also dig why a thirty-second network commercial in prime time (8:00–11:00 P.M.) in 1981 averaged $70,000. The rate for special events was even higher. Each sponsor on the Super Bowl XV telecast shelled out $275,000 for thirty seconds (for Super Bowl XVI in 1982, the price went up to $345,000), because during those precious seconds, the sponsor was granted some of the built-in believability and respect that emanates from the home screen, persuasively and automatically. They knew it was worth the price to deliver their sales pitch to tens of millions of potential customers in that span. They could also write it off as a business cost.

Now that should give you an inkling of the temptations facing news biz and everybody in it to debase our profession even more than we have. We readily sacrifice news values for entertainment values every day, which partly explains why no Emmy Award was given in 1980 in the TV news documentary category. The blue-ribbon panel that monitors and judges our efforts in the New York metropolitan area protested what the members saw as "a major failure" to produce quality news shows. A spokesman for the panel said, "Local broadcasters have been withdrawing from serious news documentaries in favor of lighter, more entertaining forms such as TV magazine shows in recent years. We could not just let this form die in obscurity."

That trend, deplored by the panel, involves more local news operations than you can count. Most of them are beginning to look and sound more and more like the typical talk show: lots of banter and forced laughter; guest stars plugging movies, TV series, and record albums; trained animals; self-help advice on everything from fixing a leaky faucet to what to look for in the perfect jogging sneakers—harmless little nothings for everybody.

In August 1981, *New York* magazine printed a puffy cover story, with pictures and salutary quotes, about "The Hottest TV Show in Town"—Channel 4's "Live at Five," infotainment from 5:00 to 6:00 P.M., which intersperses news reports among live, in-studio interviews with literary and show-biz celebrities. Citing Nielson numbers, the magazine said "Live at Five" had overtaken Channel 2's rerun dramas and Channel 7's old movie reruns in the 5:00–6:00 P.M. slot. More importantly, this growing popularity was spilling over, helping our 6:00–7:00 P.M. newscast "News 4 New York" to either consistently tie or surpass the competing early-evening news shows.

A week after that article appeared, it came as no surprise to TV news grunts when Channels 2 and 7 announced plans to elongate their early-evening newscasts within the next few months, starting at either 4:30 or 5:00 P.M., perhaps with similar formats.

In a wry commentary on this phenomenon, *Newsday*'s TV critic, Marvin Kitman, wrote the bottom line, "Call it the herd instinct."

As this homogenizing process accelerates, we are approaching the point at which local news will practically disappear as a distinctly separate entity with a unique mission. The same perversion is engulfing TV sports even faster. Nonevents are being billed as "Sports Spectaculars"—like "Battle of the Network Stars" and "Battle of the NFL Cheerleaders." To quote TV critic Willie Schatz in the *Daily News,* "Give me sports or give me entertainment. But don't come across with the latter packaged as the former. NFL cheerleaders running a football relay may be entertaining, but it's neither sports nor spectacular."

Local news biz, sadly, is sprinting down the same road, presenting entertainment under the label of news. All of us—broadcasters and viewers alike—are shortchanged by the growing lack of sharp distinctions between newscasts and variety shows.

Viewers, especially those coveted female viewers between eighteen and thirty-four, contribute to this erosion by bestowing their favors on the pseudojournalism programs. This naturally produces endless spin-offs; more of the worst, less of the best. Which is to say that the news directors, producers, and assignment editors I have complained about can be excused, given the rules of the game they are forced to play.

Network news, though declining at a slower pace, is also "becoming show business" in the judgment of Eric Sevareid, the elder statesman of CBS News. In an interview with TV critic Kay Gardella in the *Daily News,* the former commentator lamented the trend toward "checkbook journalism"—the practice of pirating newsflesh known to have high watchability quotients, and thereby creating millionaire celebrities. "If people are going to be judged or thought of in this business with dollar signs around their necks, it's the worst thing that can happen. . . . People today are acting the news, and I don't like it. Journalists are trying to be stars. It's even happening in the print medium. Reporters are really laying out themselves, not their subjects. It's a form of acting; a dangerous sympton."

It is significant, I think, that two other journalistic giants— Walter Cronkite of CBS and David Brinkley of NBC—paraphrased Sevareid in separate informal conversations with Richard Reeves of the *New York Post* and me.

According to Reeves, "Judging by a conversation we had last spring, Cronkite is as worried about that as the rest of us should be." He quoted the retiring anchorman, who said, "Up to now, those who are rising to the top in network television news are the best newspeople, not those who are seeking only the glamour. I don't have a terrible worry about the immediate future. But as it goes down the line a couple of generations or so, I'm not sure what you are going to end up with. It would be disastrous . . . disastrous if we started using the local formula of funny talk, pretty boy-pretty girl news, trivialization of the news."

In his office on the sixteenth floor of the RCA Building, Brinkley and I discussed the same topic one afternoon in the spring of eighty-one, prior to his switch to ABC. His perceptions were almost identical to Cronkite's. "There must be two thousand local news programs across this country, and I haven't seen them all. Some of those I have seen in several towns seem excessively jazzed up. I never have liked the blazer with the station's call letters on the breast pocket, and all of that nonsense. I don't see any reason for it.

Network news shows, for the most part, I'm happy to say, have stayed away from that sort of thing up to now. As for the future, I couldn't agree with you more when you say those of us who care about good journalism ought to do whatever we can to protect it, network or local. I think local stations might take a look around at what's happening.

"One of the most successful people in broadcast journalism is Walter Cronkite. Walter and I are good friends. I've known him since we both started, a long time ago. He has many charms, but he is not exactly a male model. He is sixty-four, looks fine, and people obviously like him. And it can't be because he is a matinee idol. I don't mean to be critical of Walter. I mean, I think people who are attracted to the news are attracted to newscasters who they feel know what they're talking about. They want to be told the truth as far as we know it. I even think—again using Cronkite as an example—I think they're inclined to trust newscasters who have been around long enough to have seen and heard it and to have been there—newscasters who have seen big stories come and go, politicians come and go, social crises come and go; who have developed a little understanding and a little perspective of how this country works.

"So if I were running a news program, local or network, I certainly wouldn't be looking for the handsome men and best-looking women I could find. I would look for the most talented and experienced I could find. I think that's what the public wants. All the evidence seems to me to prove that. After all, we are not just storytellers. We are also watchdogs—an important element in a country as big as this, three thousand miles long, and as diverse as this. Watching news is one of the very few things that all of the American people do together. I mean, they sit down together at six or seven P.M. and again at ten or eleven to look at the news, ours or somebody's. And they do it at the same time. The only other thing I can think of that we all do together is electing a president and paying federal income taxes. It has become a kind of national rite, something we all do. I think it is very important, and it certainly should not be corrupted.

"I'm not sure it's such a great idea, but from the polls we have seen in recent years, television is where most people get most of their news. I have always said, and I'm sure you'll agree, that that's not enough. If they really want to know what's going on, they should do some reading in addition—newspapers and magazines. On the other hand, I suspect that if television news didn't exist, a lot of those people who look at it wouldn't get any news anywhere. I think we have enlarged the audience for news, increased interest in it, which is what we ought to be doing. TV news is very important to this country, as a country.

"One of the things that has pleased me about being in this business is the letters I receive from people who have moved to this country from Europe and elsewhere overseas. They tell me they have learned English from listening to me, listening to others in our profession. One of the things I don't like about this business is— well, let me put it this way. Every night, as you know, we have a half hour to fill on the network news show. If there is *tremendous* news, we have a half hour. If there is *no* news, we still have a half hour. Yet no one is going on the air and saying, 'Well, there's no news tonight.' I did it once, years ago, on the 'Huntley-Brinkley Report.' There wasn't any. So I said, 'There's no news tonight in Washington.' Caught hell for it. I also got a letter from an older lady who said, 'What do you mean there's no news tonight in Washington? Don't you know the local Safeway supermarket is on strike?'

"So we fill the half hour every day, even on Christmas day and New Year's Eve when there's nothing stirring. We still have to put on a half hour of something that looks like news whether there is any or not.

"Let me go back a minute to what I was saying earlier about the kind of news show I would try to put on it if I were in charge. I don't want to sound like an older, experienced person being critical of younger people. Some of them are very good. But I think—and I don't know who makes these decisions—that their news judgment is rather poor. In too many instances—I'm talking about the local news shows I have seen around the country—they spend half the program on some minor incident, like a bus having a flat tire out on Highway Sixteen. The passengers are held up on their journey for an hour or so. Except for the people on the bus, I think nobody really cares.

"There's a tendency to put on something that looks like news simply because it is accessible; because they can get to it, get a picture of it. I think news is what is worth knowing. I really don't give a damn and I can't believe anyone else does about a lot of the things they put on the air. It has no effect on people's lives. There's no meaning. It has no significance. I can't imagine anyone who would want to sit there and look at it. So I think that very often the definition of news is whatever they're able to get to and get back to the studio and on the air by six o'clock.

"Yes, no question about it, a lot of this does come about under the pressure of trying to build up an audience. There's nothing wrong with building up an audience. However, I think if you want to build an audience, the better way to do it is to put on an interesting program about the things that matter and about the people the public cares about. Trivia is trivia, whether it's on the street or on the air. If you want to develop an audience and have it stay with you over a period of time, I think the way to do it is to put on a program of news that has some meaning. It doesn't always have to be about the national budget, the gross national product, and foreign trade, which is not very entertaining. But news that means something to people. And when the story is over, they will be interested and pleased to have heard about it."

I goaded Brinkley with Sevareid's denunciation of network news correspondents who "are really laying out themselves, not their subjects."

"There are a few who do that," David agreed. "I don't like it at all. I might point out that the people who have been highly successful over a long period in this business do not do that. When I see a story that's more about the reporter than the event he or she is supposed to be covering, I am appalled. I hate that. I don't think the reporter should be the story. Again I would say that beginning with—going all the way back to Ed Murrow, to Chet Huntley, to Cronkite, and the rest of us—nobody has ever made it in television news and lasted—anybody can be a big flash in the pan for a year, it's not hard—but anyone who has done it and lasted has not done any of that. You can't fool the public with that stuff. They know what you're doing. People don't tune in to see you. They tune in to see the news. And if you can tell it well, fine; and give the impression that you know what you're talking about, fine. I would hope, of course, not a false impression. No, I don't like this, 'Look at me, folks. I'm a big reporter standing at Mount Vesuvius or Mount Saint Helen's'—whatever it is—'and aren't I great?' No, that makes me sick. I can't stand it."

Now the bad news: we have not yet seen the worst. That disturbing reality became apparent to me during recent interviews with New York television executives and private media consultants. They all agreed that the competition for big audiences and the temptation to play the whore will escalate sharply because of new technology.

TV broadcasting is on the verge of proliferating to the point of being an inescapable adjunct to our lives from the time we get up in the morning until we go to sleep. A respected TV consultant in New York, Mike Dann, says, "I believe totally that man's lifestyle will change because of the new wired society. . . . We really are just starting out. The full range of cable [TV] has hardly been touched."

Dann was alluding to the not so distant future when you will be able to tune in a hundred different channels on the ordinary TV set in your living room: to closed-circuit TV programs in banks, beauty parlors, and supermarkets. These are not wild possiblities, nor the whole scope of the lucrative future. Most of the technology for such innovations is already in production. The rest is in the research and development stage.

By dramatically lowering the cost of telecasting, the new technology will encourage massive expansion of the industry. In 1982, most telecasting is accomplished through leased telephone lines and microwave radio transmitters, which carry the signal along a network of relay towers all over the country. The towers have to be positioned in a direct line of sight, one to another. Building and maintaining them costs a lot of money. Communications satellites are going to make the entire operation simpler and cheaper. Only a few satellites are up there now. (New York Telephone has three.)

More will come. With additional satellites, it will become more practical for a TV station in Kansas City, for example, to forget about all those relay towers and Telco lines, tuning instead to one or more satellites bouncing TV programs all over that geographic region. The big TV networks will have to revise their game plans to survive. That is why all three networks or their parent corporations are investing heavily now in the hardware of tomorrow. ABC has made a deal with Warner Communications to set up the Alpha Network on cable TV, specializing in the performing arts and other cultural programming. In a separate contract, ABC and the Hearst Corporation are building the Beta Network for cable TV—a so-called women's network specializing in programs on beauty, health, child rearing, and related subjects. Much of the programming for the Beta Network will be provided by the Hearst empire's twenty-one magazines, thirteen newspapers, three book publishing houses, four TV stations, and ten radio stations.

The satellite explosion is just around the corner now that Astronauts John Young and Robert Crippen have successfully tested the space shuttle *Columbia* in orbit. NASA predicts that this will eventually make going into space less expensive and more common. After *Columbia's* first lift-off, Senator John Glenn of Ohio—the first American to orbit the earth in the early sixties—said the shuttles will be going up perhaps once a week, "fifty times a year."

By the mid-eighties, NASA expects four or five of those hybrids to be in service. The shuttlecraft is designed to blast into space like a rocket ship and come back to earth like an airplane, making it possible to haul communications satellites into orbit and to fly back when necessary to make repairs on them. The shuttlecraft will park alongside. Mechanics will get out their tool kits and go to work, replacing burned-out circuits, power cells, or damaged antennae. Therefore, a malfunctioning satellite won't have to be replaced entirely at enormous costs. Furthermore, if a "bird" falls into a decaying orbit, facing a flaming finish in the earth's atmosphere, the space shuttle can tow it back up.

Now add those technological advances to the federal government's current bent toward further deregulation of television. Experts in the industry say the Federal Communications Commission, within the next couple of years, will authorize low-powered regional TV stations—with a broadcasting radius of perhaps twenty-five miles—to augment the thirteen VHF channels now on the tube. This will open the door to many entrepreneurs who cannot afford the millions of dollars it now takes to set up a TV station from scratch. The cost of launching a low-powered station is estimated at between $100,000 and $200,000. Operational costs also will be affordable, since the low-powered stations will not tie into those expensive relay transmitters and Telco lines. The satellites can carry so many different programs to so many places simultaneously that the cost per station for that service will be at least ten times cheaper than the present soon-to-be-discarded system.

Investors will gallop into low-powered television because owning a TV station in this country is like having a license to print money.

My friend Larry Forray, a New York TV consultant, predicts that, by 1990, the average viewer in America will be able to flip the dial on his set to forty or fifty channels; by the year 2000, a hundred channels. Programs for all those new stations will be packaged and peddled by an expanded movie industry, by existing and projected independent production companies, and by middlemen who specialize in mass distribution of videotape cassettes.

Aside from TV stations, the middlemen will also supply cassettes and playback equipment to many areas of private industry not yet tapped. Forray, one of the early pioneers in closed-circuit playback in hotel rooms, says successful experiments already have been made in beauty parlors in Boston, New York, Atlanta, Detroit, and San Francisco.

"It's a captive audience," Forray declared. "A woman sits under the hair dryer an average of forty-five minutes. By putting up a single screen and inserting an audio receiver in each of those big helmets, with volume controls on the armrest, we played twenty-eight-minute cassettes of entertainment and commercials that would interest women. The sponsors were backed up around the corner. The beauty parlor and barbershop market will definitely be tapped very soon. We've also seen promising experiments in banks. And right now, three hundred forty-two supermarkets are running closed-circuit TV commercials for people waiting in the checkout line—silent pictures with large captions. Department stores like Macy's and Gimbels's will get into it eventually. I can see in the future, not too far away, when you can dial a certain low-powered station on your TV set, see commercials for your local supermarket or department store, and order what you want by phone. The store will deliver what you want and debit your account there or your bank account. That's why the telephone company also has a good shot in this kind of shopping. It could work out that the store would bill your telephone number instead of your bank account. Either way, it's coming. The technology for it has already been tested by Warner Communications out in Ohio. And it works."

Forray didn't say so, but you can easily envision more closed-circuit transmissions in bus depots, airports, and subway stations— wherever large numbers of potential consumers have to wait with nothing in particular to occupy their minds.

Additionally, you will have all of those new channels on your home set. Channel 81 might be the place you can turn to twenty-four hours a day to learn about cooking. Channel 83 could be a full-time service that instructs you about household economics and solving family problems. Study yoga on Channel 91. Learn a new language on Channel 96.

Warner Communications is testing an all-children's programming channel in the Midwest, charging ten cents a month per home. A joint venture by Warner and American Express already has introduced a twenty-four-hour all-music channel on cable TV— MTV-Music Television. In New York City, where only Manhattan had cable TV in 1982, sixteen private cable TV companies are competing for franchises to install their systems in the four other boroughs—Brooklyn, Queens, Staten Island, and the Bronx. Part of the delay in granting these franchises stems from a desire among several city officials to create a municipally owned cable TV system. The director of the Bureau of Franchises, Morris Tarshis, advised Mayor Koch, "There's a good bit of money to be made from cable TV. It would work just like the city taking over a building and leasing it to someone else. I think it can pay for itself and make a profit for us. It's worth consideration."

If and when New York succeeds in such a venture, other financially strapped municipalities will certainly try to follow suit.

In Forray's words, "There's no end to the possibilities for specialization, and making money at it. Big business firms will also be able to buy time on low-powered public-access channels at certain times of the night to broadcast information to their employees right in their homes after dinner."

All of which means that we are going to be surrounded and bombarded by television wherever we go. The competition for mass audiences will be fiercer than ever. Gimmicks and hype will abound as never before. Whatever it takes to capture our attention will be attempted.

My fear is that news biz, under that kind of pressure, will bend itself so far out of shape as to lose what is left of its character and its purpose.

But I think something can be done to prevent that.

First, I would like to see television executives all over the country agree among themselves to take news programs out of the traditional rating system. Instead, let the news shows compete for qualitative ratings by an independent city or state monitoring board composed of former journalists, educators, and a representative cross section of the population in that particular broadcasting area. The monitoring board would establish criteria such as accuracy, clarity, scope, sensitivity, grammar, initiative, and the ratio of stories that viewers really need to know compared with nonstories— like silly live remotes—or simple-minded entertainments. On a monthly basis, the monitoring panel would grade each station's news programs in that viewing area: excellent, good, fair, or poor. Each program's current quality rating should be flashed on the screen at the top of each broadcast, the way movies display their content rating before the list of credits. The result, I think, would be heightened competition for journalistic excellence instead of numbers. Viewers who want to know what's going on could then make intelligent choices as to which station's news program to watch, instead of blindly tuning to the one that Nielsen or Arbitron say more people are watching, perhaps for the wrong reasons.

My second radical proposal, endorsed by Forray, would eliminate head-to-head competition among news programs in the same time slot. A newscast is not supposed to be just another vehicle for peddling underarm deodorants. The public needs to know. There is no good reason why the three flagship stations in New York should all be providing essentially the same information simultaneously at six and eleven. Why not let each station take a different time slot? After all, everybody's lifestyle is not geared to being in front of the TV set at the same time every day. Suppose in 1983, WABC put on its local news between six and seven; WNBC between seven and eight; WCBS between eight and nine. In the years to follow, they could rotate the three time slots.

When Forray first heard that idea, he balked momentarily. "Why should a station give up an hour of its prime time in the evening when it normally runs its big money-making entertainment shows? Local news commercials don't produce profits as huge as the network sitcoms."

Forray dropped his objections whem I amplified. "We are talking about giving up only one hour for a year on a rotating basis. If you have five or six stations in the same city, as we certainly will have all over the country before long, each station would make the same sacrifice the same number of times. Consider, too, how much money each station might save or put to better purposes if it no longer had to spend megabucks on gimmicks, on ceaseless promotional campaigns, and on exorbitant salaries for newsflesh. The way things are right now, even a weatherman or a sportscaster with attractive demographic numbers in his or her dossier can stick up a TV station and get away with it. The CBS affiliate in Washington, D.C., WDVM-TV, recently signed a sportscaster named Glenn Brenner to a five-year contract worth three and a half million dollars. The deal includes a college education for Brenner's kids, a million-dollar insurance policy, and ten years of retirement pay at a hundred grand a year—for telling people about games, for Christ's sake."

The elimination of head-to-head newscasts—network and local—would also mean a much more stable and professional cadre. Journalists could afford to concentrate more on the news instead of cosmetics. And the good ones would stay on their beats longer—being less inclined to run to the next town and less likely to be eighty-sixed on a whim. Local TV newsflesh was described by Neil Hickey in *TV Guide* as "probably the most nomadic, peripatetic, and rootless bunch of rolling stones in the entire American work force."

The same could be said of news managers. As they leapfrog one another in town after town, the quality of their decisions and the news shows they run decline more often than not. A principal reason is the fact that the nomads—talents and managers alike—come and go before they have time to absorb important background references they ought to have about the problems, history, traditions, and folklore in their new theater of operations.

I am thinking now about a big story that almost got away from WNBC-TV because of that kind of ignorance. While the night shift was organizing our 11:00 P.M. newscast, the AP Teletype spelled out a bare-bones bulletin:

DAVID KENNEDY, SON OF THE LATE SEN. ROBERT F. KENNEDY, HAS BEEN MUGGED IN A HOTEL AT 116TH STREET AND 8TH AVENUE.

It was ripped off the machine by Len Tepper, a deputy assistant to assignment editor Doug Spiro. Being dues-paying New Yorkers, both recognized in a flash that there had to be much more to that story than met the eye, demanding a full-blown report from the scene because of its location. "It could lead the show," Tepper suggested. However, when he brought the bulletin to the assistant news director, the executive producer, and the producer of the eleven o'clock show, all three—being recent immigrants to the metropolitan area—disagreed. Yes, they said, since a Kennedy was involved, it should be mentioned on the air, but only in copy to be read by the anchorman in ten or twelve seconds; no film or tape. Luckily, Tepper recovered from his astonishment as he realized that he was dealing with out-of-towners. "Don't you understand? That location—One-Hundred Sixteenth and Eighth Avenue—it's in

Harlem: A notorious supermarket for narcotics. The Kennedy kid had to be up there making a buy. Why else would a rich kid like him go into a joint like that?"

Because of Tepper's persistence, we covered the story in detail—as did all the other New York channels—that night and for the next two days. Sure enough, David Kennedy had gone to Harlem to get a fix.

Had we missed the full implication of the AP bulletin, I grant you, no irreparable harm would have been done; just another embarrassment for our news team. By simple extrapolation, however, you can see how easily, under those circumstances, we could also miss important developments in political, economic, or ethnic stories of wide concern. Management seems to give little thought to the inevitable handicap that imported messiahs bring with them, being more concerned about a possible quick fix for The Ratings.

In light of these denigrating realities, Forray said thoughtfully, "I see your point. It's a good concept you're trying to sell: an hour of local news on different stations at six, seven, eight, ten, or even later, depending on the number of stations in a given area. Yes, I can see the big wheels at TV stations sitting down and making that kind of arrangement. It would solve one of their problems. They've got to compete with one another for audiences on so many other fronts, it would be a big relief—one less headache—to run their news operations as more of a public service and still make money on them. I like it."

The changes I have suggested up to now would help to "deglorify" anchorpersons, as Walter Cronkite has proposed, and deemphasize glamour—perhaps to a point where female talents could be appreciated for their abilities rather than their dimples and bustlines. At a New York symposium for women broadcasters in 1981, a former ABC reporter, Ellen Burstein MacFarlane, said newswomen were now regarded as "the electronic equivalent of the *Playboy* centerfold." Another speaker, anchorwoman Jessica Savitch of NBC, looked forward to the day when TV audiences would accept female journalists who were "as gray and wrinkled" as Cronkite.

It is my belief that TV audiences will make that adjustment if given the chance, as proved by commentator Dorothy Fuldheim of WEWS-TV in Cleveland. A former freelance print journalist, Fuldheim—now eighty-six years old—has been broadcasting continuously since 1949, a record unmatched by any other television talent of either sex. Her wit and wisdom perennially produce high ratings.

Such could be the future of news biz. As for the interregnum—Well, if I were applying for the job of local news director today, I would offer a few common-sense policies to improve the state of broadcast journalism. Above all, I would concentrate on eighty-sixing fear and bullshit instead of covering my ass and looking for scapegoats. I would regularly consult with grunts as well as department chiefs to learn where and why nonsense was rampant. Where negotiations failed to wipe it out, I would act with hard-line ultimatums.

In screening job applicants—men or women—their expertise, experience, and credibility would count more heavily in my selections than their age, good looks, or sex appeal. Neither would I be overly concerned about pear-shaped tones or standard midwestern accents. I just want newspeople who know what the hell they are talking about every day. My anchors would also serve as reporters, spending at least four months a year in the field.

Another priority would be the crisp presentation of a hard-nosed hour of news interspersed with human-interest side bars and features. I would establish an investigative unit, expecting—realistically—only one or two hard-hitting series a month.

Moving right along, I would authorize live remotes only when something newsworthy was happening at the site; not to chew the fat about something that had happened hours before and should have been covered on tape. My reporters would always be on videotape or live in the field; they'd never be in the studio except to tell the rare big story that could not be covered with pictures and sound bites.

Once a week the newscast would carry a fifteen- or twenty-minute segment of updates on the big stories we had aired weeks or months ago, then forgotten. Sure, updates are done now once in a while, but on a very haphazard basis. I would assign at least two associate producers and a research staff to focus on that project.

Next, I would plan on covering fewer stories on a given show—especially the traditional half-hour newscast at 11:00 P.M.—so that more time could be allotted to important, complex matters that need background inserts or analysis, live or on tape from the archives.

I would personally spend more time in face-to-face confabs and critiques with members of my team, less time in guessing games with numbers-watchers in the Golden Ghetto. Every man and woman on the team, I feel, should have a sense of being respected, appreciated, and listened to, and confidence that concrete steps will be taken by their leaders to eradicate the problems that sabotage the operation and cripple their morale.

Valuable air time would not be squandered on studio skits, gossip, or family jokes. The weekly "Sixty Minutes" on CBS has proved conclusively, in prime-time competition against fluff, that millions of viewers like their news without frills.

I would *not* build a new studio set.

That is all. Everything else would fall into place.

I like to think—in a way, this is the closest thing in my cynical heart to a prayer—I like to think that we can make news biz better. What we have to do, first of all, is jettison the excess baggage that hampers our pursuit of excellence.

Index